THE NORTH CAROLINA
Justice Reinvestment Act

James M. Markham

2012

The School of Government at the University of North Carolina at Chapel Hill works to improve the lives of North Carolinians by engaging in practical scholarship that helps public officials and citizens understand and improve state and local government. Established in 1931 as the Institute of Government, the School provides educational, advisory, and research services for state and local governments. The School of Government is also home to a nationally ranked graduate program in public administration and specialized centers focused on information technology and environmental finance.

As the largest university-based local government training, advisory, and research organization in the United States, the School of Government offers up to 200 courses, webinars, and specialized conferences for more than 12,000 public officials each year. In addition, faculty members annually publish approximately fifty books, book chapters, bulletins, and other reference works related to state and local government. Each day that the General Assembly is in session, the School produces the *Daily Bulletin*, which reports on the day's activities for members of the legislature and others who need to follow the course of legislation.

The Master of Public Administration Program is a full-time, two-year program that serves up to sixty students annually. It consistently ranks among the best public administration graduate programs in the country, particularly in city management. With courses ranging from public policy analysis to ethics and management, the program educates leaders for local, state, and federal governments and nonprofit organizations.

Operating support for the School of Government's programs and activities comes from many sources, including state appropriations, local government membership dues, private contributions, publication sales, course fees, and service contracts. Visit www.sog.unc.edu or call 919.966.5381 for more information on the School's courses, publications, programs, and services.

Michael R. Smith, DEAN
Thomas H. Thornburg, SENIOR ASSOCIATE DEAN
Frayda S. Bluestein, ASSOCIATE DEAN FOR FACULTY DEVELOPMENT
L. Ellen Bradley, ASSOCIATE DEAN FOR PROGRAMS AND MARKETING
Todd A. Nicolet, ASSOCIATE DEAN FOR OPERATIONS
Ann Cary Simpson, ASSOCIATE DEAN FOR DEVELOPMENT
Bradley G. Volk, ASSOCIATE DEAN FOR ADMINISTRATION

FACULTY

Whitney Afonso	Joseph S. Ferrell	Janet Mason	Jessica Smith
Gregory S. Allison	Alyson A. Grine	Christopher B. McLaughlin	Karl W. Smith
David N. Ammons	Norma Houston	Laurie L. Mesibov	Carl W. Stenberg III
Ann M. Anderson	Cheryl Daniels Howell	Kara A. Millonzi	John B. Stephens
A. Fleming Bell, II	Jeffrey A. Hughes	Jill D. Moore	Charles Szypszak
Maureen M. Berner	Willow S. Jacobson	Jonathan Q. Morgan	Shannon H. Tufts
Mark F. Botts	Robert P. Joyce	Ricardo S. Morse	Vaughn Upshaw
Michael Crowell	Kenneth L. Joyner	C. Tyler Mulligan	Aimee N. Wall
Leisha DeHart-Davis	Diane M. Juffras	David W. Owens	Jeffrey B. Welty
Shea Riggsbee Denning	Dona G. Lewandowski	William C. Rivenbark	Richard B. Whisnant
James C. Drennan	Adam Lovelady	Dale J. Roenigk	
Richard D. Ducker	James M. Markham	John Rubin	

This project was supported by Grant No. 2010-RR-BX-K071 awarded by the Bureau of Justice Assistance. The Bureau of Justice Assistance is a component of the Office of Justice Programs, which also includes the Bureau of Justice Statistics, the National Institute of Justice, the Office of Juvenile Justice and Delinquency Prevention, the SMART Office, and the Office for Victims of Crime. Points of view or opinions in this document are those of the author and do not represent the official position or policies of the United States Department of Justice.

Contents

Chapter 2

Introduction

The Justice Reinvestment Act of 2011 (the JRA)[1] made substantial changes to the law of sentencing and corrections in North Carolina—the most sweeping changes since the enactment of Structured Sentencing itself. This book summarizes and analyzes those changes, with an eye toward helping judicial officials, lawyers, corrections officials, and others do their work in a post-JRA world.

The legislation takes its name from the national-level Justice Reinvestment project spearheaded by the nonprofit Council of State Governments (CSG) Justice Center. The goal of the project is to encourage states to reduce prison populations and spending on corrections and then to reinvest the savings in community-based programs. More than fifteen states have taken part in the program as of this writing.

In 2009, CSG analysts began collecting data and focus group input on North Carolina's criminal justice system. In early 2011 they issued a report of their findings and gave recommendations on how the justice reinvestment concept could be applied in the state. Among other things, they found that

- North Carolina's prison population was projected to increase by 10 percent between 2010 and 2020,[2]

---

1. North Carolina Session Law (hereinafter S.L.) 2011-192.

2. More recent projections that take into account 2009 legislative changes and the prison system's decision to award earned time more quickly estimated that the prison population would grow by less than 2 percent between 2011 and 2021. *See*

- most felons (all Class F–I offenders, who account for 85 percent of all felons) had no community supervision upon release from prison,
- more than half of new prison admissions were revoked probationers,
- community-based treatment programs were not allocated in an evidence-based way, and
- North Carolina was unusual in the number of misdemeanants housed in its prison system instead of local jails.[3]

With those findings in mind, the CSG group helped write House Bill 642, the Justice Reinvestment Act. The bill passed virtually unanimously and was signed into law by the governor as North Carolina Session Law (hereinafter S.L.) 2011-192 on June 23, 2011. Before most of the law came into effect, it was amended by S.L. 2011-412 (the 2011 Technical Corrections Act).[4] Several parts of the JRA were amended again the following year by S.L. 2012-188, referred to hereinafter as the 2012 Clarifications Act.

Chapter 1 of this book discusses the changes the JRA made to the felony sentencing law in North Carolina. Those changes include the expansion of post-release supervision (PRS) to include all felons, the creation of a new early release program called Advanced Supervised Release, and modifications to the habitual felon law. The JRA did not make any changes to the minimum sentences on the front of the felony sentencing grid, but it did change the maximums on the back. Related legislation also changed the rules for maximum sentences for certain sex offenders. As a result, court and corrections officials should take care to use the proper sentencing grid for the offense in question—as always, dictated by the date of the offense.

"Current Population Projections: Fiscal Year 2012 to Fiscal Year 2021," North Carolina Sentencing and Policy Advisory Commission (2012), www.nccourts.org/Courts/CRS/Councils/spac/Documents/2012-popproj.pdf.

3. "Justice Reinvestment in North Carolina: Analysis and Policy Framework to Reduce Spending on Corrections and Reinvest in Strategies to Increase Public Safety," Council of State Governments Justice Center (2011), http://justicereinvestment.org/files/JR_North_Carolina_policy_framework_v8mg_mc.pdf (hereinafter "Framework").

4. Readers should note that the changes made by the 2011 Technical Corrections Act became law after LexisNexis issued the 2011 versions of *North Carolina Criminal Law and Procedure* (the unannotated collections of statutes related to criminal law, sometimes referred to as the "Red Book") and the *Annotated General Statutes of North Carolina*. As a result, some of the statutes printed in those books do not reflect the final version of the law.

Chapter 2 covers changes related to probation, the most noteworthy of which is the substantial limitation on a judge's authority to revoke probation. Chapter 2 also addresses the blending of community and intermediate punishment and the expansion of delegated authority, which gives probation officers more authority to add certain probation conditions, including short periods of jail confinement, without court action.

Chapter 3 discusses the expansion of the conditional discharge available for certain drug offenders under G.S. 90-96. Most notably, the JRA makes that discharge mandatory for consenting defendants, raising a variety of legal and logistical issues.

Chapter 4 of the book covers the changes the JRA made to the rules about the proper place to serve a sentence. In general, those changes were designed to transition most misdemeanants from the prison system to the local jails. To help the counties absorb the cost of that transfer, the legislation created the Statewide Misdemeanant Confinement Program, through which a county can be reimbursed for voluntarily agreeing to house certain inmates. Chapter 4 provides a full discussion of the post-JRA rules for where a sentence should be served, including a refresher on the place-of-confinement rules that were unaffected by the legislation.

Not all of the JRA's many changes had the same effective date. Some portions were made effective for offenses committed on or after December 1, 2011 (for example, the expansion of post-release supervision). Some were made effective for probation violations occurring on or after December 1, 2011 (such as the limitation on the court's authority to revoke probation). And some were made effective for sentences imposed on or after January 1, 2012 (for example, the changes to the place-of-confinement rules). More effective-date issues arose with the passage of the 2012 Clarifications Act, which was effective when it became law on July 16, 2012. Additionally, some of the changes apply only to cases sentenced under Structured Sentencing while others apply to sentences for impaired driving as well. And finally, some of the dates have unanticipated interactions with one another. For instance, a court may revoke for violations of the new statutory absconding condition for violations that occur on or after December 1, 2011, but only persons on probation for an offense that occurred on or after December 1, 2011, are actually subject to the revocation-eligible condition. These nuances require careful attention if the law is to be applied correctly. The summary chart in Appendix A notes the effective date of each change and whether it applies in DWI cases.

The first step in following the law is often choosing the proper form to use. The JRA (and other recent legislation) required the creation of multiple versions of the boilerplate judgment forms issued by the Administrative Office of the Courts. In general, those forms adhere to the following convention:

- "A" series forms (for example, AOC-CR-603A) are for offenses committed before December 1, 2009.
- "B" series forms are for offenses committed from December 1, 2009, to November 30, 2011.
- "C" series forms are for offenses committed on or after December 1, 2011.

The entire forms library is available at the AOC's webpage at www.nccourts.org/Forms/FormSearch.asp.

The JRA requires the Division of Adult Correction and the Judicial Department, through the North Carolina Sentencing and Policy Advisory Commission, jointly to conduct ongoing evaluations of the implementation of the new law. The Sentencing Commission must report on the law to the General Assembly by April 15 of each year. The first annual report is available on the Commission's web page at www.nccourts.org/Courts/CRS/Councils/spac/Documents/JRIReports-2012.pdf.

One of the few things that is certain about the changes made by the JRA is that they will be subject to further amendment in the future. The appellate courts will also inevitably add an interpretive gloss, just as they have with Structured Sentencing over the course of nearly two decades. Updates to the law will be covered on the School of Government's North Carolina Criminal Law Blog[5] and collected on the School's Justice Reinvestment Resource Page.[6]

5. http://nccriminallaw.sog.unc.edu.
6. www.sog.unc.edu/node/2044.

Chapter 1

Changes to Felony Sentencing

A. Post-Release Supervision for All Felons

Post-release supervision (PRS) is a period of supervised release, similar to probation, that an inmate serves in the community upon release from prison. Under prior law only Class B1–E felonies received PRS. Analysts from the Council of State Governments recommended expanding PRS after noting that felons who leave prison with no community supervision had slightly higher re-arrest rates than supervised offenders.[1]

The Justice Reinvestment Act (JRA) broadens the post-release supervision law so that all felons receive PRS.[2] The JRA lengthens the period of PRS for Class B1–E felons and for the first time adds PRS for Class F–I felons. The changes are effective for offenses committed on or after December 1, 2011.[3]

---

1. The North Carolina Sentencing and Policy Advisory Commission has analyzed offender recidivism, including a comparison of post-release supervision (PRS) and non-PRS offenders, for many years. *See, e.g.,* "Correctional Program Evaluation: Offenders Placed on Probation or Released from Prison in Fiscal Year 2003/04," North Carolina Sentencing and Policy Advisory Commission (2008), www.nccourts.org/Courts/CRS/Councils/spac/Documents/recidivismreportR_2008.pdf, 53–74.

2. N.C Gen. Stat. (hereinafter G.S.) § 15A-1368.1. The law excludes Class A and Class B1 felons sentenced to life imprisonment without parole.

3. North Carolina Session Law (hereinafter S.L.) 2011-192, § 2.(j). When a crime has allegedly been committed over a range of dates both before and after December 1, 2011, the defendant generally should be sentenced under the law that results in the less severe sentence. *See* State v. Poston, 162 N.C. App. 642, 651 (2004) (applying that

Under the new law, Class F–I felons serve a 9-month term of PRS upon their release from prison. Class B1–E felons serve a 12-month term of PRS, up from the 9-month period required under prior law.[4] All felon sex offenders serve a longer period of PRS upon release, described below.

Class F–I felons are automatically released onto PRS 9 months before reaching their maximum term of imprisonment, less any earned time the inmate may have accrued. Class B1–E felons are released 12 months before attaining their maximum, less earned time. Offenders sentenced under the JRA will not, however, serve any less time in prison than pre-JRA offenders. Rather, to accommodate PRS, the JRA added time equivalent to the length of the early release onto every felony maximum sentence. Maximum sentences for Class F–I felonies are thus 120 percent of the imposed minimum plus 9 months (9 months longer than under prior law), while Class B1–E maximums are 120 percent of the imposed minimum plus 12 months (3 months higher than under prior law).[5]

The extra time added on to each sentence operates like a suspended sentence during the offender's period of PRS. It is, in other words, the time

---

rule to a crime committed over a range of dates that crossed the transition from Fair Sentencing to Structured Sentencing).

4. G.S. 15A-1368.2(c).

5. Three of the maximum sentences set out in G.S. 15A-1340.17(e) depart from the standard formula for calculating a maximum sentence for a Class B1–E offense (120 percent of the minimum, rounded to the next highest month, plus 12 months). The maximum sentence corresponding to a 66-month minimum should be 92 months, not 91. The maximum corresponding to an 86-month minimum should be 116 months, not 115. And the maximum sentence corresponding to a 216-month minimum should be 272 months, not 271. Despite the apparent errors, court officials who select an affected minimum sentence should use the maximum sentence set out in the chart in G.S. 15A-1340.17(e); they should not correct the maximum so that it follows the standard formula. The formula, set out in G.S. 15A-1340.17(e1), technically applies only to sentences with a minimum of 340 months or more.

The errors do not render the affected sentence inadministrable. Rather, they simply result in the defendant being released onto PRS slightly earlier than he or she would had the maximum sentence been set out according to the standard 120-percent-of-the-minimum-plus-12-months rule. A judge could avoid the issue by not selecting one of the affected minimum sentences.

Another error that appeared in the Justice Reinvestment Act (JRA) as initially enacted—the maximum sentence corresponding to a 328-month minimum—was corrected from 408 months to 406 months by Section 2.4.(a) of the 2011 Technical Corrections Act (S.L. 2011-412).

that hangs over the offender's head during PRS, subject to activation by the Post-Release Supervision and Parole Commission (the Commission) upon certain findings of violation, discussed below.[6] For example, a Class H felon that received a 5–6 month sentence under prior law would receive a 5–15 month sentence under the new law. This felon will be released when he or she is within 9 months of the maximum sentence, which would be at some point between 5 and 6 months, depending on earned time. He or she will then be on PRS for 9 months, with the possibility of serving the 9 remaining months on that 15-month maximum sentence if he or she violates the terms of supervision. An inmate may not refuse PRS.[7]

The reverse side of the felony sentencing grid, showing the maximum sentence that corresponds to each minimum, has been updated to reflect the longer maximum sentences created by the JRA.[8] Court officials should be sure to use the grid that corresponds to the offense date of the crime being sentenced. The JRA made no changes to the ranges of permissible minimum sentences set out on the front of the sentencing grid.

Although added onto maximum sentences to accommodate the defendant's eventual release onto PRS, the extra time carries additional consequences. For example, the inflated maximum allows for a longer term of special probation, as the maximum term of confinement in a split sentence is one-fourth of the maximum imposed sentence.[9] Thus, a 6–8 month sentence that allowed for a 2-month split sentence under prior law becomes a 6–17 month sentence that allows for a 4.25-month split.

The increased maximum may also trigger additional collateral consequences for certain offenses under federal law. For instance, some federal sentencing enhancements and crimes hinge on whether a person has any prior convictions for crimes punishable by imprisonment for a term exceeding one year.[10] Under prior law, many low-level state offenses did not qualify as federal felonies when committed by defendants who, based on their prior record level and the absence of aggravating factors, faced

---

6. *See infra* notes 39–42 and accompanying text.

7. G.S. 15A-1368.2.

8. G.S. 15A-1340.17(d) and (e).

9. G.S. 15A-1351(a).

10. *E.g.,* 21 United States Code § 802(44) (*felony drug offense* defined for purposes of the federal Controlled Substances Act).

a maximum sentence of 12 months or less.[11] Under the JRA every felony maximum sentence now exceeds one year—even the lowest sentence from the mitigated range for a first-time Class I offender has a maximum of 13 months—meaning all offenses committed on or after December 1, 2011, may trigger additional federal consequences.

The law setting out the applicability of PRS says that it applies to all felons "sentenced to an active punishment."[12] *Active punishment* is a defined term under Structured Sentencing, referring to a sentence that requires an offender to serve a sentence of imprisonment that is not suspended.[13] If those statutes are read together, a question arises as to whether PRS applies to felons sentenced to community or intermediate punishments whose suspended sentences are later activated. The issue arose only rarely under prior law because few Class B1–E felons could and did receive nonactive sentences.[14] It will arise with great frequency for offenses committed on or after December 1, 2011, because two-thirds of Class F–I felons are initially sentenced to probation.[15]

If the PRS law applies to defendants initially sentenced to probation whose probation is later revoked, a practical issue arises in the administration of their sentences. Many offenders with short suspended sentences will, after taking applicable jail credit into account, be eligible for release onto PRS immediately upon revocation of probation. For instance, an offender with a 5–15 month sentence who has already served two 90-day periods of

---

11. *See* United States v. Simmons, 649 F.3d 237 (4th Cir. 2011) (en banc) (holding that a prior conviction only meets the definition of an offense punishable by more than one year in prison if the defendant in question faced a sentence that long in light of his or her criminal record and the presence of aggravating factors). *Simmons* overruled United States v. Harp, 406 F.3d 242 (4th Cir. 2005), *cert. denied*, 546 U.S. 919 (2005), which had directed federal district courts to consider the hypothetical worst-case defendant when evaluating whether an offense was punishable by imprisonment in excess of one year.

12. G.S. 15A-1368.1.

13. G.S. 15A-1340.11(1).

14. The only Class B1–E felons for whom intermediate punishment is authorized are those convicted of Class E offenses with prior record level I or II. In fiscal year 2010–11, 666 felons in those cells received an intermediate punishment. "Structured Sentencing Statistical Report for Felonies and Misdemeanors, Fiscal Year 2010/11," North Carolina Sentencing and Policy Advisory Commission (2012), www.nccourts.org/Courts/CRS/Councils/spac/Documents/statisticalrpt_fy10-11.pdf (hereinafter "2010/11 Statistical Report"), 13.

15. In fiscal year 2010–11, 15,876 Class F–I felons received a community or intermediate punishment. *Id.*

confinement in response to violation (CRV or "dunks," described in Chapter 2)[16] will already be within 9 months of his or her maximum sentence—and thus due for release from prison immediately upon revocation. It would appear to be inappropriate to incarcerate such a person for any longer than necessary to set his or her conditions of PRS. When such situations arise, it may be possible to arrange for a direct release from the revoking court to PRS by coordinating with the Division of Adult Correction (DAC) and the Post-Release Supervision and Parole Commission.

B. Changes to Sentencing and Post-Release Supervision for Sex Offenders

Defendants convicted of reportable sex crimes that require PRS receive a 60-month PRS period instead of the 9- or 12-month period applicable to nonreportable crimes.[17] The 60-month supervised release period applies to any PRS-eligible offense, regardless of offense class.

Effective for offenses committed on or after December 1, 2011, legislation outside of the JRA amended G.S. 15A-1340.17(f) to provide that for sex offenders convicted of Class B1–E felonies, the maximum sentence is 120 percent of the minimum, rounded to the next highest month, plus 60 additional months.[18] The law makes a parallel change to G.S. 15A-1368.2(a)

---

16. *See infra* "H. Changes to the Court's Authority to Revoke Probation" in Chapter 2.

17. G.S. 15A-1368.2(c).

18. S.L. 2011-307.

In limited circumstances, adding time onto a defendant's maximum sentence for a reportable sex crime may infringe on his or her Sixth Amendment right to a jury trial. Under *Blakely v. Washington*, 542 U.S. 296 (2004), any fact that increases a person's punishment must be admitted to by the defendant or proved to a jury beyond a reasonable doubt. In general, the obligation to register as a sex offender flows from a reportable conviction itself; no additional court finding is required. And if no additional finding is required, *Blakely* is not implicated. Certain crimes, however, are only reportable if the court makes additional findings beyond the conviction itself. Kidnapping is only reportable if committed against a minor by a person who is not the victim's parent. G.S. 14-208.6(1m). Aiding and abetting a reportable offense is only reportable if the sentencing judge finds that registration would further the purposes of the registry. G.S. 14-208.6(4)a. If those offenses are reportable, their maximum sentence is 120 percent of the minimum plus 60 months instead of 120 percent of the minimum plus 12 months. To the extent that 48 months of additional imprisonment to provide that those offenders will be released from prison onto PRS 60 months before attaining their maximum, less earned time. The changes were designed to make the time remaining on an offender's sentence of imprisonment match the length of his or her period of PRS and to give those offenders an increased incentive to avoid revocation. Under prior law Class B1–E sex offenders had a 60-month PRS period but faced only 9 months of imprisonment if revoked, leading some to attempt to refuse PRS or to violate on purpose.

The changes apply only to Class B1–E sex offenders. They do not apply to Class F–I felons convicted of reportable crimes, even though those lower-level felons are now subject to a 60-month supervised release period under G.S. 15A-1368.2(c). For example, a defendant convicted of indecent liberties with a child for an offense occurring on or after December 1, 2011, will have a maximum sentence that is 120 percent of the minimum sentence, plus 9 months; the defendant will be released from prison 9 months before attaining that maximum sentence, less earned time; the defendant will then be on supervised release for five years, with the 9 remaining months of imprisonment to be served in the event of revocation. In other words, Class F–I sex offenders are sentenced under the new law in the same manner Class B1–E sex offenders were sentenced under prior law.

Even these lower level offenders, however, will have an incentive to complete their PRS in the community. Effective June 27, 2011,[19] the law provides that willful refusal to accept or comply with the terms of PRS by an offender under supervision for a reportable offense is punishable as criminal contempt of court.[20] A willful refusal to accept or comply with the terms of PRS includes but is not limited to "knowingly violating the terms of post-release supervision in order to be returned to prison to serve out the remainder of the prisoner's sentence."[21] The Post-Release Supervision and Parole Commission is empowered under the law to act as a judicial official would under

---

are triggered by a finding that makes the convictions reportable, *Blakely* might require that the finding be made by a jury or admitted to by the defendant.

19. The contempt provisions in S.L. 2011-307 were made effective when they became law on June 27, 2011, (§ 10), with no exclusion for offenders under supervision for offenses committed before that date. The prospect of additional punishment through the contempt provision for offenders whose offenses occurred before the law's passage may run afoul of the Ex Post Facto Clause.

20. G.S. 15A-1368.2(b).

21. *Id.*

Chapter 5A. The Commission can, after holding a plenary contempt proceeding under G.S. 5A-15 and finding beyond a reasonable doubt that an offender willfully refused to accept or comply with PRS, punish a person by up to 30 days' imprisonment under G.S. 5A-12. Under G.S. 15A-1368.2(b), notwithstanding any other provision of law, any contempt punishment does not count for credit for time served against the underlying sentence.[22] The new law also provides that any time spent imprisoned "due to the prisoner's resistance to . . . release" must "toll the running of the period of supervised release."[23] "Tolling" in this context appears to mean that time does not run off the offender's period of supervised release while he or she is imprisoned for the contempt.

In light of the changes to maximum sentences for Class B1–E sex offenders, the North Carolina Sentencing and Policy Advisory Commission issued a new table of maximum punishments exclusively for those offenses.[24] Table 1.1 summarizes the PRS laws for nonreportable offenses (those that do not require registration as a sex offender) and reportable offenses, based on offense class and offense date.

C. Sentencing Multiple Convictions after the JRA

Consecutive Sentences

Under G.S. 15A-1354(b), when a person is sentenced to consecutive felonies, the Division of Adult Correction treats that person as though he or she has been committed for a single, aggregate term. The minimum of the aggregate term is the sum of all the individual minimum sentences in the string of consecutive judgments. The aggregate maximum is the sum of all the individual maximums, reduced as needed to account for the fact that additional time was built into the maximum sentence of every PRS-eligible offense.[25] That subtraction is necessary because the defendant will serve only one period of

---

22. That provision may conflict with *State v. Belcher*, 173 N.C. App. 620 (2005), in which the court of appeals held that a revoked probationer was entitled to credit for time spent jailed for contempt in response to a violation of probation under G.S. 15A-1344(e1).

23. G.S. 15A-1368.2(b).

24. The chart is available at www.nccourts.org/Courts/CRS/Councils/spac/Documents/SexOffenderTable_12_01_11.pdf.

25. G.S. 15A-1354(b).

post-release supervision upon release from prison, even if subject to multiple PRS-eligible judgments. This rule of sentence administration, a statutory requirement since the inception of Structured Sentencing, is referred to as the single-sentence rule.

Under prior law there was only one type of PRS: 9 months of supervised release for Class B1–E felonies. Thus, the subtraction necessary to account for duplicate post-release terms in a string of consecutive judgments was relatively straightforward. When a court imposed consecutive terms of imprisonment for more than one Class B1–E felony, the prison system subtracted 9 months from the aggregate maximum for each second or subsequent Class B1–E felony. The defendant was released from prison to PRS 9 months before attaining the adjusted aggregate maximum to serve a 9-month period of supervised release.

Under the new law there are three types of post-release supervision: 60-month PRS for Class B1–E reportable felonies, 12-month PRS for Class B1–E nonreportable felonies, and 9-month PRS for Class F–I felonies.[26] Consecutive sentences are, as a result, more complicated to administer. As under prior law, the consecutive sentence is treated as a single term whose aggregate minimum sentence is the sum of the individual minimums.[27] The aggregate maximum sentence is the sum of all the individual maximums, "less 12 months for each of the second and subsequent sentences imposed for Class B through Class E felonies, or less 60 months for each second or subsequent [reportable] Class B1 through E felony . . . , and less nine months for each of the second and subsequent sentences imposed for Class F through Class I felonies."[28]

Parallel changes to G.S. 15A-1368.2(a) state that prisoners will be released from prison 60, 12, or 9 months before attaining their maximum sentence, less earned time, depending on whether they are serving a Class B1–E reportable offense, a Class B1–E nonreportable offense, or a Class F–I offense, respectively.

The new aggregate maximum provision—amended twice in 2011 by two different bills—is susceptible to multiple interpretations. It is unclear,

---

26. There is actually a fourth type of post-release supervision, 4-month PRS for aggravated level one impaired driving under G.S. 20-179(f3), but it is not mentioned in G.S. 15A-1354(b).

27. G.S. 15A-1354(b).

28. *Id.*

Table 1.1.   Post-release supervision for nonreportable and reportable offenses

	Maximum Sentence	Mandatory release to PRS	PRS period
Nonreportable			
Class B1–E felonies Committed before Dec. 1, 2011	120% of minimum plus 9 months	Maximum less 9 months, less earned time	9 months
Class B1–E felonies Committed on/after Dec. 1, 2011	120% of minimum plus 12 months	Maximum less 12 months, less earned time	12 months
Class F–I felonies Committed before Dec. 1, 2011	120% of minimum	No PRS	None
Class F–I felonies Committed on/after Dec. 1, 2011	120% of minimum plus 9 months	Maximum less 9 months, less earned time	9 months
Reportable			
Class B1–E felonies Committed before Dec. 1, 2011	120% of minimum plus 9 months	Maximum less 9 months, less earned time	60 months
Class B1–E felonies Committed on/after Dec. 1, 2011	120% of minimum plus 60 months	Maximum less 60 months, less earned time	60 months
Class F–I felonies Committed before Dec. 1, 2011	120% of minimum	No PRS	None
Class F–I felonies Committed on/after Dec. 1, 2011	120% of minimum plus 9 months	Maximum less 9 months, less earned time	60 months

for example, whether the order in which the consecutive judgments are entered matters when determining which of them is "first" and which are "second and subsequent" within the meaning of the statute. (The order did not matter under prior law, when there was only one type of PRS.) The literal language of the statute also suggests that DAC should subtract for only the second and subsequent sentences imposed for each type of PRS-eligible offense.

The apparent intent of the law is that a defendant who receives consecutive sentences for multiple PRS-eligible felonies will serve a single post-release supervision period upon release from prison. The length of that PRS period, the date of release, and the imprisonment time to be served in the event of revocation will be dictated by the defendant's most serious offense. The most serious offense controls regardless of the order in which the judgments are imposed, and the additional time built into the maximum sentences for all but the most serious offense is subtracted from the aggregate maximum. Thus, a defendant serving consecutive sentences for a Class B1–E sex crime, a Class B1–E nonreportable crime, and a Class F–I crime would be released from prison 60 months before attaining the maximum sentence, less earned time, to serve a single 60-month period of PRS with 60 months of remaining imprisonment to be served in the event of revocation. The prison system would subtract a total of 21 months from his aggregate maximum sentence: 12 months for the Class B1–E nonreportable offense and 9 months for the Class F–I offense.

Court officials should note that the single-sentence rule is a rule of sentence administration, not a rule of sentencing. Judges should not, when imposing consecutive felony sentences, deduct any time from the maximum sentence entered on the judgment for the "second and subsequent" felonies.

Should the court inform the defendant of the impact of the single-sentence rule when accepting a plea to consecutive felonies? Under G.S. 15A-1022(a)(6), the court must inform the defendant of the maximum possible sentence on the charge, including the maximum possible from consecutive sentences. The Transcript of Plea form from the Administrative Office of the Courts, AOC-CR-300, has a place for the court to note the maximum punishment for each offense and a line at the bottom to record the total maximum punishment. If the defendant is pleading guilty to multiple PRS-eligible offenses, that total maximum will overstate the defendant's maximum exposure to imprisonment if it fails to account for the subtraction rule of G.S. 15A-1354(b). That overstatement may, depending on its scope, call into question whether the defendant's plea was knowing, voluntary, and intelligent.[29] Thus, the court may wish to inform the defendant that, in light of G.S. 15A-1354(b), the

---

29. *See* Jessica Smith, "Overstating Possible Punishment and the (In)voluntary Nature of the Plea," *North Carolina Criminal Law, UNC School of Government Blog* (Mar. 27, 2012), http://nccriminallaw.sog.unc.edu/?p=3440.

maximum possible total sentence may be less than the sum of the individual sentences.

Consolidation of Offenses

Especially for the next few years, many defendants will be before the court for sentencing on multiple offenses, some of which will have occurred before December 1, 2011, and some on or after that date. May a pre–December 1, 2011, offense be consolidated with a more recent offense subject to the revised sentencing provisions under the JRA? Under Structured Sentencing, if an offender is convicted of more than one offense at the same time, the court generally may consolidate the offenses for judgment and impose a single judgment for the consolidated offenses. That single judgment will contain a sentence for the class of offense and prior record level of the "most serious offense."[30] But can acts sentenced under different versions of Structured Sentencing be consolidated for judgment? Some authority suggests they may not. In *State v. Branch*, 134 N.C. App. 637 (1999), the court of appeals considered whether it was permissible to consolidate an offense sentenced under the Fair Sentencing Act (the sentencing law in effect from 1981 to 1994) with a Structured Sentencing offense. The defendant initially received a consolidated Structured Sentencing judgment for multiple offenses with offense dates that spanned the Fair Sentencing–Structured Sentencing divide. After being informed by the Department of Correction that Fair Sentencing and Structured Sentencing cases could not be combined, the trial court resentenced the defendant, entering two separate judgments under the law applicable to each. The defendant argued on appeal that there was no prohibition on consolidating offenses committed before and after the implementation of Structured Sentencing. The court of appeals disagreed, saying that each crime should be sentenced according to its own rules and that separate judgments were therefore required.

The non-consolidation rule from *Branch* may not control for pre- and post-JRA cases. The changes made by the JRA are not as dramatic as the shift from Fair Sentencing to Structured Sentencing, and the sentences are therefore more compatible. Moreover, Structured Sentencing cases on either side of the December 1, 2011, divide are all subject to the very same version of G.S. 15A-1340.15(b) regarding consolidation. The JRA did not amend that statute.

---

30. G.S. 15A-1340.15(b).

Even if there is no per se prohibition on consolidating pre- and post-JRA cases, there may be practical reasons to avoid consolidating them. First, it may be difficult in some circumstances to gauge which is the most serious offense within the meaning of G.S. 15A-1340.15(b). For example, in light of the additional time added onto maximum sentences for PRS, a post–December 1, 2011, Class I felony might have a longer maximum sentence (17 months) than a pre–December 1 Class G offense (16 months) sentenced at the same prior record level. It is not clear which offense would be the lead offense for purposes of the consolidated judgment.

Second, different conditions of probation apply to offenses committed before and after December 1, 2011. The Justice Reinvestment Act changed the definitions of community and intermediate punishment, added a statutory absconding condition, and allowed different forms of confinement and delegated authority for offenses committed on or after December 1, 2011. The boilerplate language on the forms for different offense dates varies accordingly. To be clear about which probation conditions apply to each individual case, the judge must enter a separate judgment (using the appropriate judgment form) for each offense.

D. Post-Release Supervision after the JRA

Post-release supervision is similar to probation in some respects, but there are key differences. The same officers who supervise probationers also supervise post-release supervisees, but the controlling authority in PRS cases—the body that sets the conditions of supervision and conducts hearings on violations of those conditions—is the Post-Release Supervision and Parole Commission, not the court. Post-release supervision violation hearings are governed by G.S. 15A-1368.5, which the JRA did not amend. A supervisee alleged to have violated the conditions of supervision is entitled to a preliminary hearing, typically held in the local jail, and then a final hearing before the full Commission, held at Central Prison in Raleigh.[31]

The JRA's expansion of the PRS law will cause a sharp increase in the number of post-release supervisees in the state. The fiscal note accompanying the JRA indicated that the number of new supervisees would increase

31. G.S. 15A-1368.5.

from around 2,000 to over 14,000 each year.[32] In anticipation of a surge in PRS violation hearings, the General Assembly directed two half-time parole commissioners to transition to full-time status in 2012 and added another full-time commissioner to begin in 2013, bringing the total number of commissioners to four.[33] The legislature also authorized the Commission to conduct parole and PRS violation hearings and contempt hearings for sex offenders via videoconference, effective December 1, 2012.[34] Questions may arise as to whether a hearing conducted via videoconference satisfies constitutional due process requirements,[35] particularly in the context of a hearing on a supervisee's alleged criminal contempt.[36]

Absconding

The JRA added a new controlling condition of PRS prohibiting the supervisee from absconding by "willfully avoiding supervision or by willfully making the supervisee's whereabouts unknown to the supervising probation officer."[37] The condition is the same as the absconding condition applicable to probationers.[38]

Limits on Revocation of Post-Release Supervision

The JRA limits the authority of the Post-Release Supervision and Parole Commission to revoke offenders' PRS in much the same way that it limits courts' authority to revoke probation. Effective for offenses committed on or after December 1, 2011,[39] the Commission may only fully revoke PRS—that

---

32. "Legislative Fiscal Note: House Bill 642 (Sixth Edition)," General Assembly of North Carolina, Fiscal Research Division (June 14, 2011), www.ncleg.net/Sessions/2011/FiscalNotes/House/PDF/HFN0642v6.pdf.

33. S.L. 2012-142, § 25.1.(g).

34. S.L. 2012-188, § 7; G.S. 143B-720.

35. *See* Wilkins v. Timmerman-Cooper, 512 F.3d 768 (6th Cir. 2008) (upholding, on federal habeas review, a state parole violation hearing in which a parole officer and a witness testified against the parolee via videoconference).

36. *See* S.E.C. v. Kimnes, 759 F. Supp. 430 (N.D. Ill. 1991) (discussing a defendant's constitutional rights to be present and to confront witnesses at a criminal contempt hearing).

37. G.S. 15A-1368.4(e)(7a).

38. *See infra* "G. Absconding" in Chapter 2.

39. S.L. 2011-192, § 2.(j).

is, return the supervisee to prison to complete the entire remaining sentence of imprisonment—for

- violations of the "not commit another crime" condition in G.S. 15A-1368.4(b);
- violations of the new statutory absconding condition in G.S. 15A-1368.4(e)(7a), described above; or
- any violation by a supervisee convicted of an offense for which registration as a sex offender is required.[40]

The Commission is statutorily authorized to re-release inmates after a full revocation[41] but has, over the years, generally declined to do so.

For other types of violations the Commission may not revoke PRS. Instead, it may return the offender to prison for three months, after which the offender must be released back onto PRS. Supervisees may be returned to prison for additional 3-month stints in response to subsequent technical violations until no time remains on their maximum imposed terms. Thus, Class F–I felons (who have 9 months of imprisonment remaining when initially released to PRS) may be returned to prison three times, while Class B1–E felons (who have 12 months remaining) may be returned four times.[42]

Tolling during Re-Imprisonment

An amendment to G.S. 15A-1368.3(c)(1) in North Carolina Session Law (hereinafter S.L.) 2012-188 (hereinafter the 2012 Clarifications Act) makes clear that a person's PRS period is tolled when that person is re-imprisoned for a violation. For example, a supervisee who commits a technical violation in the eighth month of a 9-month post-release supervision period will have 1 month of PRS left to serve in the community upon release from a 3-month term of reimprisonment.[43] This amendment is effective for PRS violations that occur on or after July 16, 2012.

The amended law also adds that a supervisee is not to be re-released onto PRS if the supervisee has served all the time remaining on his or her maximum imposed term. This change applies to all supervisees, including sex offenders. Under prior law, sex offenders were sometimes kept under super-

40. G.S. 15A-1368.3(c)(1).
41. G.S. 15A-1368.3(d).
42. G.S. 15A-1368.4(c)(1).
43. S.L. 2012-188, § 4.

vision even after the conclusion of their full term of imprisonment, with the conditions of supervision enforced through the Commission's contempt power.[44] That practice is apparently not permissible under the revised law.

E. Advanced Supervised Release (ASR)

The JRA created a new early-release program called Advanced Supervised Release (ASR). Through ASR, certain inmates are eligible for release from prison before serving their minimum sentences if they complete risk reduction incentive programs while in prison. Advanced Supervised Release is effective for defendants who enter a plea or are found guilty on or after January 1, 2012, regardless of the offense date.[45] The law is the first statutory provision allowing a Structured Sentencing inmate to be released before completing his or her minimum sentence.

The sentencing judge determines in his or her discretion whether an eligible defendant will be admitted into the ASR program. When imposing an active sentence for an eligible defendant, the court may, in its discretion and without objection from the prosecutor, order DAC to admit the defendant into the ASR program. Only defendants ordered by the court may be admitted; DAC may not enroll inmates into the program without a court order. And no defendant may be ordered into the program over the prosecutor's objection.[46]

If the court orders a defendant into the program, it must impose both a regular sentence (pursuant to the ordinary felony sentencing grid) and an ASR date. The latest version of the felony active sentence judgment form, AOC-CR-601, includes space for both sentences. If the defendant completes the requisite risk reduction incentives as identified by DAC, or is unable to complete them through no fault of his or her own, then the defendant will be released on the ASR date.[47] If the defendant is terminated from the ASR program, the ASR date is nullified and the defendant's release date is determined based on the regular minimum and maximum term imposed by the court. Even a prisoner who has already completed the assigned risk

---

44. *See supra* notes 19–23 and accompanying text.
45. S.L. 2011-192, § 5.(e).
46. G.S. 15A-1340.18(c).
47. G.S. 15A-1340.18(e).

reduction incentives can see his or her ASR date nullified on account of noncompliance with DAC rules or regulations.[48]

There is no express statutory obligation for any party to consider the possibility of ASR and no requirement of notice to the defendant, the prosecutor, or the court in advance of such consideration. However, the defendant or the defendant's lawyer would probably want to ask the court for an ASR date in every eligible case in which sentencing is left to the court's discretion. In cases where ASR is ordered, the defendant must be notified at sentencing that if he or she completes the risk reduction incentives as identified by DAC, then he or she will be released on the ASR date."[49] Presumably the sentencing judge should give that notification when pronouncing judgment—page one, side two, of the AOC-CR-601 includes a check-box for doing so—although the statute provides that DAC is ultimately responsible for determining the exact ASR release date.[50]

ASR Date

The ASR date itself is not a discretionary matter; rather, it flows from the defendant's regular sentence. It is calculated differently depending on whether that regular sentence is (a) from the presumptive or aggravated range or (b) from the mitigated range. If the defendant's regular sentence is from the presumptive or aggravated range, no calculation is necessary: the ASR date is simply the shortest mitigated minimum sentence the defendant could have received based on his or her conviction offense and prior record level. Put another way, the ASR date in those cases is the number in the lower left-hand corner of the defendant's grid cell on the front of the sentencing grid. If the defendant's regular sentence is from the mitigated range, the ASR date is 80 percent of the minimum sentence imposed. Because the law does not include a rounding provision, the court should probably indicate fractional months in the "ASR date" block on the judgment form when necessary.

---

48. G.S. 15A-1340.18(f). It is unclear as a matter of statute what happens when a defendant completes his or her risk reduction incentives after the ASR date has passed but before the end of the regular sentence. It is likewise unclear whether a defendant with jail credit that exceeds his or her ASR date should be released to PRS immediately upon being sentenced.

49. G.S. 15A-1340.18(e).

50. *Id.*

Applying those rules, a Class G, prior record level III defendant who receives any sentence from the presumptive or aggravated range would have an ASR date of 10 months. If the defendant receives a sentence from the mitigated range, for instance 11–23 months, then the ASR date is 80 percent of the minimum sentence imposed, or 8.8 months.

Apparently the ASR date is served "flat"—that is, unreduced by any sentence credits (earned time) applicable to the inmate's maximum sentence. Such credits should nevertheless be recorded for an ASR inmate. They would factor into the determination of the defendant's release date if the defendant were terminated from the ASR program or returned to prison upon revocation of PRS.

ASR Eligibility

Defendants must be convicted and sentenced based upon the following felony classes and prior record levels to be eligible for ASR:

- Class D, Prior Record Level I–III
- Class E, Prior Record Level I–IV
- Class F, Prior Record Level I–V
- Class G, Prior Record Level I–VI
- Class H, Prior Record Level I–VI[51]

Table 1.2 illustrates these classes and levels in the context of the standard felony punishment chart. The law does not explicitly exclude defendants sentenced under the habitual felon law, but defendants sentenced as Class C felons under the habitual felon law apparently would be excluded under the language of the eligibility criteria set out above.

The effective date for ASR in the JRA indicates that defendants falling in the indicated grid cells who enter a plea or are found guilty on or after January 1, 2012, are eligible for the program.[52] However, it is unclear how the law works for Class F, G, and H felons convicted after January 1, 2012, based on offenses that occurred prior to December 1, 2011. Those defendants do not receive PRS and therefore have no supervised release to be released to in advance.[53] Arguably the ASR law—which assumes the defendant will be

---

51. G.S. 15A-1340.18(a)(2).

52. S.L. 2011-192, § 5.(e).

53. One could argue that G.S. 15A-1340.18(g) creates a new type of PRS for all ASR-eligible defendants. The law says that a defendant "released on the ASR date is subject

Table 1.2. ASR-eligible offenses and prior record levels

	I 0-1 Pt	II 2-5 Pts	III 6-9 Pts	IV 10-13 Pts	V 14-17 Pts	VI 18+ Pts
A	Death or Life Without Parole					
B1	A 240 - 300 192 - 240 144 - 192	A 276 - 345 221 - 276 166 - 221	A 317 -397 254 - 317 190 - 254	A 365 - 456 292 - 365 219 - 292	A Life Without Parole 336 - 420 252 - 336	A Life Without Parole 386 - 483 290 - 386
B2	A 157 - 196 125 - 157 94 - 125	A 180 - 225 144 - 180 108 - 144	A 207 - 258 165 - 207 124 - 165	A 238 - 297 190 - 238 143 - 190	A 273 - 342 219 - 273 164 - 219	A 314 - 393 251 - 314 189 - 251
C	A 73 - 92 58 - 73 44 - 58	A 83 - 104 67 - 83 50 - 67	A 96 - 120 77 - 96 58 - 77	A 110 - 138 88 - 110 66 - 88	A 127 - 159 101 - 127 76 - 101	A 146 - 182 117 - 146 87 - 117
D	A 64 - 80 51 - 64 38 - 51	A 73 - 92 59 - 73 44 - 59	A 84 - 105 67 - 84 51 - 67	A 97 - 121 78 - 97 58 - 78	A 111 - 139 89 - 111 67 - 89	A 128 - 160 103 - 128 77 - 103
E	I/A 25 - 31 20 - 25 15 - 20	I/A 29 - 36 23 - 29 17 - 23	A 33 - 41 26 - 33 20 - 26	A 38 - 48 30 - 38 23 - 30	A 44 - 55 35 - 44 26 - 35	A 50 - 63 40 - 50 30 - 40
F	I/A 16 - 20 13 - 16 10 - 13	I/A 19 - 23 15 - 19 11 - 15	I/A 21 - 27 17 - 21 13 - 17	A 25 - 31 20 - 25 15 - 20	A 28 - 36 23 - 28 17 - 23	A 33 - 41 26 - 33 20 - 26
G	I/A 13 - 16 10 - 13 8 - 10	I/A 14 - 18 12 - 14 9 - 12	I/A 17 - 21 13 - 17 10 - 13	I/A 19 - 24 15 - 19 11 - 15	A 22 - 27 17 - 22 13 - 17	A 25 - 31 20 - 25 15 - 20
H	C/I/A 6 - 8 5 - 6 4 - 5	I/A 8 - 10 6 - 8 4 - 6	I/A 10 - 12 8 - 10 6 - 8	I/A 11 - 14 9 - 11 7 - 9	I/A 15 - 19 12 - 15 9 - 12	A 20 - 25 16 - 20 12 - 16
I	C 6 - 8 4 - 6 3 - 4	C/I 6 - 8 4 - 6 3 - 4	I 6 - 8 5 - 6 4 - 5	I/A 8 - 10 6 - 8 4 - 6	I/A 9 - 11 7 - 9 5 - 7	I/A 10 - 12 8 - 10 6 - 8

released from prison to PRS upon completion of his or her risk reduction incentives—should not apply to these defendants at all.[54] In actuality, many low-level felons who are ineligible for PRS have, as of this writing, already been ordered into the ASR program. The prison system and the Commission have determined that these defendants will, upon successful completion of their risk reduction incentives, simply be released outright on their ASR date, with no supervision in the community.

The law appears to limit ASR eligibility to defendants for whom the court imposes an active sentence at the outset; defendants sentenced to probation but later revoked apparently are ineligible to be ordered into the program by the revoking judge.[55]

ASR and Drug Trafficking

The ASR law does not explicitly exclude drug trafficking offenses from its coverage, but how the law would apply to those offenses as a practical matter is unclear. The ASR date is determined based on the "shortest mitigated sentence for the offense at the offender's prior record level."[56] Neither of those determining factors makes sense as applied to drug trafficking: there are no mitigated sentences for drug trafficking under G.S. 90-95(h), and drug trafficking sentences do not take prior record level into account.

---

to post-release supervision under this Article"—meaning Article 81B, Structured Sentencing, where the ASR law is codified. Existing PRS law is set out in Article 84A of G.S. Chapter 15A, not Article 81B. If ASR is a new type of PRS under Article 81B, that statute does not specify how this new type of PRS operates.

54. G.S. 15A-1340.18(a)(1) (defining ASR as a "release from prison and placement on post-release supervision").

55. G.S. 15A-1340.18(c) ("When imposing an active sentence for an eligible defendant . . . the court . . . may order that the Department of Correction admit the defendant to the ASR program."); G.S. 15A-1340.18(a)(1) ("'Advanced supervised release' . . . means release from prison and placement on post-release supervision under this section if an eligible defendant is sentenced to active time."). *Active punishment* is a defined term under Structured Sentencing referring to an unsuspended term of imprisonment. G.S. 15A-1340.11(1). The ASR law also describes mandatory notifications to the defendant that must be completed "at sentencing," indicating that an ASR date may not be ordered for the first time upon revocation of probation. G.S. 15A-1340.18(e). On the other hand, a separate reference to "active punishment" in the JRA has been interpreted to apply to active and activated sentences alike. *See supra* notes 12–15 and accompanying text (discussing the scope of PRS).

56. G.S. 15A-1340.18(d).

Risk Reduction Incentives

New G.S. 15A-1340.18(b) authorizes DAC to create risk reduction incentives for defendants admitted to the ASR program. By statute, these incentives should consist of treatment, education, and rehabilitative programs designed to reduce participating offenders' likelihood of reoffending. According to DAC policy, the incentives fall into three categories: programs, services, and activities.[57] "Programs" include cognitive behavioral interventions, substance abuse treatment, and the like, while "services" and "activities" tend to include things that involve less direct interaction with prison staff, such as Alcoholics Anonymous.

Revocation of ASR

Inmates who obtain an early release through ASR are subject to the type of PRS ordinarily applicable to inmates with their offense dates and offense classes (9 months of PRS for Class F, G, and H felons with offense dates after December 1, 2011; 12 months of PRS for Class D and E felons with offense dates after December 1, 2011; and so on). ASR supervisees will, however, generally have more imprisonment time remaining to be served in the event of revocation than the typical non-ASR defendant, because the defendant's maximum is not reduced to correspond to the ASR date. For instance, the ASR date for a Class E, Level I, offender sentenced in the presumptive range to 20–36 months is 15 months. If the defendant completes risk reduction incentives and is released to PRS at 15 months, he or she will be on PRS for 12 months with 21 months of imprisonment (less any earned time accrued) remaining to be served in the event of revocation, instead of the typical 12 months.

Offenders released early onto PRS through ASR are subject to the revocation limitations set out in G.S. 15A-1368.3(c). That is, these offenders may be revoked for only new criminal offenses or absconding, or, if they are serving a sentence for a reportable sex crime, for any violation. For other violations they may be returned to prison for three 3-month periods of confinement and then returned to prison for the entire time remaining on their maximum term of imprisonment in the event of any subsequent violation. Once returned to prison for a fourth violation, the defendant is ineligible

---

57. STATE OF NORTH CAROLINA, DEP'T OF PUBLIC SAFETY, DIV. OF ADULT CORRECTION, SECTION OF PRISONS, POLICIES AND PROCEDURES (2012) § C.2603(a).

for further PRS release regardless of the amount of time remaining to be served.[58] Thus, the Class E offender described above could be returned to prison for three 3-month periods in response to technical violations and then returned to serve the remaining 12 months of imprisonment in the event of a fourth violation.

The law requires DAC to adopt policies and procedures for documenting an inmate's progress through the ASR program and for terminating inmates from the program due to a lack of progress or pattern of noncompliance with the program or other rules or regulations.[59] The same statute also directs DAC to adopt policies for "the assessment to occur at diagnostic processing," but there is no other reference to an assessment in the law.

Multiple Sentences

The ASR law itself does not address how an ASR sentence should be administered for a defendant subject to multiple judgments. For instance, a defendant convicted of two crimes might be ordered into the ASR program in one or both of the sentences. If the defendant is ordered into ASR in both sentences and they are run consecutively, the prison system will likely sum the ASR dates to determine the earliest possible point of release. For example, a defendant who receives two 8–19 month sentences with ASR dates of 6 months for each would have an aggregate ASR date of 12 months and would apparently be eligible for release onto PRS at that point if the defendant had completed the assigned risk reduction incentives.

Less clear is how the prison system will administer an ASR sentence run consecutively to a non-ASR sentence. In general, the single-sentence rule of G.S. 15A-1354 directs DAC to aggregate the minimum and maximum sentences of all the judgments in a consecutive string and then release the person when he or she has served the aggregate maximum, less earned time, and less a number of months equal to the PRS period that the person will serve. That approach will not work for an ASR sentence, however, because the release date is dictated by the inmate's service of the ASR term instead of by reference to the maximum sentence. Waiting to release the defendant until he or she is, for example, 9 months from the aggregate maximum sentence would negate the effect of the ASR date. The prison system has not issued regulations describing how it will administer such sentences.

---

58. G.S. 15A-1340.18(g).

59. G.S. 15A-1340.18(h). *See* Prisons, Policies and Procedures, *supra* note 57.

F. Drug Trafficking

As originally passed in 2011, the JRA did not add any time onto the maximum sentences for drug trafficking set out in G.S. 90-95(h). That omission led to confusion about whether defendants sentenced for trafficking crimes were eligible for release onto PRS. Previously, there were some indications that PRS applied to drug trafficking offenses and some indications that it did not. Under G.S. 15A-1368.1 as it existed at that time, PRS applied to all felons sentenced under Article 81B of G.S. Chapter 15A, Structured Sentencing. On the one hand, drug trafficking crimes are not sentenced under the regular sentencing grid set out in Article 81B. They are, rather, sentenced pursuant to the minimum and maximum sentences set out in G.S. 90-95(h). On the other hand, the statute setting out the applicability of Structured Sentencing says that the law applies to criminal offenses other than impaired driving and certain health control measures.[60] In other words, the law explicitly excludes certain crimes from Structured Sentencing's coverage, but drug trafficking crimes are not excluded. If the relevant provisions are read together, drug trafficking appears to be a Structured Sentencing offense that happens to have an alternative punishment provided for by law—a possibility expressly allowed for by G.S. 15A-1340.17(d) and (e).[61] As a practical matter, maximum sentences for class C, D, and E traffickers have long been 120 percent of the minimum plus 9 months, indicating an expectation that traffickers would, like other Class B1–E felons from that timeframe, be released onto PRS 9 months before attaining their maximum sentences.

By requiring PRS for all felons but not increasing maximum sentences for trafficking, the JRA created a statutory conflict. Class G and H traffickers will be due for release onto PRS when they are 9 months from completing their maximum sentence under G.S. 15A-1368.2(a). But because their maximum is only 120 percent of their minimum (instead of 120 percent plus 9 months, like other Class F–I felons), that PRS release date necessarily will come before they have served the minimum sentence, as required by G.S. 15A-1340.13(d). For example, a Class H drug trafficker who receives a 25–30 month sentence would, at the very latest, be due for release on PRS after serving 21 months. Thus, G.S. 15A-1368.2(a) will command the offender's release well before he or she has served the 25-month minimum.

---

60. G.S. 15A-1340.10.

61. G.S. 15A-1340.17(d) ("Unless provided otherwise in a statute establishing a punishment for a specific crime, [punishment] is as specified in the table . . . .").

The 2012 Clarifications Act resolved the confusion for drug trafficking offenses committed on or after December 1, 2012.[62] First, the act amended G.S. 15A-1368.1 to provide explicitly that the PRS law applies to drug trafficking offenses sentenced under G.S. 90-95(h). The act then added 3 months to the maximum sentences for Class C, D, and E trafficking (so that maximum sentences in those cases are 120 percent of the minimum plus 12 months) and 9 months to the maximum sentences for Class F, G, and H trafficking (so that maximums in those cases are 120 percent of the minimum plus 9 months). With that additional time built into the maximum sentences, the PRS release date will not arrive before the defendant has served the minimum.

As for trafficking offenses that occurred after the passage of the JRA but before the effective date of the Clarifications Act (between December 1, 2011, and November 30, 2012), there are different ways to reconcile the conflict between the PRS-release rule and the minimum sentence rule. The best way to preserve as much as possible of both rules might be to release a person to PRS when the person is within 9 months of his or her maximum sentence and has served the minimum. If that rule is applied to the Class H trafficker described in the example above, the inmate would be released from prison after serving 25 months to serve 9 months of PRS, with the possibility of reimprisonment for 5 months (or less, depending on earned time) in the event of revocation. Other interpretations are also possible.

G. Changes to the Habitual Felon Laws

The JRA made two changes related to recidivist sentencing provisions. It softened the sentencing provision of the existing habitual felon law and created a new habitual breaking and entering status offense. The discussion that follows uses the term "substantive felony" to describe the offense sentenced under the habitual sentencing provision and the term "previous felony" to describe the prior offenses that qualify the person as a habitual offender. The terms "underlying felony" and "predicate felony" will be avoided.[63]

---

62. S.L. 2012-188.

63. *See* Jeffrey B. Welty, *North Carolina's Habitual Felon and Violent Habitual Felon Laws*, ADMIN. OF JUSTICE BULLETIN No. 2008/04 (UNC School of Government,

Amendments to the Existing Habitual Felon Law

The JRA amended the sentencing provisions of the existing habitual felon law—the first such changes since the enactment of Structured Sentencing. The changes were a downward adjustment (making many habitual felon sentences less severe from the defendant's viewpoint) largely in response to the fact that many habitual felon sentences under prior law were sentenced in the mitigated range.[64]

Under the revised law, effective for substantive felonies committed on or after December 1, 2011,[65] a habitualized substantive felony is punished "at a felony class level that is four classes higher than the principal felony . . . but under no circumstances . . . higher than a Class C felony."[66] In summary, the practical effect of that change is as follows:

If the substantive felony is	It is sentenced under the habitual felon law as
Class I	Class E
Class H	Class D
Class G or more serious	Class C

The revised law makes no change to the counting or weighing of previous felonies.

Under the revised law, some Class I felons habitualized to Class E will fall into "I/A" cells on the sentencing grid, making it possible that a habitual felon could be sentenced to probation. Any suspended sentence ordered for

2008), http://sogpubs.unc.edu/electronicversions/pdfs/aojb0804.pdf (adopting the same terminology).

64. Under prior law all substantive felonies sentenced under the habitual felon law, regardless of their offense class, were sentenced as Class C felonies. With that rule in place, 70 percent of all habitual felons received sentences from the mitigated range, compared to 33 percent of felonies generally. *See* "2010/11 Statistical Report," *supra* note 14, at 23.

65. S.L. 2011-192, § 3.(e).

66. G.S. 14-7.6. The new four-class enhancement is similar to a three-class alternative proposed by the North Carolina Sentencing and Policy Advisory Commission in 2002. *See* "Report on Study of Structured Sentencing Pursuant to Session Law 2001-424, Section 25.8," North Carolina Sentencing and Policy Advisory Commssion (2002), www.nccourts.org/Courts/CRS/Councils/spac/Documents/finalreport-2002.pdf, 6.

a habitualized felony probably must be set to run at the expiration of any other sentence being served by the defendant in the event of revocation.[67]

The revised law applies to substantive felonies that occur on or after December 1, 2011, but expressly does not affect prosecutions based on offenses committed before that date.[68] Thus, defendants being prosecuted for substantive felonies committed prior to December 1, 2011, and inmates already serving sentences imposed under the habitual felon law are apparently not entitled to relief on account of the revised law.

New Habitual Breaking and Entering Status Offense

The JRA created a new status offense of habitual breaking and entering. The law was enacted in response to prosecutors and law enforcement officials who said in Council of State Governments focus groups that breaking and entering crimes were a particular public safety concern. They "expressed frustration at having to wait until a fourth felony conviction to sentence a [breaking and entering] offender to a lengthy [habitual felon] prison sentence."[69]

Under the new law, a defendant may, in the discretion of the district attorney, be charged with the status offense of habitual breaking and entering upon the defendant's second or subsequent conviction of felony *breaking and entering* (defined below). In other words, the defendant is eligible for an enhanced sentence upon his or her second "strike" instead of the fourth as under the regular habitual felon law. A defendant convicted of a new substantive offense and found to be a habitual breaking and entering status offender is sentenced as if the substantive felony were a Class E offense.[70] The law is effective for substantive breaking and entering felonies committed on or after December 1, 2011.[71]

---

67. G.S. 14-7.6 ("Sentences imposed under this Article shall run consecutively with and shall commence at the expiration of any sentence being served by the person sentenced under this section.").

68. S.L. 2011-192, § 3.(e).

69. "Justice Reinvestment in North Carolina: Analysis and Policy Framework to Reduce Spending on Corrections and Reinvest in Strategies to Increase Public Safety," Council of State Governments Justice Center (2011), http://justicereinvestment.org/files/JR_North_Carolina_policy_framework_v8mg_mc.pdf, 16.

70. G.S. 14-7.31(a).

71. S.L. 2011-192, § 3.(e).

Qualifying offenses. The following felony offenses are defined as *breaking and entering* for purposes of the habitual breaking and entering law:

- First-degree burglary (G.S. 14-51)
- Second-degree burglary (G.S. 14-51)
- Breaking out of dwelling house burglary (G.S. 14-53)
- Breaking or entering buildings generally (G.S. 14-54(a))
- Breaking or entering a building that is a place of religious worship (G.S. 14-54.1)
- Any repealed or superseded offense substantially equivalent to any of the offenses listed above
- Any offense committed in another jurisdiction substantially similar to any of the offenses above[72]

This list doubles as the list of eligible previous and substantive felonies for purposes of the habitual breaking and entering law. However, some of the offenses on the list were obviously included primarily to be used as previous felonies. For example, the State would be unlikely to indict a person charged with a substantive offense of first-degree burglary as a habitual breaking and entering status offender. First-degree burglary is already a Class D offense, and sentencing as a habitual breaking and entering status offender would thus result in a lesser sentence.

Using language borrowed from the existing habitual felon law, the new law says that "felony offenses of breaking and entering committed before the person is 18 years of age shall not constitute more than one felony of breaking and entering."[73] Given that only one previous felony (not three) is necessary to qualify a defendant as a breaking and entering status offender, the practical effect of this rule is simply that a person's substantive felony must be committed after his or her eighteenth birthday.

A defendant's second breaking and entering felony qualifies for habitualization only if it is committed after the conviction of the first felony breaking and entering offense. In that regard, the new law is clearer than the regular habitual felon law, which prohibits overlapping first, second, and third prior

72. G.S. 14-7.25(1).
73. G.S. 14-7.26.

felonies but never explicitly says that a fourth or subsequent felony—the substantive felony—must occur after conviction of the third.[74]

Procedure. Operationally, the new habitual breaking and entering status offense is very similar to the regular habitual felon law. Like being a habitual felon, it is a status, not a crime. A person cannot be prosecuted simply for having a covered previous felony. Rather, there must be a conviction for a new substantive breaking and entering felony, to which the status offender sentencing provisions may then attach.

The new law clearly states that the indictment charging the defendant as a habitual breaking and entering status offender "shall be separate" from the indictment charging the substantive breaking and entering crime.[75] The statute thus avoids the longstanding inconsistency in G.S. 14-7.3, which apparently requires both a single and separate indictments in regular habitual felon cases.[76] The required contents of the breaking and entering status offender indictment are virtually the same as those required in a regular habitual felon indictment, and the defendant is similarly entitled to a 20-day waiting period before going to trial on the charge.[77] Other provisions regarding evidence of prior convictions and trial procedure likewise mirror the regular habitual felon law.

Sentencing. A defendant convicted under the habitual breaking and entering law is sentenced as a Class E felon. Any previous conviction used to establish a person's habitual breaking and entering status does not count toward that person's prior record level.[78]

Any sentence imposed under the new habitual breaking and entering law must run consecutively with any sentence "being served" by the defendant.[79] Similar language in other statutes, including the regular habitual felon law, has been interpreted to allow consolidated or concurrent sentences for convictions sentenced at the same time.[80]

---

74. Welty, *North Carolina's Habitual Felon and Violent Habitual Felon Laws, supra* note 63, at 6.

75. G.S. 14-7.28.

76. Welty, *North Carolina's Habitual Felon and Violent Habitual Felon Laws, supra* note 63, at 7–8.

77. G.S. 14-7.28(b).

78. G.S. 14-7.31(b).

79. *Id.*

80. State v. Haymond, 203 N.C. App. 151 (2010).

Under G.S. 14-7.31(c), a "conviction as a status offender under this Article shall not constitute commission of a felony for the purpose of either Article 2A or Article 2B of Chapter 14 of the General Statutes." Articles 2A and 2B are the habitual felon and violent habitual felon laws, respectively. The precise meaning of that provision is not clear, but it apparently restates the rule that being a habitual breaking and entering offender is a status, not a crime. Thus, a person's conviction as a status offender cannot itself qualify as a previous or substantive felony for other recidivist sentencing provisions.

Chapter 2

Changes to Probation

A. Community Punishment and Intermediate Punishment Redefined

Under Structured Sentencing there are two types of nonactive sentences: intermediate punishment and community punishment. Under prior law intermediate punishment was supervised probation that was required to include at least one of six specific conditions of probation: special probation (a split sentence), assignment to a residential program, electronic house arrest, intensive supervision, assignment to a day-reporting center, or drug treatment court.[1] A community punishment was defined by exception as any other nonactive sentence that did not include one of those six intermediate conditions.[2]

The Justice Reinvestment Act (JRA) made important changes to the definitions of community and intermediate punishment—changes generally intended to lessen the distinction between the two types of sentences. The changes are effective for "persons placed on probation based on offenses which occur on or after December 1, 2011"[3]—meaning the old definitions continue to apply to many thousands of probationers already on probation or yet to be placed on probation for offenses that occurred before that date.

The terms "community" and "intermediate" are part of Structured Sentencing under Article 81B of North Carolina General Statute (hereinafter G.S.)

---

1. N.C Gen. Stat. (hereinafter G.S.) § 15A-1340.11(6).
2. G.S. 15A-1340.11(2).
3. North Carolina Session Law (hereinafter S.L.) 2011-192, § 1.(*l*).

Chapter 15A. They thus apply only to Structured Sentencing cases and not to impaired driving under G.S. 20-138.1, failure to comply with health measures under G.S. 130A-25, and of course any offense committed before October 1, 1994.[4]

Intermediate Punishment

The JRA amended the definition of an intermediate punishment so that the court is no longer required to impose any particular conditions to make the sentence intermediate. Rather, the only mandatory component of an intermediate sentence is that the defendant must be placed on supervised probation. Aside from that, the new definition provides that the sentence may include drug treatment court,[5] special probation, or one or more of the "community and intermediate probation conditions" set out in new G.S. 15A-1343(a1), discussed below.[6] The revised definition does not reference intensive supervision or assignment to a residential program or a day-reporting center because, as discussed below, each of those conditions is repealed.

Community Punishment

Community punishment is redefined under the JRA as a sentence that does not include an active punishment, assignment to a drug treatment court, or special probation. The definition also now provides that community sentences may, like intermediate sentences, include any one or more of the new "community and intermediate probation conditions" set out in new

---

4. G.S. 15A-1340.10. Though G.S. 15A-1340.10 only expressly mentions impaired driving under G.S. 20-138.1, all of the crimes sentenced under G.S. 20-179 are generally thought to be excluded from Structured Sentencing. The other crimes sentenced under G.S. 20-179 are impaired driving in a commercial vehicle (G.S. 20-138.2) and second or subsequent convictions of operating a commercial vehicle after consuming (G.S. 20-138.2A) and operating a school bus or child care vehicle after consuming (G.S. 20-138.2B). *See* Shea Riggsbee Denning, *Sentencing for Impaired Driving under G.S. 20-179*, ADMIN. OF JUSTICE BULLETIN No. 2012/02 (UNC School of Government, 2012), http://sogpubs.unc.edu/electronicversions/pdfs/aojb1202.pdf, 4.

5. Drug treatment court remains in the law as a permissible condition of probation in spite of separate budgetary provisions ending state funding of the program. Some jurisdictions have found alternative funding sources for their drug treatment courts.

6. *See infra* C. New "Community and Intermediate Probation Conditions."

G.S. 15A-1343(a1). As under prior law, a community punishment can include supervised or unsupervised probation.

B. Repeal of Certain Intermediate Punishment Conditions

Effective for persons placed on probation based on offenses that occur on or after December 1, 2011, the JRA repealed several Structured Sentencing provisions related to intermediate punishment.

Intensive Supervision

The JRA repealed G.S. 15A-1340.11(5), the definition of intensive supervision, and the corresponding condition of probation in G.S. 15A-1343(b1)(3b) that required a probationer to submit to intensive supervision and abide by related departmental rules. Offenders ordered to intensive supervision generally were subject to multiple contacts by a probation officer each week, a curfew, and a requirement that they work or participate in a course of study or training. Intensive supervision was the most commonly imposed of the six intermediate conditions, used in over half of intermediate sentences.[7] Defendants with offense dates after December 1, 2011, may no longer be ordered to intensive supervision as part of their probation. A judge may, however, impose ad hoc conditions similar to those that would apply to a person under intensive supervision, such as a curfew.

The JRA did not repeal intensive supervision as a condition of post-release supervision (PRS) or the requirement that the Post-Release Supervision and Parole Commission make rules for the Intensive Post-Release Supervision Program.[8]

---

7. "Structured Sentencing Statistical Report for Felonies and Misdemeanors, Fiscal Year 2010/11," North Carolina Sentencing and Policy Advisory Commission (2012), www.nccourts.org/Courts/CRS/Councils/spac/Documents/statisticalrpt_fy10-11.pdf (hereinafter "2010/11 Statistical Report"), 25.

8. G.S. 15A-1368.4(e)(14); G.S. 143B-704(c).

Day-Reporting Center

The JRA also repealed G.S. 15A-1340.11(3), the definition of a day-reporting center (DRC). A DRC was a facility to which assigned offenders were required to report each day for a variety of activities, including counseling, treatment, and skills or employment training. The state's eighteen DRCs were funded principally through the Criminal Justice Partnership Program (CJPP), which the JRA also repealed.[9] Assignment to a DRC was a condition that would qualify a probationary sentence as an intermediate punishment under prior law, although less than 5 percent of all intermediate sentences required assignment to a DRC.[10] Because of the repeal of CJPP, DRCs generally ceased to accept new offenders on May 1, 2012, and closed on June 30, 2012. Some districts have chosen to continue operating their DRCs using local funds. In those areas DRC is a valid and enforceable intermediate punishment for persons on probation for offenses that occurred before December 1, 2011, and a valid special condition of probation under G.S. 15A-1343(b1)(10) for all offenders, regardless of offense date.

Residential Program

Third, the law repealed G.S. 15A-1340.11(8), which defined a residential program. The repeal of that definition does not, however, mean that probationers may no longer be ordered to attend residential programs such as DART-Cherry, Black Mountain Substance Abuse Treatment Center for Women, Triangle Residential Options for Substance Abusers (TROSA), or other similar programs. Rather, the repeal of the residential program definition, coupled with the amendment to the definition of an intermediate punishment, means that assignment to a residential program no longer carries the additional significance of converting a probationary sentence into an intermediate punishment. In that sense, the repeal of the statutory definition is an enabling change, allowing the court to assign any probationer—community or intermediate—to a residential program pursuant to the statutory special condition of probation in G.S. 15A-1343(b1)(2).[11]

---

9. See infra "J. Repeal of Criminal Justice Partnership Program and Creation of Treatment for Effective Community Supervision" for a discussion of the CJPP repeal.

10. "2010/11 Statistical Report," supra note 7, at 25.

11. Defendants ordered to submit to residential treatment at DART-Cherry or Black Mountain Substance Abuse Treatment Center for Women still must undergo a

Given the prospective offense date–based effective date applicable to the repeal of these provisions, thousands of probationers are still validly subject to each condition, and defendants sentenced today for offenses that occurred before December 1, 2011, can still validly be placed on intensive supervision, ordered into a residential program, or ordered to a day-reporting center as part of an intermediate punishment.[12]

C. New "Community and Intermediate" Probation Conditions

The JRA creates a new pool of community and intermediate probation conditions that may be imposed as part of a community punishment or an intermediate punishment. The conditions may be imposed in addition to any special conditions of probation imposed under G.S. 15A-1343(b1). The community and intermediate probation conditions are

- house arrest with electronic monitoring;
- performance of community service;
- submit to a short-term period or periods of confinement in a local confinement facility for a total of no more than 6 days per month during any 3 separate months during the period of probation. The 6-days-per-month confinement may only be imposed as 2-day or 3-day consecutive periods. When a defendant is on probation for multiple judgments, the short-term periods must run concurrently and may total no more than 6 days per month;
- substance abuse assessment, monitoring, or treatment;
- abstain from alcohol consumption and submit to continuous alcohol monitoring (CAM) when alcohol dependency or chronic abuse has been identified by a substance abuse assessment;
- participation in an educational or vocational skills development program, including an evidence-based program; and

---

screening and assessment to determine chemical dependency prior to entering those programs. G.S. 15A-1343(b3).

12. According to the Division of Adult Correction (DAC), over 1,500 probationers were still subject to intensive supervision as of this writing.

- submission to satellite-based monitoring, pursuant to Part 5 of Article 27A of G.S. Chapter 14, if the defendant is described by G.S. 14-208.40(a)(2).[13]

The court may impose one or more of these six conditions in any case under Structured Sentencing but not in a case sentenced under G.S. 20-179, where the terms "community" and "intermediate" do not apply. The conditions may be imposed at sentencing or as a modification of probation for persons on probation for offenses that occurred on or after December 1, 2011.[14] Each of the conditions is discussed in greater detail below.

House Arrest with Electronic Monitoring

The JRA added electronic house arrest (EHA) as a community and intermediate condition of probation. The act did not, however, repeal the existing special condition of probation in G.S. 15A-1343(b1)(3c), which also describes electronic house arrest. Thus, there are now two statutory EHA conditions, the existing special condition under G.S. 15A-1343(b1)(3c) and the new community and intermediate condition available under G.S. 15A-1343(a1)(1). The two conditions are virtually identical, with the details of the former spelled out in the condition itself and the latter defined by reference to the definition of "house arrest with electronic monitoring" in G.S. 15A-1340.11(4a). The only difference between the two conditions appears to be that the new community and intermediate version does not include the one-time $90 electronic monitoring device fee described by G.S. 15A-1343(c2). As such, it seems that only EHA ordered under the existing statutory special condition in G.S. 15A-1343(b1)(3c) should include the fee—although it may still be waived in those cases for good cause and upon motion of the probationer. The addition of EHA as a community and intermediate condition of probation, coupled with the condition's removal from the definition of an intermediate punishment, means that EHA may, for the first time, be ordered in community cases at sentencing.

Community Service

The new "perform community service" community and intermediate condition of probation in G.S. 15A-1343(a1)(2) is, to a certain degree, duplicative of the existing statutory special condition of probation set out in

---

13. G.S. 15A-1343(a1).
14. S.L. 2011-192, § 1.(*l*).

G.S. 15A-1343(b1)(6) requiring the defendant to "[p]erform community or reparation service." As initially enacted in 2011, the new community service condition differed from the existing special condition in that it made no reference to the one-time $250 community service fee required by G.S. 143B-708. As a result, some defendants ordered to complete community service as a special condition of probation under G.S. 15A-1343(b1)(6) were required to pay the fee, while defendants ordered to perform community service as a community and intermediate condition under G.S. 15A-1343(a1)(2) may not have been required to pay it. S.L. 2012-188 (referred to hereinafter as the 2012 Clarifications Act) amended the community and intermediate version of the condition to say that the fee is required under the community and intermediate condition, too. The change was effective July 16, 2012, and applies to any community service ordered as a community and intermediate condition on or after that date. For cases after that date, court personnel should disregard the usage note on the judgment forms saying that the community service fee should not be assessed for the community and intermediate version of the condition unless specifically ordered by the court.

The revised law's reference to the fee probably forecloses any argument that the community and intermediate version of the probation condition allowed for informal community service arrangements outside of the Community Service Work Program of the Division of Adult Correction (DAC).

Short-Term Jail Confinement

The JRA adds a community and intermediate probation condition allowing short-term jail confinement for no more than 6 days per month during any 3 separate months during a period of probation. The confinement must be imposed as 2-day or 3-day consecutive periods, with "consecutive" apparently intended to mean continuous. Because the confinement must be served in 2- or 3-day increments, it has been referred to by some as a "dip"—as in a "dip in the jail"—although it is not to be confused with another portion of the JRA that allows probation officers to impose "quick dips" in the jail through delegated authority in certain circumstances.[15] This short-term confinement may be ordered by the judge at sentencing or as a modification of probation, but only after a proper sentencing or violation

---

15. *See infra* "F. Delegated Authority" for a discussion of the "quick dip" confinement that a probation officer may impose through delegated authority.

hearing. In that sense, there is nothing "quick" about this type of confinement when it is ordered by a judge.

Given the permissible length of each dip and the total amount of confinement that may be ordered, the maximum number of individual dips a person could face in a single probation case is nine (three 2-day dips in 3 separate months). Thus, the latest probationary judgment forms include a nine-cell chart in the "Community and Intermediate Probation Conditions" section where the judge can spell out exactly when and how any dip confinement it orders is to be served. If the defendant is on probation for multiple judgments, dip confinement periods must run concurrently and may total no more than 6 days per month. In other words, dip confinement periods may not be "stacked" or "boxcarred" to create a confinement period longer than 3 days.

Dips did not replace special probation (split sentences). The JRA did not amend the special probation law set out in G.S. 15A-1351(a), and split sentences are still available as a sentencing option. Dip jail confinement is, however, similar in some ways to special probation; like a split, a dip is a condition of probation that requires a short period of incarceration. But a dip is different from a split sentence. It is not, for example, subject to the rule for split sentences that the total active component may not exceed one-fourth of the defendant's maximum imposed sentence.[16] Thus, an entire 16-day misdemeanor sentence could be served through dips (assuming the time were appropriately spread across 3 months), whereas only 4 days of it could be served as a split sentence. Nor are dips listed among the probation conditions that may not be imposed on a community-punished case. The only prohibited conditions under the new definition of a community punishment are special probation and drug treatment court.[17] Thus, the dip condition is the first and only way under Structured Sentencing that a judge may impose jail confinement at sentencing as part of a community punishment. There is some argument that a community punishment should not include imprisonment because community punishment is defined as a

---

16. G.S. 15A-1351(a); G.S. 15A-1344(e) (setting out the rules for special probation ordered as a modification of probation).

17. G.S. 15A-1340.11(2). Both before and after the Justice Reinvestment Act (JRA), the court may add intermediate conditions to a community case upon a finding that the probationer has violated one or more conditions of probation. G.S. 15A-1344(a).

sentence that "does not include an active punishment."[18] But "active punishment" is a term of art under Structured Sentencing, defined as one that requires service of a sentence of imprisonment that is not suspended at all.[19] A sentence can therefore still meet the definition of a community punishment despite the inclusion of a dip in the jail as a condition of probation under G.S. 15A-1343(a1).

Dip confinement is served in a "local confinement facility," which almost certainly means the local jail.[20] Because the confinement is ordered as a condition of probation, it would seem to fit within the language of the second paragraph of G.S. 7A-313, which allows (but does not require) the court to impose jail fees for time spent in the jail "pursuant to a probationary sentence." The amount of that jail fee, if ordered, is $40 per day of confinement.[21] Any time a probationer spends in the jail as a dip undoubtedly counts for credit against the probationer's suspended sentence if that sentence is activated.[22]

---

18. G.S. 15A-1340.11(2).

19. G.S. 15A-1340.11(1).

20. *See* G.S. 153A-217 (defining a local confinement facility as a "county or city jail, a local lockup, a regional or district jail, a juvenile detention facility, a detention facility for adults operated by a local government, and any other facility operated by a local government for confinement of persons awaiting trial or serving sentences . . .").

21. G.S. 7A-313 describes two types of jail fees. The first, set out in the first paragraph of that statutory section, is a fee for time spent in jail awaiting trial. The law says that a person who is eventually convicted shall be liable to the county in the sum of $10 for each 24 hours of confinement or fraction thereof. No fee is assessed if a person is acquitted or the case is dismissed. The second fee, set out in the second paragraph of G.S. 7A-313, is for "persons who are ordered to pay jail fees pursuant to a probationary sentence." The amount of the probationary-sentence jail fee is set at the "same per diem rate paid by the Department of Correction to local jails for maintaining a prisoner, as set by the General Assembly in its appropriations acts." *Id.* Before 2009 that reference was ambiguous, as there were two DOC-to-jail per diem reimbursement rates set out in the budget. There was an $18-per-day rate, authorized by G.S. 148-32.1(a), for jail inmates serving criminal sentences of 30 days or longer, and there was a $40-per-day "jail backlog" rate, authorized by G.S. 148-29, for convicted inmates awaiting transfer from a jail to DOC. In 2009, however, the reimbursement for 30-day inmates was repealed (S.L. 2009-451, § 19.22A), leaving the $40 rate as the only one to which the jail fee could be pegged. Since then the probationary-sentence jail fee has been $40.

22. *See* State v. Farris, 336 N.C. 553 (1994) (holding that imprisonment served under a split sentence counts for credit under G.S. 15-196.1, which requires that a "defendant be credited with all time . . . in custody and not at liberty as the result of the charge").

Substance Abuse Assessment, Monitoring, or Treatment

The new community and intermediate conditions of probation allow the court to impose substance abuse assessments, monitoring, or treatment. The condition is similar to and contains elements of several existing conditions, including the regular condition requiring a probationer to supply a breath, urine, or blood specimen when instructed[23] and the special condition requiring a probationer to attend treatment.[24]

Continuous Alcohol Monitoring (CAM)

Legislation passed in 2012 added another community and intermediate probation condition, allowing the court to require the defendant to abstain from alcohol consumption and to submit to continuous alcohol monitoring (CAM) if alcohol dependency or chronic alcohol abuse has been identified by a substance abuse assessment.[25] The same legislation added a similar condition as a permissible special condition of probation under G.S. 15A-1343(b1). The new conditions do not reference a required fee for CAM, but another statute, G.S. 15A-1343.3(b), states that probationers must pay CAM fees directly to the monitoring provider.[26] The provider may not, however, terminate CAM services for nonpayment without court authorization.[27]

Participation in an Educational or Vocational Skills Development Program

This new condition is likewise similar to existing conditions (for example, the special condition requiring a probationer to attend skill or employment training). The condition's reference to "evidence-based" programs tracks the emergence of a new supervision policy within DAC that emphasizes tailoring an offender's supervision to the offender's assessed risk and needs.[28]

---

23. G.S. 15A-1343(b)(16).

24. G.S. 15A-1343(b1)(2).

25. G.S. 15A-1343(a1)(4a); S.L. 2012-146 (effective for offenses committed on or after December 1, 2012).

26. The vendor currently authorized to provide continuous alcohol monitoring charges an installation fee of $75 plus $12 for each day of monitoring. *See* Shea Denning, "Authorization for Continuous Alcohol Monitoring Expanded by S.L. 2012-146," *North Carolina Criminal Law, UNC School of Government Blog* (July 17, 2012), http://nccriminallaw.sog.unc.edu/?p=3726.

27. G.S. 15A-1343.3(b).

28. *See infra* "E. Risk Assessment" for a discussion of the risk assessment process.

Literally, any program that research shows will help reduce an offender's likelihood of reoffending or will promote some other measure of success could be characterized as an "evidence-based" program, but recent correctional literature generally uses the term to refer to motivational interviewing, therapeutic programs, cognitive behavioral interventions, and the like.[29] Exactly what evidence-based programming will be available on a statewide basis in North Carolina will depend in part on the progress of the Treatment for Effective Community Supervision program, the successor to the Criminal Justice Partnership Program, discussed below.[30]

Satellite-Based Monitoring

The final community and intermediate probation condition allows the court to impose satellite-based monitoring (SBM) if the probationer is a sex offender described by G.S. 14-208.40(a)(2). To be described by that subdivision, an offender must (1) have been convicted of a reportable sex crime; (2) be required to register as a sex offender; (3) have committed an "offense involving the physical, mental, or sexual abuse of a minor"; and (4) require the "highest possible level of supervision and monitoring" based on the results of a DAC risk assessment. That category of offender may be ordered to enroll in SBM for a period of time specified by the court.[31] The court determines whether an offender fits within that category at a determination hearing under G.S. 14-208.40A (for hearings held at sentencing) or G.S. 14-208.40B (for offenders for whom a determination was not held at sentencing, sometimes referred to as a "bring-back hearing").

Whether the new community and intermediate probation condition referring to SBM should be used at all is a matter of debate. Any offender the court has determined (through the hearing procedure described above) to be a sex offender described by G.S. 14-208.40(a)(2) and ordered to enroll in SBM should already be enrolled. If the court held a determination hearing and decided in its discretion that the person should not enroll, a subsequent court probably should not alter that decision by adding SBM as a

---

29. *See generally* Roger K. Warren, "Evidence-Based Practice to Reduce Recidivism: Implications for State Judiciaries," U.S. Department of Justice, National Institute of Corrections (2007), http://static.nicic.gov/Library/023358.pdf.

30. *See infra* "J. Repeal of Criminal Justice Partnership Program and Creation of Treatment for Effective Community Supervision."

31. G.S. 14-208.40A(e); G.S. 14-208.40B(c).

condition of probation. In *State v. Clayton*,[32] a defendant who initially was not ordered to enroll in SBM after a proper SBM determination hearing was later ordered to enroll after a probation violation hearing. The court of appeals vacated the latter order, noting that "the SBM statutes do not provide for reassessment of [a] defendant's SBM eligibility based on the same reportable conviction, after the initial SBM determination is made based on that conviction."[33] If no formal determination hearing has been held for a person who appears to fit the eligibility requirements, DAC should make an initial determination as to whether the person requires SBM and, if so, bring the person before the court for a determination hearing.[34]

Moreover, SBM is (and has been for years) a mandatory condition of probation for any defendant in the category described by G.S. 14-208.40(a)(2).[35] With a mandatory condition in place, the need for a discretionary condition is unclear.

D. The Impact of Blending Community and Intermediate Punishment

The blending of the community and intermediate punishment definitions is an intentional outcome of the JRA. Findings by the Council of State Governments (CSG) indicated that the sentencing grid's distribution of C and I dispositions—requiring a particular type of punishment in certain grid cells and prohibiting it in others—led to an inefficient allocation of scarce correctional resources. For example, if a judge wished to put an I or I/A defendant on probation, he or she was required under the former law to impose one of the six conditions that allowed the sentence to fit within the definition of an intermediate punishment. CSG analysts reported that people sentenced to an intermediate punishment often turned out to be low-risk offenders who probably did not merit the cost of an intermediate condition (typically, a split-sentence jail bed or intensive supervision). In some cases, their report continued, applying that attention to low-risk offenders is "counterproduc-

---

32. 206 N.C. App. 300 (2010).
33. *Id.* at 305–06.
34. G.S. 14-208.40B(a).
35. G.S. 15A-1343(b2)(8).

tive and can actually increase recidivism rates."[36] Conversely, some offenders in C only cells on the sentencing grid turn out to be high risk, deserving of more focused supervision than a community punishment would allow. The new definitions of community punishment and intermediate punishment remove some of those constraints (never is the court required under the new law to impose any particular conditions to make a sentence intermediate), and the availability of a common pool of community and intermediate conditions gives the court more flexibility to shape the defendant's supervision.

That flexibility could raise issues in the interpretation of judgments. Under prior law, whether a sentence was one of community punishment or intermediate punishment was obvious. If the sentence included one of the six intermediate conditions, it was intermediate; if it did not include any of those six conditions, it was community. After the JRA, the distinction will not be so apparent. For example, a sentence to supervised probation with electronic house arrest (or any other condition from the pool of community and intermediate probation conditions) could be either community punishment or intermediate punishment. Only sentences that initially include special probation or assignment to a drug treatment court will be unambiguously intermediate.

Even if that blending is to some extent intentional, there are still at least three legal distinctions between the two types of punishment. First, whether

---

36. "Justice Reinvestment in North Carolina: Analysis and Policy Framework to Reduce Spending on Corrections and Reinvest in Strategies to Increase Public Safety," Council of State Governments Justice Center (2011), http://justicereinvestment.org/files/JR_North_Carolina_policy_framework_v8mg_mc.pdf (hereinafter "Framework"), 14.

That same line of thinking motivated the repeal of intensive supervision. Intensive supervision was the most frequently ordered of the six intermediate conditions under prior law, ordered in over half (53 percent) of all cases in which an intermediate punishment was imposed. "2010/11 Statistical Report," *supra* note 7, at 25. There was, however, a sense that intensive supervision was sometimes being ordered because some intermediate sanction was required in order for the sentence to meet the definition of an intermediate punishment and intensive supervision was the easiest to impose, not because the court had actually determined that the defendant merited more focused supervision. By repealing intensive supervision, the JRA steers judges—who generally do not have access to any sort of presentence report when they sentence defendants—toward a more vanilla form of probation at sentencing. The law envisions that additional conditions may be added later, either by the court or through the probation officer's exercise of delegated authority, in response to the risk and needs assessments completed during the first two months of the defendant's probation.

a sentence is a community punishment or an intermediate punishment dictates how long the period of probation can be (without findings that a longer or shorter period is required) under G.S. 15A-1343.2(d). For instance, a community-punished felon may be placed on probation for up to 30 months, whereas an intermediate-punished felon may be placed on probation for up to 36 months. Second, under G.S. 15A-1343(b4), four additional conditions of probation apply to any defendant subject to intermediate punishment (perform community service if required; not use, possess, or control alcohol; remain within the county; and participate in any evaluation, counseling, treatment, or educational program as directed by the probation officer). Third, whether the sentence is community or intermediate punishment has a slight bearing on what conditions a probation officer can add through delegated authority, discussed below. Given those differences, judges and clerks should be sure to check the box in the upper right-hand corner of the suspended sentence judgment forms indicating whether the sentence is a community or intermediate punishment.

E. Risk Assessment

For probationers sentenced under Structured Sentencing, the JRA requires DAC to use a validated instrument to assess each probationer's risk of reoffending.[37] The law further requires DAC to place probationers into different supervision levels based on the results of that risk assessment and offenders' "criminogenic needs."[38] DAC refers to the assessment process collectively as the "Risk-Needs Assessment," or RNA. By DAC policy the RNA must be completed within the first 60 days of an offender's probation.[39]

---

37. Though the new statutory risk assessment requirement technically applies only to offenders sentenced under Structured Sentencing (it is included in G.S. 15A-1343.2, which only applies to persons sentenced under Article 81B of G.S. Chapter 15A), DAC uses the assessment on all probationers, including DWI offenders.

38. G.S. 15A-1343.2(b1).

39. State of North Carolina, Dep't of Public Safety, Div. of Adult Correction, Section of Community Corrections, Policy and Procedure Manual (2012) (hereinafter Community Corrections Policy) § D.0503.

Table 2.1. DAC projections of the likelihood of re-arrest within 1 year

OTI-R score range	Risk level	Percentage re-arrested within 1 year
0–10	Minimal	7
11–25	Low	16
26–49	Moderate	31
50–65	High	47
66–100	Extreme	57

Risk Level

DAC has for many years assessed offenders' risk using a risk assessment instrument called the Offender Traits Inventory, or OTI. More recently, DAC has begun to use a revised version of the instrument called the OTI-R. The OTI-R predicts a person's probability of re-arrest through an algorithm that takes into account aspects of his or her criminal record and certain personal characteristics, such as age, employment, and education. The instrument assigns the person one of five risk levels ranging from Extreme to Minimal. Table 2.1 shows DAC's projection of the likelihood of re-arrest within 1 year for offenders in each risk level.

Needs Level

Two assessment tools make up the needs portion of the RNA: the "Officer's Interview/Impressions Worksheet" and the "Offender Self-Report." These tools ask a battery of questions designed to flag a person's criminogenic needs. Criminogenic needs are aspects of an offender's life linked to criminal behavior, such as association with criminal peers, a dysfunctional family, and substance abuse.[40] DAC sorts offenders into one of five needs levels ranging from Extreme to Minimal depending on the particular needs identified by the assessment tools and other factors, such as the offender's record of juvenile delinquency.

---

40. *See* James Bonta, *Offender Risk Assessment: Guidelines for Selection and Use*, 29 CRIMINAL JUSTICE & BEHAVIOR 355 (2002).

Supervision Level

The results of the risk and needs assessments are blended together to determine an overall supervision level for the probationer. Figure 2.1 represents this relationship.

DAC sorts offenders into five supervision levels. Supervision Level 1 (L1) probationers are the most likely to re-offend and have the greatest need for programming, while L5 probationers are those who are least likely to re-offend. Figure 2.2 shows in greater detail how the results of the risk assessment and the needs assessment are correlated to determine the offender's supervision level.

As a matter of Community Corrections policy, certain offenders are subject to a minimum supervision level regardless of the results of the RNA. For example, offenders under supervision for a reportable sex crime; court-identified domestic violence offenders; Level One, Two, or Three DWI offenders; and validated gang members are never supervised below Supervision Level 3 (L3). All probationers are supervised at L1 for the first 60 days of supervision.[41]

Figure 2.1. DAC determination of offender supervision level

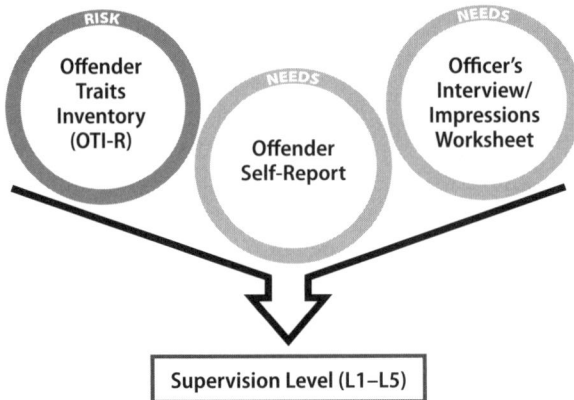

Consequences of the Supervision Level

An offender's supervision level dictates two principal aspects of the way that offender is supervised. First, the supervision level determines the frequency with which the probation officer must contact the offender. Officers must

---

41. COMMUNITY CORRECTIONS POLICY, *supra* note 39, § D.0602.

Figure 2.2. Correlation of risks and needs in determining offender supervision level

		Risk level				
		Extreme	High	Moderate	Low	Minimal
Needs level	Extreme	L1	L1	L2	L3	L3
	High	L1	L2	L3	L3	L3
	Moderate	L2	L2	L3	L4	L4
	Low	L2	L2	L4	L4	L5
	Minimal	L2	L2	L4	L5	L5

have at least one "offender management contact" (a face-to-face contact in which the officer must discuss certain things with the offender) per month with L1, L2, and L3 supervisees. By contrast, L4 and L5 offenders are generally placed on a remote reporting system called Offender Accountability Reporting (OAR), which allows supervisees to report via the Internet or mail. (OAR is not the same as unsupervised probation. OAR offenders have a probation officer and pay supervision fees, for example.) Table 2.2 shows the minimum contact standards applicable to each supervision level. Additional contacts may be required as directed by the court or in the discretion of the probation officer.[42]

Second, a probationer's supervision level influences how the probation officer responds to noncompliance by the probationer. Figure 2.3, derived from Community Corrections policy, shows the various options permissible in response to a particular type of violation by a probationer within a particular supervision level. Note, for instance, that an officer may use option B, a quick dip in the jail through delegated authority, only in response to serious violations (new criminal offenses or recurring technical violations) by L1, L2, and L3 offenders.[43] The supervision level also dictates whether a probation officer may impose certain other conditions through delegated authority without first finding a violation.[44]

42. *Id.*
43. *Id.* § E.0202.
44. *See infra* notes 55–56 and accompanying text.

Table 2.2. Minimum contact standards for supervision levels

Supervision level	L1	L2	L3	L4	L5
Minimum contact standards	1 home contact and 1 offender management contact per month	1 home contact every 60 days and 1 offender management contact per month	1 home contact every 60 days and 1 offender management contact per month	Remote report monthly and one face-to-face contact every 90 days	Remote report monthly

Caseload Goals

The JRA amended the existing statute on probation caseloads to say that the goal of the General Assembly is that no probation officer will supervise more than an average of 60 high- and moderate-risk offenders.[45] Prior law set the caseload goal at 90 offenders but did not distinguish between offenders of different risk levels. The lower goal takes into account that many offenders assessed as low risk are, because of recently enacted DAC policy, monitored through OAR. As before, the new caseload goal is advisory, subject to the availability of funds, and not tied to any legal requirements.

F. Delegated Authority

For cases sentenced under Structured Sentencing, the law allows a probation officer to impose certain additional probation conditions on an offender without action by the court.[46] That power, referred to as delegated authority, has been a part of North Carolina law since Structured Sentencing first became effective in 1994. As the law was initially enacted, authority to add additional conditions was not granted to the probation officer unless the court expressly delegated it. Under changes made to the law in 1997,[47] however, the default position was reversed so that delegated authority applied unless the judge specifically said it did not.

---

45. G.S. 15A-1343.2(c).
46. G.S. 15A-1343.2(e) and (f).
47. S.L. 1997-57.

Figure 2.3. Options for responses to probation noncompliance according to violation type and supervision level

		Supervision level					Response options
		L1	L2	L3	L4	L5	A Probation violation report and arrest
	Public safety	A	A	A	A	A	B Delegated authority: quick dip
	New crime	A/B/C	A/B/C	B/C	C	C	C Probation violation report and cite
	Recurring / multiple	A/B/C	B/C	B/C	D	D	Contempt, Modify/extend probation, Delegated authority: non–quick dip, Increase searches
	Nonrecurring	C	C	D	D	D	Increase contacts, Increase drug screens
	Non-willful	D	D	D	D	D	D Refer to treatment

Type of noncompliance

Response options

A Probation violation report and arrest

B Delegated authority: quick dip

C Probation violation report and cite
Contempt
Modify/extend probation
Delegated authority: non–quick dip
Increase searches
Increase contacts
Increase drug screens

D Refer to treatment
Reprimand by probation officer
Reprimand by chief probation officer
Modify payment schedule
Initiate contact

Applicability

Delegated authority applies only to cases sentenced under Structured Sentencing;[48] it does not apply in impaired driving cases or any case sentenced under older law. Because an offender must be sentenced to a community or intermediate punishment for delegated authority to apply, it is questionable whether a probation officer may exercise delegated authority in deferred prosecution or G.S. 90-96 cases. In those cases, the defendant has not yet been sentenced and thus has not yet received a community or intermediate punishment—a classification necessary for determining which delegated authority conditions would be permissible under G.S. 15A-1343.2(e) (community) or (f) (intermediate).

Effective for persons placed on probation based on offenses that occurred on or after December 1, 2011,[49] the JRA expanded the authority delegated to probation officers in two ways: first, it added to the list of conditions an

---

48. G.S. 15A-1343.2(a) ("This section applies only to persons sentenced under Article 81B of this Chapter.").

49. S.L. 2011-192, § 1.(*l*).

officer may impose and second, it broadened the circumstances in which the officer may impose them. As under prior law, the court may find in any case that it is not appropriate to delegate authority to a probation officer. Probationary judgment forms include a check-box for the court to withhold delegated authority. The probation modification form (AOC-CR-609) likewise includes check-boxes for the court to delegate authority that was previously withheld or to withhold authority previously delegated. The statute does not directly address whether judges are permitted to delegate authority to impose some conditions but not others, but it seems reasonable to assume they may.

Conditions a Probation Officer May Impose

Under the new law, a probation officer may require an offender sentenced to community punishment to

- perform up to 20 hours of community service and pay the fee prescribed by law;
- report to the offender's probation officer on a frequency to be determined by the officer;
- submit to substance abuse assessment, monitoring, or treatment;
- submit to house arrest with electronic monitoring;
- submit to "quick-dip" confinement, a period or periods of confinement in a local confinement facility, for a total of no more than 6 days per month in any 3 separate months during the period of probation. This confinement may be imposed only as 2- or 3-day consecutive periods;
- submit to an electronically monitored curfew; or
- participate in an educational or vocational skills development program, including an evidence-based program.[50]

Under prior law, the only conditions a probation officer could impose in a community case were community service; increased reporting frequency; and substance abuse assessment, monitoring, and treatment.

In keeping with the JRA's blending of community and intermediate punishment, the list of conditions an officer may impose through delegated

---

50. G.S. 15A-1343.2(e).

authority in an intermediate case is largely the same as in a community case. The officer may require the offender to

- perform up to 50 hours of community service and pay the fee prescribed by law;
- submit to an electronically monitored curfew;
- submit to substance abuse assessment, monitoring, or treatment;
- participate in an educational or vocational skills development program, including an evidence-based program;
- submit to satellite-based monitoring (SBM), if the defendant is described by G.S. 14-208.40(a)(2);
- submit to "quick-dip" confinement;
- submit to house arrest with electronic monitoring; or
- report to the offender's probation officer on a frequency to be determined by the officer.[51]

Under prior law, the conditions an officer could impose in an intermediate case were community service; an electronically monitored curfew; substance abuse assessment, monitoring, and treatment; participation in an educational or skills development program; and satellite-based monitoring.

The list of conditions probation officers may impose through delegated authority is similar to the list of community and intermediate probation conditions a judge may impose. Special rules, discussed below, apply to quick dips in the jail imposed by a probation officer through delegated authority. Regarding SBM, probation officers should be wary of imposing it through delegated authority for the same reasons that judges should avoid adding it as a community and intermediate condition of probation.[52]

If an officer imposes any of the conditions set out above, the officer may subsequently reduce or remove them.[53]

Circumstances in Which Probation Officers May Impose Conditions

The circumstances in which officers may exercise delegated authority are identical for community cases and intermediate cases. An officer may exercise delegated authority upon a determination that the offender has failed to comply with one or more court-imposed conditions. An officer may not

---

51. G.S. 15A-1343.2(f).
52. *See supra* notes 32–35 and accompanying text.
53. G.S. 15A-1343.2(e) and (f).

exercise delegated authority in response to violations of officer-imposed conditions.[54]

Under the JRA a probation officer may also add delegated authority conditions other than quick dips without a violation if the offender is determined to be high risk based on the results of the risk assessment discussed above.[55] The statute does not define *high risk*, but DAC has determined as a matter of policy that it will mean offenders in Supervision Levels 1 and 2.[56]

Whether acting in response to a violation or to a probationer's risk level, the probation officer must obtain administrative approval from a chief probation officer prior to exercising delegated authority.

When a probation officer imposes a delegated authority condition other than a quick dip, the probationer may file a motion with the court to review the new condition. The law does not describe the exact nature of that hearing or set any time line for how quickly it must be held. The offender must be given notice (presumably by the probation officer) of the right to seek court review of any officer-imposed conditions.[57] Apparently the probationer is subject to the condition during the pendency of the review hearing, although the statute does not expressly say so.

Whether a violation to which a probation officer has responded through delegated authority may later serve as the basis for a violation found by the court is not clear. The statutes say that "nothing in [the delegated authority] section shall be construed to limit the availability of the procedures authorized under G.S. 15A-1345"[58] (the probation violation hearing statute), but this provision is susceptible to multiple interpretations. It may, for example, simply mean that a probation officer is not required in any case to exercise delegated authority but rather may always bring violations before the court for review in the first instance. Alternatively the provision could be read to mean that violation proceedings before the court under G.S. 15A-1345 are available without limit even in cases where the officer has already exercised delegated authority.[59]

54. *Id.*

55. *See supra* "E. Risk Assessment."

56. COMMUNITY CORRECTIONS POLICY, *supra* note 39, § E.0205(b)(1).

57. G.S. 15A-1343.2(e) and (f).

58. *Id.*

59. Oregon law is clearer on this point, expressly stating that a judge may not impose additional sanctions after a probationer has completed a sanction imposed by the Oregon Department of Corrections. OR. REV. STAT. ANN. § 137.595.

Quick Dips through Delegated Authority

The JRA allows a probation officer to impose a short term of jail confinement, referred to colloquially as a "quick dip," in response to a violation. The purpose of the law is to allow a probation officer to impose a "swift and certain" sanction for a violation without a lengthy period of pre-hearing confinement or a hearing process.

Quick-dip confinement ordered by a probation officer is similar in many respects to the short-term confinement a judge may impose as a community and intermediate condition of probation. The officer may impose up to 6 days of confinement per month during any 3 separate months of a period of probation. The time must be served in the local jail in 2- or 3-day increments. When a defendant is on probation for more than one judgment, any quick-dip confinement periods imposed must run concurrently and may total no more than 6 days per month. The probation officer's authority to impose quick-dip confinement is identical in community and intermediate cases, but officers may not impose quick dips in impaired driving cases.

Several special procedural rules apply to the imposition of jail confinement through delegated authority. First, unlike other delegated authority conditions under the new law, quick dips may not be imposed by a probation officer based on the offender's risk level alone. Rather, a probation officer can impose a quick dip only when the Section of Community Corrections has determined that the offender has failed to comply with one or more of the conditions imposed by the court (not a condition imposed earlier by a probation officer).

Second, before imposing a quick dip, the officer must present the probationer with a violation report[60] noting the alleged violations and designating the confinement period the officer plans to impose. The law apparently allows the officer to impose the entire 18-day complement of quick-dip time in response to a single violation (provided it is served in the appropriate 2- or 3-day increments across 3 separate months), but DAC has instructed officers as a matter of policy to impose only one 2- or 3-day dip per incident of noncompliance.[61] The statute does not limit the types of violations for which quick dips may be used in response, but DAC has chosen as a matter

---

60. The DAC form used for delegated authority violations is DCC-10B.
61. COMMUNITY CORRECTIONS POLICY, *supra* note 39, § E.0205(b).

of policy to use them only for serious violations committed by Supervision Level 1, 2, and 3 offenders.[62]

Third, the probation officer must advise the probationer of several rights before imposing a quick dip: (1) the right to a "hearing before the court on the alleged violation, with the right to present relevant oral and written evidence"; (2) the right "to have counsel at the hearing, and that [counsel] will be appointed if the probationer is indigent"; (3) the right "to request witnesses who have relevant information concerning the alleged violations"; and (4) the right "to examine any witnesses or evidence."[63]

If the probationer signs a written waiver of all of those rights, the officer can impose the quick dip. The waiver must also be signed by two probation officers acting as witnesses. As initially enacted in 2011, the statute provided that one of the witnessing officers should be the offender's probation officer and the other had to be a "supervisor," which probably referred to a chief probation–parole officer. Effective July 16, 2012, the 2012 Clarifications Act amended that procedure in both G.S. 15A-1343.2(e) (for community cases) and (f) (for intermediate cases), allowing a probation officer other than a supervisor to witness the waiver.[64] The other officer must be designated by the chief of the Section of Community Corrections in the written policy of DAC. That policy directs that any officer, chief probation–parole officer, surveillance officer, or judicial district manager may serve as a witness.[65] The change was a logistical concession to DAC; in some districts, the supervisor does not work in the same county as some of the officers he or she supervises, making it inconvenient for the supervisor to witness a probationer's waiver of rights.

Offenders who waive their right to a hearing and counsel will be taken to the jail and confined for the period designated in the violation report. Magistrates and sheriffs' personnel should be aware that probation officers have this new authority to order confinement without any action or

---

62. *See supra* note 43 and accompanying text. Initially, DAC limited quick dips to Supervision Level 1 and 2 offenders. Effective October 9, 2012, the chief of the Section of Community Corrections approved quick dips for Supervision Level 3 offenders. Memorandum by W. David Guice, section chief of the Division of Adult Correction, Section of Community Corrections (Oct. 9, 2012), on file with the author.

63. G.S. 15A-1343.2(e) and (f).

64. S.L. 2012-188, § 8.

65. Community Corrections Policy, *supra* note 39, § E.0205(b)(1)c.

approval by a judicial official and with no paperwork beyond the DCC-10B violation report. If the probationer does not waive his or her rights, the probation officer will choose whether to bring the violation to the court's attention through the regular violation process, to respond to the violation through another form of delegated authority, or to take some other action. Unlike other delegated authority conditions, for which the offender can file a motion with the court to review action taken by the probation officer, the JRA expressly states that the offender "shall have no right of review" of quick-dip confinement after signing the waiver of rights described above.[66]

Whether probation officers and judges draw from a common pool of 18 days when imposing quick dips as a condition of probation is not clear. For example, if a judge imposes 3 days of dip confinement at sentencing as a "community and intermediate" condition of probation, does a probation officer have only 15 days of quick-dip confinement remaining at his or her disposal? To the extent the probation officer's authority flows from the judge, there is some sense that the time is shared—and DAC has chosen to operate under the assumption that it is. On the other hand, there is no explicit connection between the community and intermediate probation condition and the delegated authority condition. Thus, a trial judge probably should not feel that his or her authority to impose dip time is limited by any confinement previously imposed by a probation officer (except to the extent that the prior quick-dip confinement imposed by a probation officer counts for credit against the defendant's suspended sentence and thus reduces the balance on the overall sentence available for the court to impose). Of course, a judge could always use a different form of short-term confinement, such as special probation, contempt, or, in appropriate cases, confinement in response to violation (CRV).

There is no clear basis or mechanism for assessing jail fees for confinement imposed by a probation officer.

Though the effective date of the JRA authorizes use of quick dips for persons placed on probation for offenses committed on or after December 1, 2011, DAC delayed use of the condition until July 2, 2012, to allow for policy development and training.

Finally, the question of effectiveness arises. Apparently no state has an existing delegated authority law precisely like the one in the JRA, so finding a

---

66. G.S. 15A-1343.2(e) and (f).

model for predicting the law's success in North Carolina is difficult. Similar efforts in Hawaii and Georgia have been successful in reducing the total number of days probationers spend in jail on account of violations.[67] However, a study of Oregon's intermediate sanctions program, after controlling for demographic and crime-related attributes, showed that offenders who served jail time imposed by a probation officer were more likely to have their supervision revoked and were more likely to be convicted for future crimes.[68] Given the differences between North Carolina's new law and the laws in other jurisdictions, it is unclear what lessons can be drawn from these out-of-state programs.

Constitutional Concerns

No North Carolina cases have considered the baseline question of whether allowing probation officers to impose certain conditions of probation is permissible as a matter of constitutional due process or separation of powers. A variety of statutory delegation regimes have been reviewed and, for the most part, upheld in other states.[69] Case law from around the country indicates that a judge generally may not delegate to a probation officer a core judicial function,[70] such as deciding whether a probationer will be required to abide by a condition at all.[71] Judges may, however, delegate logistical or ministerial

---

67. *See, e.g.,* Angela Hawken and Mark Kleiman, "Managing Drug Involved Probationers with Swift and Certain Sanctions: Evaluating Hawaii's HOPE," (research report submitted to the U.S. Department of Justice, 2009), www.ncjrs.gov/pdffiles1/nij/grants/229023.pdf.

68. Andres F. Rengifo and Christine S. Scott-Hayward, "Assessing the Effectiveness of Intermediate Sanctions in Multnomah County, Oregon," Vera Institute of Justice (2008), www.vera.org/download?file=1790/Final%2BMultnomah%2BReport.pdf.

69. *See, e.g.,* State v. Merrill, 999 A.2d 221, 225–26 (N.H. 2010) ("The trial court retains the power to sentence defendants, and although the executive branch may be authorized by the court to impose conditions of probation, the judiciary retains the ultimate authority to review those conditions and to vacate them if they are unreasonable. Thus, the separation of powers is not violated by the judiciary's delegation of authority to probation officers to impose conditions of probation."); State v. Johnson, 817 A.2d 708 (Conn. Ct. App. 2003).

70. United States v. Johnson, 48 F.3d 806 (4th Cir. 1995) (holding that determination of a restitution amount was a judicial function that could not be delegated to a probation officer).

71. United States v. Esparza, 552 F.3d 1088 (9th Cir. 2009) (vacating a condition that allowed a probation officer to choose whether a defendant would participate in inpatient or outpatient treatment); United States v. Heath, 419 F.3d 1312, 1314 (11th

matters such as where or when a particular condition will be satisfied.[72] An important factor in any arrangement appears to be that the court has authority to review any officer-imposed conditions.[73] Delegated authority conditions like curfews or program participation are probably permissible so long as the probationer retains the right to petition the court for review of the condition.[74]

The quick-dip condition may test the boundaries of what punishments a nonjudicial officer can permissibly impose. A leading treatise on the law of probation and parole describes as "universal" the view that "a sentencing court may not under any circumstances delegate to the department of corrections or to a probation officer authority to order a period of additional incarceration for a probationer who is under their supervision."[75] Appellate courts in other jurisdictions have stricken conditions purporting to allow a probation officer to decide whether a probationer will serve additional jail time.[76] The North Carolina Department of Justice issued similar guidance in response to a question about whether a judge could impose a 30-day split

---

Cir. 2005) (striking a condition stating that a defendant was required to participate in mental health programs "*if* and as directed by the probation office").

72. United States v. Stephens, 424 F.3d 876, 884 (8th Cir. 2006) ("[T]he court does not improperly shirk its responsibility to impose the conditions of release merely by allowing the drug treatment professionals to design the course of treatment, where the court has specifically required that the treatment include testing.").

73. United States v. Kerr, 472 F.3d 517 (8th Cir. 2006).

74. *See* State v. Deese, 222 P.3d 647 (Mont. 2009) (unpublished) (upholding a trial judge's delegation of authority to impose a curfew to a probation officer).

75. 1 NEIL P. COHEN, LAW OF PROBATION AND PAROLE § 7:23 (2d ed. 1999).

76. State v. Fearing, 619 N.W.2d 115 (Wis. 2000) (holding that a trial court exceeded its authority in authorizing a probation officer to determine whether a probationer would be required to serve three additional months in jail); State v. Hatfield, 846 P.2d 1025 (Mont. 1993) (holding that a trial court erred in sentencing a defendant to 180 days of jail time to be served—or not served—in the discretion of the probation officer); State v. Lee, 467 N.W.2d 661, 662 (Neb. 1991) (invalidating a condition purporting to allow a probation officer to "waive" some of the defendant's jail days, noting that "[j]ail time is to be imposed by judges" and that a "court may not delegate the authority to impose a jail sentence, or to eliminate a jail sentence, to a nonjudge"); State v. Paxton, 742 N.E.2d 1171 (Ohio Ct. App. 2000) (reversing a 60-day period of imprisonment imposed by a probation officer on due process and separation of powers grounds); People v. Thomas, 217 Ill. App. 3d 416, 418 (1991) (vacating a condition allowing a probation officer to remit a 30-day jail sentence if a probationer completed a treatment program because that authority was "not a function that could properly be delegated when the question of further incarceration is at stake").

sentence to be used in the discretion of the probation officer "if deemed necessary for minor infractions or technical violations." In a formal opinion letter, the attorney general advised against the practice, concluding that it would violate constitutional due process and the statutory probation violation framework set out in G.S. 15A-1345.[77] However, those courts and the state attorney general might evaluate the delegation differently in light of the new enabling statute.

Even with the statute in place, however, several issues may arise. First, unlike other delegated authority conditions, an offender cannot seek court review of an officer-imposed quick dip. Instead, the statute explicitly states that the probationer has no such right of review if he or she has signed a written waiver of rights. Quick dips were probably excluded from the judicial review process on the rationale that the probation officer could not have imposed the confinement in the first place without the offender waiving his or her right to a hearing before a judge. But the lack of a judicial review process may bear on the separation of powers and due process analyses. By way of comparison, a defendant's failure to object when a judge imposes a probation condition does not constitute a waiver of the right to object to it at a later time.[78] Second, the JRA apparently places North Carolina in a very small minority of states that allow a probation officer to respond administratively to a violation with full-blown jail confinement. Delaware allows its corrections department to respond administratively to certain violations with sanctions less restrictive than "Accountability Level V" (incarceration), including up to 5 consecutive days of supervision at "Accountability Level IV" (house arrest, a halfway house, or residential treatment).[79] Georgia's system includes similar limitations, allowing probation officers to impose conditions such as intensive supervision and electronic monitoring administratively but reserving to administrative hearing officers and judges the authority to impose more restrictive conditions such as confinement in a probation detention center or placement in a residential facility.[80] Oregon, on the other hand, allows an officer to impose jail confinement under its

---

77. 60 N.C. Op. Atty. Gen. 110 (1992).
78. G.S. 15A-1342(g).
79. Del. Code. Ann. tit. 11, § 4334; § 4204.
80. Ga. Code. Ann. § 42-8-155; § 42-8-153(c).

law, and there do not appear to be any reported cases challenging the law's constitutionality.[81]

In general, before a probationer may be confined in response to a violation of probation, he or she has certain rights as a matter of constitutional due process.[82] Instead of involving a judge or an administrative hearing officer in the procedure (as is generally the case in Hawaii and Georgia), the JRA's approach to quick dips relies on the probationer's written waiver of rights. The statutorily required elements of the waiver, described above, appear to track the minimum requirements of due process for probation violation hearings set out by the United States Supreme Court. But it is questionable whether an interested party (a probation officer) can properly ensure that a probationer's waiver is knowing, voluntary, and intelligent, especially when a defendant who decides not to waive could nonetheless be arrested and jailed in advance of a probation violation hearing before the court. Moreover, to the extent that the waiver incorporates a waiver of counsel, it is unclear whether it comports with North Carolina's statutory requirement for a judge to conduct a "thorough inquiry" of defendants who elect to proceed without a lawyer[83]—a statute that is already a common source of errors for waiver inquiries conducted by judges in criminal trials[84] and probation violation hearings.[85] The form probation officers will use when taking a waiver, a DCC-10B, may be problematic in that it only requires the probationer to acknowledge the waiver of the right to a hearing, not to counsel.

A judge concerned about the constitutionality or effectiveness of delegated authority may choose to withhold the delegation by checking the appropriate box on the judgment form.

---

81. Or. Rev. Stat. Ann. § 137.595; Or. Admin. R. 291-058-0045.

82. Gagnon v. Scarpelli, 411 U.S. 778 (1973) (holding that a probationer is entitled to, among other things, notice of the alleged violations, an opportunity to be heard and to present evidence, a neutral hearing body, and, in some cases, counsel); Morrissey v. Brewer, 408 U.S. 471 (1972) (setting out what process is due in a parole revocation hearing).

83. G.S. 15A-1242; State v. Warren, 82 N.C. App. 84 (1986) (holding that G.S. 15A-1242 applies to waiver of counsel in probation matters).

84. State v. Seymore, ___ N.C. App. ___, 714 S.E.2d 499 (Aug. 16, 2011).

85. State v. Sorrow, ___ N.C. App. ___, 713 S.E.2d 180 (July 19, 2011).

Probation Officer's Finding of Violation Not an Aggravating Factor

A probation officer's determination that a probationer has failed to comply with a condition of probation is not an aggravating factor for sentencing a future felony under G.S. 15A-1340.16(d)(12a). Under the language of that subdivision, only findings of a willful violation by "a court" or by the Post-Release Supervision and Parole Commission qualify a defendant for the aggravating factor.

G. Absconding

Effective for offenses committed on or after December 1, 2011, the JRA makes it a regular condition of probation that a defendant not "abscond, by willfully avoiding supervision or by willfully making the defendant's whereabouts unknown to the supervising probation officer."[86] The new regular condition is the first true absconding condition in North Carolina. In fact, aside from a brief mention of absconding in the Crime Victims' Rights Act,[87] "abscond" in the new condition is the first appearance of the word in the criminal law statutes. Under prior law, offenders alleged to be absconders were generally violating one of two statutory conditions of probation, the "remain within the jurisdiction"[88] condition or the "report as directed . . . to the officer"[89] condition. The absconding terminology was derived from Community Corrections policy, not the law.

Though the new absconding condition appears to refer principally to supervised probationers, unsupervised probationers are not exempted from it.[90]

---

86. G.S. 15A-1343(b)(3a). The condition was initially made effective for "probation violations occurring" on or after December 1, 2011, S.L. 2011-192, § 4.(d), but that effective date was amended by S.L. 2011-412, § 2.5. The latter session law also reversed changes made to G.S. 15A-1343(b)(2), the "remain within the jurisdiction of the court" condition, by S.L. 2011-62, § 1, returning that condition to its form before any changes came into effect.

87. G.S. 15A-837(a)(6).

88. G.S. 15A-1343(b)(2).

89. G.S. 15A-1343(b)(3).

90. G.S. 15A-1343(b).

H. Changes to the Court's Authority to Revoke Probation
No Revocation for Technical Violations

Prior to Justice Reinvestment, the longstanding rule in North Carolina was that a single violation of any condition of probation was a sufficient basis for a judge to revoke probation.[91] Seeking to reduce the number of offenders revoked and imprisoned for minor violations, the JRA placed substantial limitations on a judge's ability to revoke. These limitations apply in both supervised and unsupervised probation cases, both Structured Sentencing and impaired driving cases, and to all probationers regardless of the date of the offense for which they are on probation.[92] For probation violations occurring on or after December 1, 2011,[93] a court may revoke probation only for

- violations of the "commit no criminal offense" condition set out in G.S. 15A-1343(b)(1);
- violations of the new statutory "absconding" condition set out in G.S. 15A-1343(b)(3), described above;[94] and
- any violation by an offender who has previously received a total of two periods of "confinement in response to violation," described below.[95]

For other violations—hereinafter referred to as "technical violations"—a court may not revoke probation. It may instead impose a period of "confinement in response to violation" (CRV) under G.S. 15A-1344(d2), a new form of confinement created by the JRA. Some have referred to CRV informally as a "dunk," as it is a period of confinement generally shorter than a revocation but longer than a "quick dip." The terminology is useful, but there is no express statutory connection between "dips" and "dunks." It is not, for example, a prerequisite to a dunk that a person have already served a dip, and different procedures apply to each type of confinement.

---

91. *See, e.g.*, State v. Tozzi, 84 N.C. App. 517 (1987).

92. G.S. 15A-1341(a) (stating that probation under Article 82 of G.S. Chapter 15A applies to cases under Structured Sentencing and impaired driving under G.S. 20-138.1).

93. S.L. 2011-192, § 4.(d), as amended by S.L. 2011-412, § 2.5.

94. G.S. 15A-1344(a).

95. G.S. 15A-1344(d2). There is no exception to these limitations for probationers under supervision for a reportable sex crime. By contrast, offenders on PRS for a reportable sex crime may be revoked for any violation, including technical violations. *See supra* notes 39–41 in Chapter 1 and accompanying text.

The JRA limitation on judges' revocation authority was made effective for probation violations occurring on or after December 1, 2011. The exact meaning of the phrase "probation violations occurring" in the effective date clause is not entirely clear, but it almost certainly refers to the alleged offending behavior itself—not to the date the violation report was filed, the date of the violation hearing, or any other triggering event. In the short term a single violation report may include a mix of pre– and post–December 1, 2011, violations. A judge must know the date of each alleged violation to determine the permissible response options. Prior law—allowing revocation for any violation but not authorizing CRV—applies to any violation that occurred before December 1, 2011.

The court should use a modification order, Form AOC-CR-609, to impose CRV.

Felony CRV

For a person on probation for a felony, a CRV period must be a flat 90 days, no more and no less.[96] If the person has 90 days or less remaining on his or her suspended sentence, the duration of the CRV period is for that remainder of the suspended sentence.[97] A CRV period entered pursuant to this 90-days-or-less-remaining rule is sometimes referred to as a "terminal CRV" or "terminal dunk" because it brings the person to the end of his or her sentence.[98]

Misdemeanor CRV

For misdemeanants, the CRV period is "up to 90 days," allowing a judge to impose a period shorter than 90 days in the judge's discretion.[99] As initially enacted in 2011, the rule requiring a CRV period to be for the length of the defendant's remaining suspended sentence if 90 days or less remained on the sentence apparently applied to felonies and misdemeanors alike.

---

96. If the court wishes to impose a period of confinement shorter than 90 days, it may impose special probation or contempt. These other types of confinement will not, however, count as prior confinement in response to violation (CRV) periods for purposes of qualifying the defendant for revocation. *See infra* notes 104–05 and accompanying text.

97. G.S. 15A-1344(d2).

98. Rounding out the "dip" and "dunk" metaphor, some have referred to a terminal dunk as getting "drowned."

99. G.S. 15A-1344(d2).

Because almost 90 percent of misdemeanor sentences are 90 days or less to begin with, the rule virtually always trumped the court's authority to order a shorter CRV period. That led to the peculiar result that a judge could impose a short CRV period (5 days, for example) for a defendant with a suspended sentence in excess of 90 days, whereas any CRV period ordered for a defendant with a suspended sentence of 90 days or less was required to be a "terminal dunk," using up the entirety of the remaining sentence. That formulation also apparently frustrated one of the main purposes of the JRA—reducing the number of offenders incarcerated for technical violations of probation—in that most misdemeanants' first CRV period was the functional equivalent of a revocation.

Under changes made in the 2012 Clarifications Act, misdemeanors are excluded from the 90-days-or-less-remaining rule, meaning the judge can, in his or her discretion, impose a shorter CRV period in a misdemeanor case.[100] The new version of the misdemeanor rule simply says the court may impose a CRV period of up to 90 days in a misdemeanor case. The law does not explicitly address how long the CRV period may be when the offender has less than 90 days remaining on his or her suspended sentence, but given that the confinement must be credited under G.S. 15-196.1, it may be no longer than the defendant's suspended sentence. The amendment was effective when it became law on July 16, 2012, and probably applies to any CRV-eligible violation heard on or after that date—regardless of the date the violation actually occurred or the date the violation report was filed.

Terminal CRV Periods

"Terminal CRV" periods or "terminal dunks" are CRV periods that are the last action in the defendant's probation case. Two circumstances where terminal CRV periods arise are (1) when the CRV period uses up the entirety of a defendant's suspended sentence and (2) when the person's period of probation expires during CRV confinement. The first type is discussed above in the sections on felony and misdemeanor CRV. The modification order form, AOC-CR-609, includes boilerplate language indicating that the defendant's probation is terminated upon completion of a CRV period when that confinement period uses up the remainder of the suspended sentence. That finding of termination is a prerequisite for the execution upon any

---

100. *Id.*, as amended by S.L. 2012-188.

civil judgment docketed for restitution in cases covered under the Crime Victims' Rights Act.[101]

Regarding the second type of terminal dunk, there is no statutory provision tolling a probationer's period of probation during service of a CRV period. For example, if a felon with 1 month remaining on his probation period is ordered to complete a 90-day CRV period, the felon's period of probation will expire one month into the CRV. (By contrast, a person's PRS period is tolled if that person is reimprisoned for a violation of PRS.)[102] Whether the offender should be required to complete the remaining two months of the CRV or be released upon expiration of the probation period is unclear. DAC has adopted the former interpretation, requiring the offender to complete any imposed CRV period regardless of whether the underlying probation period has expired. The issue has not arisen in the past with split sentences ordered as a condition of probation because G.S. 15A-1344(e) expressly provides that no split sentence confinement may be required beyond the period of probation. There is no similar statutory provision for CRV. A judge seeking to ensure that a person returns to probation upon completion of a CRV period may wish to extend the period of probation before imposing the CRV.

A judge also may order that a person's probation is terminated upon completion of a CRV period, even if the suspended sentence and probation period will not otherwise be complete at that point. A judge may terminate a period of probation at any time if warranted by the defendant's conduct and the ends of justice.[103] Termination is never required, but in some cases there may be a shared sense that service of one CRV period without the prospect

---

101. G.S. 15A-1340.38(c) ("[T]he docketed judgment for restitution may not be executed upon the property of the defendant until . . . the judge presiding at the probation termination or revocation hearing has made a finding that restitution in a sum certain remains due and payable, that defendant's probation has been terminated or revoked, and that the remaining balance of restitution owing may be collected by execution on the judgment."). The court may use Form AOC-CR-612 to make findings that restitution remains owed.

102. *See supra* notes 43–44 in Chapter 1 and accompanying text.

103. G.S. 15A-1342(b). An indication that the probation has been terminated "unsuccessfully" or "unsatisfactorily" carries no legal significance. *See* Jamie Markham, "Unsatisfactory Termination of Probation," *North Carolina Criminal Law, UNC School of Government Blog* (June 30, 2009), http://nccriminallaw.sog.unc.edu/?p=479.

of additional probation supervision or violation hearings is an appropriate response to the violation at hand.

Reduction of a Sentence when Ordering CRV

Under G.S. 15A-1344(d) and (d1), a court can, "before activating a sentence," reduce a defendant's sentence within the same sentencing grid cell. For felons, the reduced sentence must also be within the same sentencing range (presumptive, aggravated, or mitigated) as the initial sentence. These provisions clearly allow the court to reduce a defendant's sentence when revoking his or her probation. Whether they also allow the court to reduce a person's suspended sentence when imposing CRV is uncertain. To the extent that CRV can be styled as a partial activation, the reduction may be permissible. If it is, any suspended sentence for a misdemeanor may be sufficiently reduced to the point that a terminal CRV is permissible. To reach the same result without the questionable sentence reduction, a court could order a defendant's probation terminated upon completion of a CRV period, as described in the preceding paragraph.

Revocation after Two CRV Periods

When a defendant has previously received two periods of confinement in response to violation, the court may revoke probation for any subsequent violation, including a technical violation.[104] The law thus operates as a sort of "three strikes" provision, such that a person may not be revoked for a technical violation until the third strike. Only the prior receipt of CRV periods qualifies a person for revocation for a technical violation, not the prior findings of violations themselves. In other words, violations responded to in some other way (by a term of special probation, for example) do not count as "strikes." As a result, a prosecutor or a judge may be inclined to impose CRV even when 90 days might be a longer confinement period than anyone thinks is necessary. For felonies, however, the law does not allow a shorter CRV period. Conversely, a defendant may wish to argue for non-CRV responses to early violations so as not to have CRV strikes that place the defendant on the path toward revocation. The statute's use of the phrase "previously received" in reference to prior CRV periods indicates that the court may not

---

104. G.S. 15A-1344(d2).

satisfy multiple CRV strikes by finding multiple violations of probation in the same case at the same time.

A defendant may receive only two CRV periods in a particular probation case.[105] A defendant may not receive a third CRV period for a third or subsequent technical violation. At that point the court must either revoke probation or impose some other form of modification, including special probation or contempt, for example, if the court is inclined to use a form of non-revocation confinement.

The court is never allowed to impose CRV in response to a new criminal offense violation under G.S. 15A-1343(b)(1) or absconding under G.S. 15A-1343(b)(3a).[106] Nor may the court impose CRV for violations of probation that took place before December 1, 2011, the effective date of the portion of the JRA creating the new form of confinement. For those violations the court can either revoke probation or modify it in all the ways it could under prior law.

CRV versus Special Probation

CRV confinement is similar to special probation (a split sentence) but statutorily distinct from it. For instance, CRV is not subject to the one-fourth rule of G.S. 15A-1351(a) or G.S. 15A-1344(e), which caps the maximum permissible confinement period of a split sentence at one-fourth of the defendant's imposed sentence of imprisonment. Additionally, there is no statutory provision allowing CRV to be served in noncontinuous periods (on weekends, for example), as there is for split sentences under G.S. 15A-1351(a). In the absence of such a provision, CRV periods should probably be served continuously.[107]

Jail Credit Issues Related to CRV

Pre-hearing confinement. If a defendant is detained in advance of a violation hearing at which CRV is ordered, the judge must first credit that pre-hearing confinement to the CRV period, with any excess time to be applied

105. *Id.*

106. *Id.*

107. *See* State v. Miller, 205 N.C. App. 291 (2009) (holding that, absent statutory authorization, a judge lacks authority to allow a defendant to serve an active sentence on weekends in a Structured Sentencing case).

in the event the suspended sentence is activated.[108] In other words, the court may not bank the pre-hearing jail credit (leaving it to be applied only in the event of revocation) the way it can bank pre-trial confinement when it orders a split sentence. For instance, if a felony probationer is jailed for 20 days in advance of a probation violation hearing and the result of that hearing is a CRV period, the court will order a 90-day CRV period with 20 days credit applied to that 90-day period. The defendant will be imprisoned for 70 days. If the defendant has already been held in pre-hearing confinement in excess of 90 days, any CRV ordered would be to time served, with the remainder of the credit to be applied to the suspended sentence in the event of activation.

Only confinement awaiting the probation violation hearing is covered by the mandatory crediting rule. The law does not require—or expressly allow—the court to credit any pretrial confinement or other creditable time (such as a quick dip in the jail or residential treatment at DART-Cherry) toward a CRV period. It appears, however, that the court must consider that prior confinement to avoid ordering confinement in excess of the defendant's remaining suspended sentence. For example, if a judge ordered CRV for a probationer with a 100-day misdemeanor sentence and 20 days of pre-trial confinement, there would be no requirement that the CRV period be reduced by the 20 days of jail credit. Nevertheless, the longest CRV period the court could order would be 80 days, as that is all that remains on the defendant's suspended sentence. In felony cases, a proper accounting of all jail credit is likewise necessary to determine whether the defendant falls within the scope of the 90-days-or-less-remaining rule.

Credit for CRV periods already served. CRV confinement served in jail or prison counts for credit against a probationer's suspended sentence under G.S. 15-196.1.[109] When a person serves concurrent CRV periods for violations of multiple probation judgments, it appears that he or she gets credit against each suspended sentence, regardless of whether those sentences were set to run consecutively in the event of revocation. That is a departure from G.S. 15-196.2, which says that time spent in pretrial confinement for more than one pending charge is only applied once if those charges result in consecutive sentences.

---

108. G.S. 15A-1344(d2).
109. *Id.*

Many defendants, especially misdemeanants, will not have suspended sentences long enough to allow for two complete 90-day CRV periods before revocation. For instance, a misdemeanant with a 150-day suspended sentence who received a 90-day CRV for his or her first technical violation could receive only 60 days of CRV confinement for a second technical violation. The judge must consider the effect of the first dunk when determining how much time remains on the suspended sentence for the second.

Keeping track of credit. The increase in the number of types of creditable confinement under the JRA has raised questions about who will keep track of the credit. In addition to tallying prior CRV periods (described immediately above), quick dips ordered by probation officers are a particular concern, as they may be imposed without the court's knowledge. Community Corrections has decided as a matter of policy to file copies of delegated authority violation reports (Form DCC-10B) with the clerk in the county of supervision and, if it is different, the county of origin.[110] If that policy is followed, there should be a record of all confinement in the court's file. In anticipation of additional questions about credit, DAC computer systems have been programmed to offer a more complete accounting of all types of prior confinement. Ultimately the statutory responsibility for determining the credit rests with the court.[111]

Multiple CRV Periods

When a defendant is on probation for multiple offenses, G.S. 15A-1344(d2) requires CRV periods to run concurrently on "all cases related to the violation." Confinement is to be "immediate unless otherwise specified by the court," suggesting a preference—but not an absolute requirement—for immediate service of the confinement. Read together, those provisions indicate that CRV periods for multiple cases should not be "stacked" to create a confinement period of longer than 90 days. The law is silent as to whether CRV periods may be run consecutively to other probation sanctions, such as a term of special probation, a period of contempt confinement, or active sentences (perhaps for a shorter misdemeanor, for instance) ordered in response to some other violation. A judge wishing to do that would pre-

---

110. COMMUNITY CORRECTIONS POLICY, *supra* note 39, § E.0205(b)(1)g.

111. G.S. 15-196.4 ("Upon sentencing or activating a sentence, the judge presiding shall determine the credits to which the defendant is entitled and shall cause the clerk to transmit to the custodian of the defendant a statement of allowable credits.").

sumably specify on the modification order ordering the CRV period that it is to begin at a future date to coincide with the completion of the first sanction or sentence (or, conversely, that the other sanction is to begin at the conclusion of the CRV).

Place of Confinement for CRV

G.S. 15A-1344(d2) specifies that CRV periods are served "in the correctional facility where the defendant would have served an active sentence." That rule was made applicable to probation violations occurring on or after December 1, 2011. The simplest reading of that rule is that any CRV period ordered in a case should be served in the place of confinement ordered on the original judgment suspending sentence. Under that approach, in cases with sentences initially imposed on or after January 1, 2012, the proper place of confinement for a felony CRV period is DAC, which has identified six facilities that will house CRV inmates.[112] The proper place of confinement for a misdemeanor CRV period will be the local jail, the Misdemeanant Confinement Program, or, in some cases, prison, depending on the length of the suspended sentence and whether it was for a crime sentenced under Structured Sentencing or an impaired driving offense. Chapter 4 discusses the new place-of-confinement rules in detail.

Jail Fees for CRV

A judge may order a $40 per day jail fee for time spent in the jail "pursuant to a probationary sentence."[113] That authority applies to special probation confinement (a split sentence) and probably also to dip confinement imposed by a judge as a community and intermediate condition of probation. The fee probably may not be ordered for a CRV period served in a jail. Though CRV arises only in probationary sentences, it is not a condition of probation like special probation or a dip. It is, rather, more akin to a partial activation of a suspended sentence, and a defendant is never required to pay a jail fee for time spent in jail pursuant to an active sentence.

---

112. Those facilities are Dan River, Greene, Odom, Tyrrell, Western Youth Institution, and, for women, Fountain Correctional.

113. G.S. 7A-313.

No Sentence Reduction Credit during CRV

The Secretary of Public Safety is empowered to issue regulations allowing for the award of earned time for Structured Sentencing sentences and good time for impaired driving sentences.[114] As of this writing, the secretary has not issued rules regarding credit against CRV confinement periods, meaning each day of the imposed term must be served. In that regard CRV is similar to special probation, for which no sentence reduction credits are allowed.[115] With that in mind, revocation may be preferable to CRV for some defendants, particularly impaired driving offenders, whose activated sentences are cut in half by good time. For example, a DWI defendant with a 30-day suspended sentence would serve every day of a 30-day CRV period but would serve only 15 days if the sentence were activated.

CRV Appeals

The JRA did not include an explicit statutory provision for appealing a CRV period, either from district to superior court for a de novo violation hearing or from superior court to the appellate division for review. Under G.S. 15A-1347 and existing case law, there is no provision for appeal of probation matters other than revocation or imposition of special probation.[116] Strictly speaking, CRV is neither of those things. And because the right to appeal in North Carolina is purely statutory, there is a sense that CRV may not be appealed.[117]

There may, however, be an argument that imposition of a CRV period—especially a terminal CRV period—fits within the language of G.S. 15A-1347 as an activation or partial activation, although other provisions in that law reference "judgments revoking probation." Even if that statute is not applicable, other avenues for review may be possible. For appeals from superior court to the appellate division, either G.S. 15A-1442(6) (providing that a defendant may appeal other prejudicial errors of law) or G.S. 7A-27(b) (granting jurisdiction to the court of appeals to review any final judgment of a

---

114. G.S. 148-13.

115. G.S. 148-13(f) excludes special probation from the secretary's sentence reduction credit authority. There is no such statutory exclusion for CRV.

116. *See* State v. Edgerson, 164 N.C. App. 712, 714 (2004) ("Defendant's sentence was neither activated nor was it modified to 'special probation.' Defendant therefore has no right to appeal." (citations omitted)).

117. State v. Joseph, 92 N.C. App. 203, 204 (1988), *cert. denied*, 324 N.C. 115 (1989).

superior court)[118] may be a sufficient basis for appeal. Aside from those provisions, a defendant might also seek review through a petition for a writ of certiorari, motion for appropriate relief, petition for a writ of habeas corpus, or other extraordinary writ, depending on the nature of the alleged error.

Revocation-Eligible Violations after Justice Reinvestment

For violations occurring on or after December 1, 2011, the court may (but is not required to) revoke a person's probation for two types of probation violations: new criminal offenses and absconding under G.S. 15A-1343(b)(3a).[119] Issues associated with each category of revocation-eligible violation are discussed below.

New criminal offense. Under G.S. 15A-1343(b)(1), it is a regular condition of probation that a person "commit no criminal offense in any jurisdiction." For many years there has been a division of opinion on whether that condition is violated only when a person is convicted of a new criminal offense, or whether a pending charge or even uncharged criminal conduct could be the basis of a violation. Practice is divided around the state, with some districts routinely holding violation hearings on unconvicted conduct and others having a per se rule against holding a probation violation hearing on a new criminal offense until the defendant is convicted. Nothing in the JRA directly changes the analysis, but the law puts pressure on the issue by making a new criminal offense one of the only revocation-eligible violations.

The rule that emerges from a patchwork of cases decided over the past century is that a person's probation should not be revoked based on a new criminal offense until the person is convicted of that charge,[120] unless the probation court makes an independent finding, to its "reasonable satisfaction," that the defendant committed a crime.[121] Probation should never be revoked based on the mere fact that a new criminal charge is pending; rather, there must be a conviction or some inquiry by the probation court into the alleged criminal behavior itself.

It is apparently permissible for a probation court to find that a probationer has committed a new criminal offense regardless of the State's decision to

---

118. *See* State v. Singleton, 201 N.C. App. 620, 625–26 (2010) (holding that a defendant had a right to appeal the superior court's satellite-based monitoring determination under G.S. 7A-27(b)).

119. G.S. 15A-1344(a) and (d2).

120. State v. Guffey, 253 N.C. 43 (1960).

121. State v. Monroe, 83 N.C. App. 143 (1986).

drop the new criminal charge[122] or not to bring a charge at all.[123] There is also support for the idea that the probation court may revoke probation based on its independent findings of a criminal act even if the defendant is acquitted of the new criminal charge,[124] but the appellate courts themselves describe such a revocation as against the better practice.[125] Revocation in lieu of or even in addition to a new criminal conviction does not constitute double jeopardy; the probation revocation is not new punishment for the same act but rather the activation of a punishment previously imposed for conviction of a prior crime.[126]

In the past a probation officer or the State could avoid some of the difficulties of the "new criminal offense" condition by proceeding on technical violations related to the offender's criminal behavior instead of based on the alleged crime itself. For example, a defendant charged with impaired driving might be alleged to have violated the "not use, possess, or control alcohol" condition, or a person charged with possession of a firearm by a felon might be alleged to have violated the "possess no firearm" condition. Case law supported the court's authority to revoke probation based on a technical violation instead of waiting for a conviction in the related criminal case,[127] even for defendants acquitted of the related criminal act.[128] After Justice Reinvestment, however, those related technical violations are not a sufficient basis to revoke probation. Rather, the court is empowered to revoke only for a violation of the commit no criminal offense condition itself. As a result, the

---

122. *See* State v. Debnam, 23 N.C. App. 478 (1974) (upholding the trial court's revocation based on a nolle-prossed charge).

123. *See Monroe*, 83 N.C. App. at 145–46.

124. *See* State v. Greer, 173 N.C. 759 (1917) (holding that a jury verdict acquitting the defendant of a new criminal charge was not binding on the probation court so long as the court found facts based on the evidence before it).

125. *See Debnam*, 23 N.C. App. at 481 ("It may not be desirable for a judge to activate a suspended sentence upon conduct where a jury has found the defendant not guilty of a charge arising out of that conduct, but it appears to be within the power of the judge to do so.").

126. State v. Monk, 132 N.C. App. 248 (1999).

127. State v. Coffey, 255 N.C. 293 (1961) (rejecting a defendant's argument that his probation could not be revoked for the technical violation of possessing alcohol while criminal charges based on the same behavior were pending).

128. *See* State v. Causby, 269 N.C. 747 (1967) (upholding a revocation based on a violation of a "possess no alcohol for any purpose" condition despite the defendant's acquittal on a new illegal possession of alcohol charge).

probation court should either wait for a conviction on the alleged criminal act or make independent findings that the acts occurred.

In light of the JRA's limits on revocation authority, some violations that were, in the past, typically handled as technical violations are now being treated as violations of the commit no criminal offense condition. For instance, a probationer with a positive drug screen might be said to have committed the criminal offense of possession of a controlled substance, or a probationer who fails to appear for a violation hearing might be said to have committed the crime of failure to appear under G.S. 15A-543. *State v. Monroe*[129] supports that general line of reasoning, but any "independent finding" of a new criminal offense must be a finding of behavior that clearly constitutes a crime.[130] For instance, a positive drug screen does not, without more, constitute evidence sufficient to prove that a defendant committed the crime of knowingly and intentionally possessing a controlled substance.[131]

The JRA made no change to the longstanding rule that probation may not be revoked solely for conviction of a Class 3 misdemeanor.[132] That prohibition stands as an exception to the rule that probation may be revoked for a new criminal offense, just as it was previously an exception to the rule that probation could be revoked for any violation.

A 2011 legislative change outside of the JRA has a collateral effect on the new criminal offense condition. Effective for persons placed on probation on or after December 1, 2011, probation tolling under G.S. 15A-1344(g) was repealed.[133] Under that law, when a person had pending criminal charges that could result in revocation proceedings (essentially, any charge other than a Class 3 misdemeanor), that person's probation was tolled, meaning time ceased to run off the period of probation. With the tolling law in place, the State and the courts could comfortably wait for a pending criminal charge to run its course before deciding whether also to bring the alleged criminal behavior as a violation of probation. There was no fear of the court losing jurisdiction over the probation matter in the meantime, because the probation period would be extended for as long as the charge was pending.

---

129. 83 N.C. App. 143 (1986).
130. *See* State v. Hardin, 183 N.C. 815 (1922) (setting aside a trial court order activating a suspended judgment when the probationer's alleged criminal act, possessing 150 gallons of wine, was not a crime).
131. State v. Harris, 361 N.C. 400 (2007).
132. G.S. 15A-1344(d).
133. S.L. 2011-62.

That was particularly important in districts with a hard and fast rule against considering pending charges as a probation violation.

Without tolling, probation officers will want to at least file violation reports based on pending criminal charges before a period of probation expires so the court can have authority over the case under G.S. 15A-1344(f). That statute gives the court jurisdiction to hear and respond to a violation of probation after the probation period has expired if the violation report is filed before expiration.

Absconding. Under the JRA the court may revoke probation for a violation of the new statutory absconding condition set out in G.S. 15A-1343(b)(3a), discussed above. However, that condition only applies to persons on probation for offenses that occurred on or after December 1, 2011.[134] The JRA empowers judges to revoke only for violations of the new statutory absconding condition; the act refers explicitly to the statutory subsection of the new condition, not to absconding generally. Thus, violations of other conditions (such as the "remain within the jurisdiction" condition or the "failure to report to the officer" condition) are ineligible for revocation, even though the Section of Community Corrections refers to them as absconders. For violations occurring on or after December 1, 2011, court and corrections officials should thus be careful to distinguish between statutory absconders and policy absconders. Only the former may be revoked, whereas the latter are technical violators subject to CRV or other non-revocation response options. If an offender allegedly absconded before December 1, 2011, that offender would be eligible for revocation under the applicable prior law.

Even for offenders actually subject to the new statutory absconding condition, the language of the condition itself is not clear about what avoiding supervision means or how long a person's whereabouts must be unknown before that person becomes an absconder. Those thresholds will, to some degree, be shaped by other conditions to which the probationer may be subject and by the contact frequency standards associated with the probationer's supervision level. Additionally, probation officers are still required as a matter of their internal policy to conduct a specialized investigation before declaring that an offender has absconded. That investigation includes attempting to contact the offender by telephone, visiting the offender's residence in the daytime and in the evening, contacting the offender's landlord and neighbors, visiting the offender's workplace or school, contacting the

---

134. S.L. 2011-412, § 2.5.

offender's relatives and associates, and contacting local law enforcement, including the jail.[135]

I. Electing to Serve a Sentence after Justice Reinvestment

Council of State Governments (CSG) analysts noted that many North Carolina defendants choose to serve prison sentences rather than complete a term of probation. Some defendants ask for active sentences in lieu of probation at the outset, while others admit to violations in order to have their probation revoked. Despite the 1995 repeal of G.S. 15A-1341(c), the law that formerly allowed probationers to "elect to serve,"[136] the CSG reported that approximately 8 percent of probationers chose to serve a short sentence in prison rather than complete a longer sentence on probation.[137] The Justice Reinvestment Act (JRA) made several changes that directly and indirectly affect the various ways defendants attempt to elect to serve a sentence.

At sentencing, a defendant who falls within a cell on the sentencing grid that allows for active punishment (that is, one that includes an "A" as a dispositional option) certainly is free to ask the judge for an active sentence. The judge is likewise free to impose one. Defendants should be aware, however, that for felony offenses committed on or after December 1, 2011, they will be released onto PRS at the conclusion of the active term, and that under G.S. 15A-1368.2(b), PRS cannot be refused. Knowing that they will eventually have to serve a period of supervised release very similar to probation, defendants may be less inclined to request active time.

Defendants who fall in a cell on the sentencing grid that does not allow for an active punishment may not, in general, receive an active sentence. There is a limited exception to that rule for misdemeanants, allowing an "active" sentence to time served even if the defendant falls in a "C" or "C/I" cell on the sentencing grid.[138] There is no parallel statutory provision for felonies, although any felon—even one who falls in a "C," "C/I," or "I" grid cell—should be sentenced to time served if that person's jail credit exceeds

---

135. COMMUNITY CORRECTIONS POLICY, *supra* note 39, § E.0503.
136. 1995 N.C. SESS. LAWS ch. 429 (effective for criminal offenses occurring on or after January 1, 1997).
137. "Framework," *supra* note 36, at 7.
138. G.S. 15A-1340.20(c1).

the maximum sentence imposed. If the maximum has already been served, there would be no sentence left to suspend. However, jail credit in excess of the *minimum* imposed sentence is not sufficient to permit a sentence to time served. And with felony maximum sentences inflated to accommodate PRS, fewer defendants will have served time in excess of the maximum. For instance, a defendant with 9 months of pretrial jail credit sentenced to 6–17 months cannot be sentenced to time served; 8 months remain on the defendant's maximum sentence.

Outside of those "time served" scenarios, an active sentence is impermissible for a defendant falling in a grid cell without an "A." Under prior law, a common work-around for those defendants was to be sentenced to probation and then immediately have that probation revoked. The basis for the revocation was the defendant's admission to a violation of probation, often regular condition G.S. 15A-1343(b)(3) requiring a person to report to the probation officer as ordered. That two-step process avoided a later challenge, raised via appeal or motion for appropriate relief, that the original sentence was unlawful.

This approach will not work after Justice Reinvestment. For probation violations occurring on or after December 1, 2011, the court may revoke a defendant's probation only for a new criminal offense, for absconding, or when the defendant has previously received two CRV periods.[139] Unless the defendant admits to one of those specific violations, the longest period of confinement the court may order is 90 days of CRV under G.S. 15A-1344(d2). For many misdemeanants the CRV period could be long enough to use up the entire remaining sentence, allowing for the functional equivalent of a revocation.[140] But that is unlikely to be the case for most felons.

For felons with offense dates on or after December 1, 2011, the two-step approach also probably does not accomplish the goal of serving time quickly without the need for supervised release. All felons with offense dates after December 1, 2011, receive PRS, which cannot be refused. As a practical matter, that supervision is very similar to the probation they sought to avoid in the first place. The analysis is the same for defendants already on probation who wish to serve their time. They must admit to a revocation-eligible violation to be revoked, but their incentive for doing so is reduced by the PRS that awaits at the conclusion of their activated sentence.

---

139. G.S. 15A-1344(a); G.S. 15A-1344(d2).

140. Unlike active sentences, CRV periods are not reduced by sentence reduction credits. *See supra* notes 114–15 and accompanying text.

Finally, defendants, lawyers, and court officials should bear in mind that G.S. 15A-1341(c) is still repealed. Defendants do not at any point have a statutory right to refuse probation or, as is sometimes said, to "invoke" their sentence. The elect-to-serve check-box does not appear on the most recent editions of the AOC judgment forms.

J. Repeal of Criminal Justice Partnership Program and Creation of Treatment for Effective Community Supervision

The Criminal Justice Partnership Program (CJPP) was a state–local partnership established as part of Structured Sentencing. Through it, local Criminal Justice Advisory Boards advised the counties on the composition and funding of local community corrections programs. The boards were made up of a variety of local stakeholders in the criminal justice system, including county commissioners, county managers, judges, prosecutors, sheriffs, and probation officers. State funds flowed to eligible counties according to a pre-established funding formula. Counties then spent the money on things like substance abuse treatment centers and day-reporting centers according to their locally developed plans. The JRA repealed CJPP (Article 6A of G.S. Chapter 143B) in its entirety, including the statutory authorization for local advisory boards. The repeal was effective July 1, 2011, but allowed DAC to continue to contract with existing providers on a sole-source basis during fiscal year 2011–12.

The JRA replaced CJPP with the centrally administered Treatment for Effective Community Supervision (TECS) program.[141] Under TECS, DAC will contract with "eligible entities" directly through a competitive procurement process to provide community-based services to offenders on probation, parole, or PRS. The contracts will be between DAC and the service providers themselves; the counties will not act as intermediaries. Local governments are, however, listed among the entities eligible to compete for contracts. Other eligible entities include regional governments, nongovernmental entities, and collaborative partnerships.[142]

---

141. In the JRA itself, the Treatment for Effective Community Supervision (TECS) program was codified as Article 6B of G.S. Chapter 143B. It was recodified as G.S. 143B-1150 through G.S. 143B-1201 at the direction of the revisor of statutes.

142. G.S. 143B-1152(4).

The types of programs eligible for TECS funding include, but are not limited to, substance abuse treatment services and cognitive behavioral programming.[143] Contracts for substance abuse treatment services must be awarded to certified or licensed substance abuse professionals, defined to include North Carolina Substance Abuse Professional Practice Board certified or licensed substance abuse professionals and Department of Health and Human Services licensed agencies.[144] Contracting service providers may spend no more than 15 percent of their TECS funding for administrative purposes.[145] The law creates a 23-member State Community Corrections Advisory Board tasked with recommending, monitoring, and evaluating programs.[146]

Offenders eligible for services through TECS are adults convicted of a misdemeanor or felony and those on probation pursuant to a conditional discharge under G.S. 90-96 who have received a nonincarcerative sentence of a community or intermediate punishment or are serving a term of parole or PRS after an active sentence of imprisonment.[147] Impaired driving defendants are thus excluded unless they are on PRS (pursuant to a sentence for an aggravated level one DWI) or parole. Unlike CJPP, TECS does not allow for funding for programs for pretrial inmates.[148] The priority populations for TECS programs are eligible misdemeanants deemed to have a "high" risk level and a "moderate" to "high" need for substance abuse treatment and felons and felony G.S. 90-96 probationers regardless of their risk or needs levels.[149]

As part of the TECS program, DAC must publish a recidivism reduction plan that articulates a goal of reducing revocations of probation and PRS by 20 percent from the rate in the 2009–10 fiscal year.[150]

143. G.S. 143B-1160.
144. G.S. 143B-1152.
145. G.S. 143B-1156(d).
146. G.S. 143B-1158.
147. G.S. 143B-1154(a). Strictly speaking, G.S. 90-96 probationers do not fit within any of these categories, as they have not yet received a sentence of community or intermediate punishment.
148. *Cf.* G.S. 143B-273.14(a)(2) (repealed).
149. G.S. 143B-1154(b). See *supra* "E. Risk Assessment" for a discussion of the risk and needs levels.
150. G.S. 143B-1155(b)(1).

Chapter 3

Changes to G.S. 90-96 and Related Provisions

North Carolina General Statute (hereinafter G.S.) 90-96 allows for a conditional discharge for certain drug and drug paraphernalia offenders. It is not a deferred prosecution. It is, rather, a process that allows certain defendants who have pled guilty or been found guilty to be placed on probation without entry of judgment in the case. If the defendant successfully completes the probation, the court must dismiss the proceedings and discharge the defendant. The discharge and dismissal is without court adjudication of guilt and does not count as a conviction. Successful defendants under age 22 at the time of their offense may be eligible to have records related to the offense expunged under G.S. 15A-145.2(a).[1] If the defendant violates probation, the court may enter an adjudication of guilt and sentence the defendant as otherwise provided by law.[2]

---

1. North Carolina General Statute (hereinafter G.S.) § 90-96(b).

2. For a more detailed discussion of the discharge and dismissal and expunction procedures related to G.S. 90-96, see JOHN RUBIN, RELIEF FROM A CRIMINAL CONVICTION: A DIGITAL GUIDE TO EXPUNCTIONS, RESTORATION OF RIGHTS, AND OTHER PROCEDURES IN NORTH CAROLINA (UNC School of Government, forthcoming 2012).

A. Eligibility

The Justice Reinvestment Act (JRA) made multiple changes to the eligibility requirements for conditional discharges under G.S. 90-96(a), 90-96(a1), 90-96(e), and related expunction provisions in G.S. 15A-145.2. Subsections (a) and (a1) of G.S. 90-96 provide for two distinct types of conditional discharge. They are therefore discussed separately below. All of the changes were effective January 1, 2012, and apply to persons entering a plea or found guilty on or after that date.[3]

Changes to G.S. 90-96(a)

The most significant JRA changes to G.S. 90-96 involve conditional discharges under G.S. 90-96(a).

Offense eligibility. The JRA expanded the offenses eligible for conditional discharge under G.S. 90-96(a). The revised law allows for conditional discharge under this section for an eligible defendant who is found guilty of or pleads guilty to

- any felony simple possession of a controlled substance offense under G.S. 90-95(a)(3),
- any misdemeanor possession of a controlled substance in any offense class schedule, or
- misdemeanor possession of drug paraphernalia under G.S. 90-113.22.

Previously, the only felony offense eligible for discharge and dismissal under G.S. 90-96(a) was possession of less than one gram of cocaine. As under prior law, only simple possession offenses under G.S. 90-95(a)(3) are eligible for conditional discharge; offenses involving intent to manufacture, sell, or deliver controlled substances continue to be ineligible.

Offender eligibility. The JRA narrowed the pool of defendants eligible for conditional discharge under G.S. 90-96(a). The revised law limits eligibility to defendants who have no prior

- felony convictions of any type under any state or federal law (previously, a felony conviction barred a discharge and dismissal under G.S. 90-96(a) only if it involved offenses under Article 5 of G.S. Chapter 90),

---

3. North Carolina Session Law (hereinafter S.L.) 2011-192, § 5.(e).

- misdemeanor controlled substance convictions under Article 5 of G.S. Chapter 90,
- misdemeanor drug paraphernalia convictions under any state or federal law relating to the paraphernalia included in Article 5B of G.S. Chapter 90, or
- misdemeanor convictions under any state or federal law relating to the substances included in Article 5A of G.S. Chapter 90, the Toxic Vapors Act (sometimes referred to as "huffing" offenses).

As under prior law, a person is barred from discharge and dismissal under G.S. 90-96(a) if that person has received any prior discharge and dismissal under G.S. 90-96 or G.S. 90-113.14 (a parallel provision that allows for the discharge and dismissal of toxic vapor convictions).

G.S 90-96(a) mandatory for certain defendants. Finally, the JRA made discharge and dismissal under G.S. 90-96(a) mandatory for eligible defendants who consent to it. Previously, the decision to place a person on probation under G.S. 90-96 was left within the discretion of the court.

The mandatory nature of revised G.S. 90-96(a) has raised a variety of legal and logistical issues since the law came into effect. For example, prosecutors have expressed concern that more defendants will risk trials on simple possession offenses, knowing that the court will be bound to place them on probation under G.S. 90-96(a) if they are convicted. Prosecutors are also less willing to reduce more serious felony charges, such as possession with intent to sell, manufacture, or deliver a controlled substance, on account of the mandatory outcome of a simple possession conviction.[4] Some district attorneys have also ended voluntary deferred prosecution programs out of concern that some defendants who fail in those programs might nonetheless receive a second opportunity for deferral through G.S. 90-96.

Defense lawyers, meanwhile, have noted that probation under G.S. 90-96(a) is in some ways a more severe punishment than other outcomes their clients may have been able to obtain for a simple possession conviction, such as a fine or a prayer for judgment continued. Of course, no defendant can be forced onto probation under G.S. 90-96(a); discharge and dismissal under that subsection is permissible only with the defendant's consent.

---

4. In some districts, a practice has emerged in which the defendant pleads to simple possession with an agreement that the defendant will not consent to the otherwise mandatory conditional discharge under G.S. 90-96(a).

Mandatory discharge and dismissal under G.S. 90-96(a) also raises issues for judges. Because proceedings may only be deferred under G.S. 90-96(a) with the consent of the defendant, questions have arisen about whether and to what degree the defendant must, upon conviction of an eligible offense, be advised about the nature of G.S. 90-96 and the consequences of refusing to consent to it. There is a related question about whether the court must document a defendant's refusal to consent. The statute does not expressly require it, but to avoid any later challenge the judge may wish to note on the sentencing judgment that the defendant did not consent to the conditional discharge. The most recent versions of the boilerplate judgment forms include a pre-printed optional finding to that effect.

An issue of concern to all parties is the proper and timely determination of a defendant's eligibility for conditional discharge under G.S. 90-96(a). When a defendant is convicted of a G.S. 90-96–eligible offense, a review of his or her criminal record will show whether the defendant has any disqualifying prior convictions of the types described above or a prior discharge and dismissal under G.S. 90-96 or G.S. 90-113.14. That review will not, however, indicate whether the defendant has a prior discharge and dismissal that has subsequently been expunged. The only record of expunged cases is maintained by the North Carolina Administrative Office of the Courts (AOC) in its confidential files.[5]

When a defendant's regular record shows no disqualifying convictions or conditional discharges, the court should order a query of the defendant's confidential file at the AOC to ensure that the defendant has not had a prior discharge or dismissal that does not appear on the defendant's record because it was expunged. The court may make the query using Form AOC-CR-237, Request for Report of Conditional Discharge. The query can be made either before or after the defendant has been convicted of a G.S. 90-96–eligible offense, but because it may take several days for the AOC to reply in a confidential manner, the parties may wish to make the query before the defendant pleads or is found guilty.[6] Otherwise, the court will likely have

---

5. G.S. 15A-151.

6. Some have expressed concern that the query will take months. That concern likely stems from confusion between the process for querying the AOC's confidential file (which takes several business days) and the expunction review process used by the State Bureau of Investigation (which can take months). The SBI is not involved in the

to continue the proceedings for a proper determination of whether placement onto probation under G.S. 90-96(a) is required, necessitating additional court proceedings. Form AOC-CR-237 includes language allowing the parties to request an advance determination of whether the defendant has a disqualifying prior conditional discharge. The request should be signed by a judge. The query is only necessary when the defendant's regular criminal record shows no disqualifications; if eligibility can be ruled out through available information, no query is needed. For defendants who might be eligible, the parties may wish to submit the advance query even when the defendant is charged with a more serious offense (for example, drug trafficking) in anticipation of the possibility that the defendant will be convicted of a lesser-included simple possession offense.

Conditional discharge is apparently mandatory even when an eligible defendant is convicted of multiple simple possession offenses at once. If the convictions arise at the same time, none is a disqualifier for the others, and the court apparently must defer proceedings and place the defendant on G.S. 90-96 probation for all of them (assuming the defendant consents). Multiple cases probably should not, however, be "consolidated" into a single G.S. 90-96 deferral. Rather, the judge's authority to consolidate multiple offenses for judgment arises when the defendant is sentenced.[7] If consolidation is to happen at all, it seems that it would properly take place after a defendant's G.S. 90-96 probation is revoked and he or she is being sentenced.

Changes to G.S. 90-96(a1)

Subsection (a1) of G.S. 90-96 provides for another type of conditional discharge separate from that set out in subsection (a). The same offenses are eligible for conditional discharge under G.S. 90-96(a1) as are eligible under subsection (a), but subsection (a1) is broader in terms of offender eligibility. A defendant is disqualified from receiving a conditional discharge under G.S. 90-96(a1) if he or she has a prior conviction for any offense that generally qualifies for conditional discharge under the provisions of subsection (a)

---

query of the AOC's confidential file. Additionally, the AOC's Court Services Division has created a process for handling expedited requests via fax.

7. G.S. 15A-1340.15(b) (consolidation of felonies); G.S. 15A-1340.22(b) (consolidation of misdemeanors).

(simple possession of a controlled substance or possession of drug paraphernalia) or a prior violation of

- G.S. 90-95(a)(1) (manufacture, sale, or delivery of a controlled substance or possession with intent to manufacture, sell, or deliver),
- G.S. 90-95(a)(2) (creation, sale, or delivery, or possession with intent to sell or deliver, a counterfeit controlled substance),
- G.S. 90-95(a)(3) (simple possession),
- G.S. 90-113.10 (inhaling toxic fumes),
- G.S. 90-113.11 (possession of toxic substances for the purpose of inhaling),
- G.S. 90-113.12 (sale of toxic substances), or
- G.S. 90-113.22 (possession of drug paraphernalia).

A prior conviction for a non-drug felony offense is not a disqualifier under G.S. 90-96(a1) as it is under G.S. 90-96(a). Nor does an out-of-state conviction disqualify a person for a conditional discharge under G.S. 90-96(a1).

G.S. 90-96(a1) also includes a seven-year look-back period for disqualifying prior convictions and prior discharges and dismissals. No prior offense occurring more than seven years before the date of the current offense can be the basis of a disqualifying prior conviction or prior discharge and dismissal under subsection (a1).

Unlike G.S. 90-96(a), conditional discharge under G.S. 90-96(a1) is discretionary with the trial court. Given the substantial overlap between the two subsections and the mandatory nature of revised G.S. 90-96(a), subsection (a1) appears to be a discretionary option for defendants who may be ineligible for the mandatory discharge under G.S. 90-96(a) on account of an older (more than seven years older) drug conviction or perhaps a prior non-drug felony conviction. A defendant may be ordered onto probation under G.S. 90-96(a1) without his or her consent.

The JRA did not make any changes to the discharge and dismissal provisions applicable to toxic vapor offenses under G.S. 90-113.14.

B. Probation under G.S. 90-96

When a defendant receives a conditional discharge under G.S. 90-96(a) or G.S. 90-96(a1), the judge defers further proceedings and places the defendant on probation. In general, probation under G.S. 90-96 is subject to the same rules as any probation case unless there is some statutory provision to the contrary.[8] In *State v. Burns*, for example, the court of appeals held that the jurisdictional rules for violation hearings held after a period of probation has expired apply in G.S. 90-96 cases just as they do in regular probation cases.

Several provisions in G.S. 90-96 depart from the regular probation rules, however. These differences are not consistent between G.S. 90-96 subsection (a) and subsection (a1).

G.S. 90-96(a)

Probation under G.S. 90-96(a) is mostly left to the discretion of the trial judge. That subsection directs the court to place defendants on probation "upon such reasonable terms and conditions as it may require"; thus, there are no mandatory conditions. The court may, however, allow the defendant to participate in a drug education program.[9] That permissive reference to drug education programs differs from the mandatory requirement for drug education school for probation cases under G.S. 90-96(a1), described below. All G.S. 90-96 probationers are eligible for services under the Treatment for Effective Community Supervision program, with G.S. 90-96 felons highlighted as a "priority population" regardless of their assessed risk and needs.[10]

Probation under subsection (a) may be supervised or unsupervised and may apparently be for any duration in the court's discretion, up to 5 years.[11] It is unclear whether the default rules on probation length applicable in Structured Sentencing cases (for example, probation may be for not less than 6 months nor more than 18 months for a community-punished misdemeanant), set out in G.S. 15A-1343.2(d), apply in G.S. 90-96 cases. A judge wishing to impose a period of probation longer than the Structured Sentencing default should probably make a finding that a longer period is required.

---

8. State v. Burns, 171 N.C. App. 759, 761 (2005) ("In the absence of a provision to the contrary, and except where specifically excluded, the general probation provisions found in Article 82 of Chapter 15A apply to probation imposed under [G.S.] 90-96.").

9. The Treatment for Effective Community Supervision program is the statutory successor to the Criminal Justice Partnership Program. *See supra* "J. Repeal of Criminal Justice Partnership Program and Creation of Treatment for Effective Community Supervision" in Chapter 2.

10. G.S. 143B-1154.

11. G.S. 15A-1342(a). The 2-year maximum period for deferred prosecution probation does not apply in G.S. 90-96 cases.

The court should use Form AOC-CR-619 (version A, B, or C, depending on the defendant's offense date) to place a person on probation under G.S. 90-96(a). That form includes all regular conditions of probation by default and then includes space for the judge to check or add special conditions in his or her discretion.

G.S. 90-96(a1)

G.S. 90-96(a1) includes several specific requirements for probation under that subsection. First, the probation must be for at least one year. (The maximum permissible period is likely the same as in a G.S. 90-96(a) case, 5 years.) Probation under subsection (a1) must include a condition that the defendant, within 150 days, enroll in, pay the $150 fee for, and successfully complete a program of instruction at a drug education school approved by the Department of Health and Human Services under G.S. 90-96.01. The court may omit the drug education school condition only if there is no school within a reasonable distance or if extenuating circumstances would make it unlikely that the defendant would benefit from it.

The court should use Form AOC-CR-627 (version A, B, or C, depending on the defendant's offense date) to place a person on probation under G.S. 90-96(a1). That form incorporates the conditions and findings specifically applicable to probation under that subsection.

Some aspects of traditional probation cases may be inapplicable in G.S. 90-96 cases. For example, whether a judge should order collection of a DNA sample from a G.S. 90-96–eligible defendant convicted of a felony possession offense is unclear. Generally, when a person convicted of a felony is placed on probation, that person must provide a DNA sample "as a condition of the sentence."[12] The defendant in a G.S. 90-96 case necessarily has pled or been found guilty but not yet been sentenced; thus, it is uncertain whether DNA collection should be ordered as a condition of the G.S. 90-96 probation.

---

12. G.S. 15A-266.4.

C. Responses to Noncompliance in G.S. 90-96 Probation Cases

Hearing Venue and Court

A person alleged to have violated G.S. 90-96 probation is, like any probationer, entitled to a hearing on the violation. A threshold issue in that regard is where the hearing should be held. Subsection G.S. 90-96(a) is silent as to the proper venue; thus, under *State v. Burns*,[13] the regular rules of G.S. 15A-1344(a) should probably apply. Therefore, the hearing could be held in the district of origin, where the offender resides, or where the alleged violation occurred. As a practical matter, however, the case should probably be returned to the district of origin—something the court is empowered to do in any probation case under G.S. 15A-1344(c)—because that court will have to enter judgment and sentence the defendant in case of revocation.

In cases where a felony plea to an eligible offense is entered in district court under authority of G.S. 7A-272(c), the district court would place the defendant on G.S. 90-96 probation. Assuming the rules applicable to regular probation cases apply, the superior court would have default jurisdiction over any violation in the case, although the district court could hear it with the consent of the State and the defendant.[14] There may be some argument, however, that "the court" referenced in G.S. 90-96(a), responsible for entering an adjudication of guilt in the event of violation, is the same court in which the defendant pled or was found guilty. Subsection (a1) includes a provision stating that a person is entitled to a hearing "before the court of original jurisdiction prior to revocation of probation," perhaps suggesting that the case should remain in the court where it began. If the violation hearing is heard in superior court and the G.S. 90-96 probation is revoked, the case probably should be remanded to district court for sentencing and entry of judgment, as that is the court that initially accepted the defendant's plea.[15]

Permissible Responses to Noncompliance

Under G.S. 90-96(a), the court may, upon violation of a term or condition of probation, revoke the probation, enter an adjudication of guilt, and proceed as otherwise provided. Revocation is not required in the event of a violation but rather is discretionary with the trial court. Apparently any type of

---

13. 171 N.C. App. 759 (2005).
14. G.S. 7A-271(e).
15. G.S. 7A-272(d).

violation may serve as a basis for revocation of G.S. 90-96 probation. These cases probably are not subject to the post-JRA rule that a person must receive two periods of confinement in response to violation (CRV) before he or she may be revoked for a technical violation. In fact, CRV is probably inappropriate in G.S. 90-96 cases in any event. The CRV law requires the court to consider how much time remains on the defendant's maximum imposed sentence when determining the length of the CRV, but there is no imposed sentence in a G.S. 90-96 case.[16] For similar reasons the court probably may not impose special probation in a G.S. 90-96 case, either at the outset or in response to a violation. There is no suspended sentence in place to serve as a benchmark for determining the permissible length of the active portion of the split sentence under the one-fourth rule of G.S. 15A-1351(a).

Subsection (a1) does not address violations generally, but it does say that a person's "failure to complete a program of instruction at a drug education school" shall constitute grounds to revoke. The subsection defines that failure broadly to include failing to attend classes without an excuse, failing to complete the course in a timely fashion, or failing to pay the required fee. If the court receives an instructor's report about a person's failure to complete the drug education school, it must revoke probation.

When a person's G.S. 90-96 probation is revoked, the revocation may be appealed—to superior court for a de novo hearing or to the appellate division, as the case may be—as in an ordinary probation case.[17] Whether the underlying conviction itself may also be appealed at that point is unclear. In *State v. Cordon,* the court of appeals held that a defendant who consents to G.S. 90-96 probation abandons the right to appeal on the issue of guilt or innocence of the underlying offense.[18] *Cordon* may be difficult to square with more recent cases regarding a defendant's waiver of the right to a jury trial.[19] But in light of *Cordon,* a defendant convicted of a G.S. 90-96–eligible

---

16. G.S. 15A-1344(d2).

17. G.S. 90-96(a) provides that "[d]isposition of a case to determine discharge and dismissal under this section at the district court division of the General Court of Justice shall be final for the purpose of appeal." That provision probably overcomes any sense that the G.S. 90-96 revocation is not yet ripe for appeal because it happened before judgment was entered on the underlying offense.

18. 21 N.C. App. 394 (1974).

19. *See, e.g.,* State v. Reynolds, ___ N.C. App. ___, 721 S.E.2d 333 (Feb. 7, 2012) (holding that a defendant's guilty plea was not knowing and voluntary when the trial court

offense who wishes to appeal the conviction may wish to refuse to consent to G.S. 90-96 at the outset.

For cases under both subsection (a) and (a1), the court may use Form AOC-CR-622 to revoke or modify G.S. 90-96 probation or to dismiss the case when a defendant has successfully fulfilled the terms and conditions of the probation.

D. Changes to Related Expunction Provisions

Offenders who succeed on G.S. 90-96 probation who were not over 21 years of age at the time of the offense (that is, they had not yet turned 22 at that time) are eligible for an expunction of records relating to the arrest, indictment or information, trial, finding of guilty, and dismissal and discharge of the conviction.[20] The JRA did not amend the expunction procedures in G.S. 15A-145(a) applicable to young offenders who obtain a discharge and dismissal under G.S. 90-96(a) or (a1).

The JRA did, however, amend G.S. 90-96(d) and the corresponding expunction procedure in G.S. 15A-145.2(b) to broaden the charges that may be expunged when a defendant not over 21 years of age at the time of the alleged offense is found not guilty or when the charges are dismissed by the State. Under the revised law, a person may obtain an expunction of any dismissed or acquitted felony controlled substance possession charge (not just felony possession of less than 1 gram of cocaine, as was the case under prior law) or any misdemeanor simple possession charge. The change was effective for persons who enter a plea or are found guilty of an offense on or after January 1, 2012.[21] That language was likely intended to apply as well to findings of not guilty and dismissals entered on or after January 1, 2012.

The JRA also amended G.S. 90-96(e) and corresponding G.S. 15A-145.2(c) regarding cancellation and expunction of certain drug convictions for offenders who were not over 21 years of age at the time of the offense. Those subsections allow (but do not require) a court to give a young defendant roughly the same relief the defendant would get upon successful completion

---

advised him that the maximum possible sentence he faced was 168 months when it was actually 171 months).

20. G.S. 15A-145.2.
21. S.L. 2011-192, § 5.(e).

of G.S. 90-96 probation—cancellation of the conviction and expunction of related records—without ever having to succeed on G.S. 90-96 probation. Similar to the changes made to G.S. 90-96(a), the JRA broadened offense eligibility under G.S. 15A-145.2(c) by allowing cancellation and expunction for any felony or misdemeanor simple possession conviction (previously, the only eligible felony offense was possession of less than 1 gram of cocaine) or possession of drug paraphernalia conviction. On the other hand, the JRA narrowed the pool of eligible offenders by providing that any prior felony conviction is a disqualifier. Under prior law, only prior drug-related felonies disqualified a person for cancellation and expunction under G.S. 15A-145.2(c). The revised law applies to persons who enter a plea or are found guilty on or after January 1, 2012.

The court may use Form AOC-CR-266 to enter the expunctions described above.

E. Deferred Judgment as a Prior Conviction

A person's conviction for a drug or drug paraphernalia possession offense counts for prior record points while that person is still on G.S. 90-96 probation. In *State v. Hasty*,[22] the court of appeals held that until the conviction is discharged and dismissed, it counts toward the person's prior record level. A defendant has necessarily pled or been found guilty before being placed on G.S. 90-96 probation, and under G.S. 15A-1331(b) it is that determination of guilt that counts as a conviction for sentencing purposes. If a person ultimately succeeds on the G.S. 90-96 probation and the conviction is dismissed, then it would not count for points. If it had already been counted for points in a new case in the interim but was later dismissed, the defendant might have an argument for resentencing of that new case if the dismissed conviction affected the sentence.[23]

---

22. 133 N.C. App. 563 (1999).

23. *See* State v. Bidgood, 144 N.C. App. 267, 276 (2001) (holding that it would be "unjust to permit an enhanced sentence to stand where . . . the Prior Record Level has been erroneously calculated due to a subsequent reversal of a conviction on appeal").

Chapter 4

Changes to the Proper Place to Serve a Sentence

The Justice Reinvestment Act (JRA) made several changes to the rules for where a sentence is served. The general aim of those changes was to shift responsibility for housing misdemeanor offenders from the prison system to the counties, albeit with financial support from a statewide fund.[1] The changes were a response to an observation by Council of State Governments analysts that North Carolina was unusual in the number of misdemeanants housed in its prisons.

---

1. Responsibility for housing misdemeanants has shifted between the state and the counties throughout North Carolina history. Until the Civil War, the state provided no correctional facilities; housing inmates was a matter of local concern. Central Prison housed the state's most dangerous inmates upon its completion in 1884, but most other inmates continued to serve their sentences in county facilities. In response to Depression-era financial strains, the state assumed responsibility for the prison system in 1931, although inmates serving short sentences still remained in the jail. The sentence-length threshold at which an inmate was transferred from the jail to prison has varied over the years. It began at 60 days in 1931, was lowered to 30 days shortly thereafter, increased to 6 months in the 1970s, and then was reduced to 90 days in the 1990s. State reimbursement to the counties for housing misdemeanants has also varied over time. Beginning in the late 1970s, the state reimbursed the counties for certain inmates at $10 per day. The reimbursement amount was $18 per day upon its repeal in 2009 as a cost-cutting measure. North Carolina Session Law (hereinafter S.L.) 2009-451, § 19.22A. Given this history, the sentence-length thresholds and reimbursement mechanism set out in the Justice Reinvestment Act (JRA) are merely the latest chapter in a long-running story. *See* James C. Drennan, "Administration of Justice," in *State-Local Relations in North Carolina: Their Evolution and Current Status*, ed. Charles D. Liner (Chapel Hill, N.C.: UNC Institute of Government, 1985), 45–46.

The changes described below apply to sentences imposed on or after January 1, 2012.[2] In general, a sentence is "imposed" when initially entered by the sentencing court. Thus, suspended sentences imposed before January 1, 2012, but activated after that date probably are not governed by the new rules.[3]

A. New Place-of-Confinement Rules under the JRA

Felons

Under the amended law, felons must be committed to the Department of Public Safety, Division of Adult Correction (DAC, formerly the Department of Correction). In other words, they must be sentenced to prison, not to the jail. The JRA removed the provision in North Carolina General Statute (hereinafter G.S.) 15A-1352(b) allowing a felon to serve a sentence in the local jail upon request of the sheriff or the board of commissioners.[4]

Misdemeanants

Under prior law, misdemeanants with a sentence of 90 days or less were required to be sentenced to the local jail, except as provided in G.S. 148-32.1. Misdemeanants with a sentence in excess of 90 days could be sentenced to prison or to the jail in the court's discretion.[5] Under the new law, misdemeanants

- with a sentence imposed of 90 days or less must be committed to a facility other than one maintained by DAC—generally, the local

---

2. S.L. 2011-192, § 7.(q).

3. If, at the point of revocation, the court changes the initial sentence—either by reducing it under North Carolina General Statute (hereinafter G.S.) § 15A-1344(d) or by deciding for the first time that it is to run consecutively to or concurrently with another sentence—there may be an argument that a new sentence has been "imposed" and that the new place-of-confinement rules therefore apply. *See* State v. Hanner, 188 N.C. App. 137 (2008) (holding that the defendant had a right to be present when the court made a substantive change to his sentence—running it consecutively to another activated sentence—upon revocation of probation, on the rationale that the defendant had a right to be present when a sentence was imposed).

4. G.S. 15A-1352(b).

5. G.S. 15A-1352(a).

jail—except as provided in G.S. 148-32.1 (described below). Inmates are housed at county expense.[6]

- with a sentence imposed that requires confinement for a period of 91–180 days, except for impaired driving (DWI) under G.S. 20-138.1 or for nonpayment of a fine under Article 84 of G.S. Chapter 15A, must be committed to confinement pursuant to the new Statewide Misdemeanant Confinement Program (SMCP), described below. Counties are reimbursed for these inmates from the new Statewide Misdemeanant Confinement Fund, also described below.[7]
- with a sentence or sentences imposed that require confinement for more than 180 days must be committed to DAC. Inmates are housed at state expense.[8]

Under G.S. 15A-1352, the court determines to whose custody a defendant will be committed to serve his or her sentence. It is unclear whether the court should consider the length of the imposed sentence (unreduced by jail credit) or the length of time remaining to be served when evaluating whether a defendant should be committed to the local jail, the SMCP, or prison. For example, should a defendant with 30 days of jail credit who receives a 100-day sentence be committed to the SMCP (because the "imposed" sentence falls within the 91–180 day range) or the local jail (because the defendant has 70 days left to serve)?

Prior to the JRA, the statute setting the jail–prison threshold at 90 days referred simply to the "sentence imposed." The revised law uses slightly different language, with eligibility determined by whether the "sentence imposed requires confinement" for a particular period. The reference to required confinement suggests that the court should consider how much time the defendant actually has left to serve. Moreover, the fiscal note accompanying the final version of the bill said that "in order to be placed in the custody of the Department of Correction, the offender must have over 180 days remaining to serve, net of any credit for time served."[9] That interpretation of the law may, however, have been based on prior drafts of

---

6. *Id.*

7. G.S. 15A-1352(e).

8. G.S. 15A-1352(a).

9. "Legislative Fiscal Note: House Bill 642 (Sixth Edition)," General Assembly of North Carolina, Fiscal Research Division (June 14, 2011), www.ncleg.net/Sessions/2011/FiscalNotes/House/PDF/HFN0642v6.pdf, 5.

the bill, which had explicitly required the court to subtract credit for time already served when determining the proper place of confinement.

Under either interpretation the court probably should disregard the possibility of sentence reduction via earned time or good time, as neither credit is guaranteed.

Effect of Consecutive Sentences

When a defendant is subject to multiple judgments, whether the court should determine the proper place of confinement by considering each sentence in isolation or considering the effect of any consecutive sentences is unclear. The place-of-confinement statutes are inconsistent in how they describe the sentence-length thresholds for each place (the local jail, the SMCP, or prison). The statutory subsection describing which defendants should be sentenced to the SMCP, G.S. 15A-1352(e), refers to "a misdemeanor" and "a sentence" in the singular, whereas subsection (a) says that a defendant should be committed to DAC if the "sentence or sentences" imposed require confinement of more than 180 days.

An interpretation that takes both of those provisions into account is that consecutive sentences should not be aggregated when determining whether the defendant meets the 91-day floor for the SMCP but should be aggregated when determining whether sentences exceed the program's 180-day ceiling. To illustrate: two consecutive 50-day sentences would each be sentenced to the local jail because neither exceeds the 90-day threshold individually, while consecutive 100-day sentences would be sentenced to DAC because the sentences together require confinement of more than 180 days. Other interpretations are also possible.[10]

---

10. As a practical matter, many defendants are subject to multiple judgments entered by different judges at different times. There may not be a single judge in a position to make a holistic determination of the proper place of confinement for each sentence. For example, a judge entering a 60-day suspended sentence for Crime A has no way of knowing that the defendant may later have that sentence revoked and run consecutively to a 150-day sentence for Crime B. Does the proper place of confinement in Judgment A change from the local jail to DAC on account of the later-arising sentence? Perhaps, although there is no express statutory provision allowing that change to happen by operation of law or specifically directing a judge to amend the judgment. Many other examples involving non-contemporaneous convictions, convictions from different counties, convictions with sentences imposed before and after January 1, 2011, probation revocations, and combinations of Structured Sentencing and impaired driving sentences could be used to illustrate the complexity of the rules.

Exceptions to the 90-Day-or-Less Misdemeanor Confinement Rules

The JRA amended the rules for when certain misdemeanants can be committed to another county's jail or to DAC. The revised law applies only to misdemeanants not housed pursuant to the SMCP (separate transfer procedures, described below, apply to them). Under G.S. 148-32.1, as amended, the custodian of a local jail may certify in writing to the clerk of superior court that the jail

- is filled to capacity;
- cannot reasonably accommodate any more prisoners due to segregation requirements for particular prisoners;
- anticipates, in light of local experiences, an influx of temporary prisoners; or
- does not meet minimum standards published pursuant to G.S. 153A-221.

If the custodian does so, any district or superior court judge of the district where the facility is located may transfer a non-SMCP prisoner to another jail with available space. If no other jail has space and the transfer is requested because of either segregation requirements or noncompliance with minimum standards, the judge may order a non-SMCP inmate transferred to DAC. In no event, however, may a prisoner whose term of imprisonment is less than 30 days be transferred to DAC.[11]

The revised procedure is slightly more restrictive than prior law in terms of who may be transferred to DAC (prior law did not limit the reasons for which a person could be transferred). Additionally, DAC has apparently been enforcing preexisting rules more strictly since the new law came into effect. For instance, DAC is no longer accepting misdemeanants pursuant to a blanket "overcrowded letter" in which a sheriff represents that his or her jail cannot accommodate misdemeanants with sentences exceeding a certain length (45 days, for example). That procedure was common but never had a clear statutory basis.

Imprisonment for Fines

The JRA amended G.S. 15A-1352(c) to provide that persons imprisoned for failure to pay a fine imposed for a misdemeanor must be committed to DAC if the sentence or sentences require confinement for more than 180 days.

---

11. G.S. 148-32.1(b).

Inmates imprisoned for nonpayment of a fine are expressly excluded from the SMCP.[12]

Confinement in Response to Violation (CRV)

CRV is served where the defendant would have served an active sentence.[13] Thus, felony CRV is served in prison.[14] Misdemeanor CRV is served in the local jail, pursuant to the SMCP, or in prison, depending on the length of the defendant's suspended sentence or sentences and when they were imposed. The varying effective dates of the JRA will likely lead to interpretive wrinkles regarding the proper place of confinement for CRV. For instance, many defendants on probation for sentences entered before January 1, 2012, will be ordered to CRV based on violations that occurred after December 1, 2011. The place of confinement originally entered in those older judgments may not comport with the new place-of-confinement rules described above. But, as the place "where the defendant would have served an active sentence," it should probably still dictate the place of confinement for the CRV.

"Quick Dips"

Short-term confinement ordered by a probation officer pursuant to delegated authority under G.S. 15A-1343.2(e)–(f) or by a judge under new G.S. 15A-1343(a1)(3) is served in the local jail.

B. The Statewide Misdemeanant Confinement Program (SMCP)

The JRA established a new program for housing non-DWI misdemeanants with sentences imposed that require confinement for a period of 91 to 180 days.[15] The law required the North Carolina Sheriffs' Association Inc. (NCSA) to develop the program in consultation with DAC. After a brief pilot in late 2011, the program began statewide operation on January 1, 2012. As of this writing, over six hundred inmates are housed in the program.

---

12. G.S. 15A-1352(e).

13. G.S. 15A-1344(d2).

14. Confinement in response to violation (CRV) periods served in prison are served in one of the following facilities: Dan River, Greene, Odom, Tyrrell, Western Youth Institution and, for women, Fountain Correctional.

15. G.S. 148-32.1(b2).

Program Overview

When the court commits an inmate to the Statewide Misdemeanant Confinement Program (SMCP), the NCSA finds space for the inmate in a jail that has voluntarily agreed to provide space to the program. No county is required to participate as a "receiving county." As of this writing, approximately half of all counties (49) have volunteered space (see Figure 4.1 for a representation of these counties). The counties that participate in the program as receiving counties do so pursuant to a written agreement with DAC. Under that agreement and its related terms and conditions,[16] receiving counties are reimbursed at the rate of $40 per inmate per day for inmates housed through the program and receive additional money for out-of-jail medical expenses and certain transportation and supervision costs. The money comes from the Statewide Misdemeanant Confinement Fund, described below.

As the program has been implemented by the NCSA, all counties participate in the SMCP as "sending counties." That is, a misdemeanant from any county can be sentenced to the SMCP, and the county of conviction is expected to transport the inmate to a volunteer receiving county identified by the NCSA. (If the county of conviction is itself a volunteer receiving county, then the inmate will in all likelihood remain in that county's jail to serve the sentence.) Sending counties are reimbursed for transportation and supervision expenses related to the transfer of SMCP inmates according to the terms and conditions set by the NCSA.

If the NCSA determines that the jails available for housing misdemeanants under the SMCP are filled to capacity, a misdemeanant housed under the program may be transferred to DAC. DAC is then reimbursed for the costs of housing the inmate (including costs of "care, supervision, and transportation") from the Statewide Misdemeanant Confinement Fund.[17]

SMCP Funding Issues

The JRA established the Statewide Misdemeanant Confinement Fund (the Fund) to be used to cover the costs of managing the SMCP.[18] The program operates only as long as sufficient moneys are available in the Fund.[19] The

---

16. Memorandum by Eddie Caldwell, executive vice president and general counsel of the N.C. Sheriffs' Association (Mar. 21, 2012), www.ncsheriffs.org/documents/Memo%20Sheriffs%20SMCP%20Terms%20and%20Conditions%2003-21-2012.pdf.

17. G.S. 148-32.1(b4).

18. G.S. 148-10.4.

19. G.S. 148-32.1(b2).

Figure 4.1.   Counties that have vounteered beds to the Statewide Misdemeanant Confinement Program (SMCP) as of Sept. 30, 2012

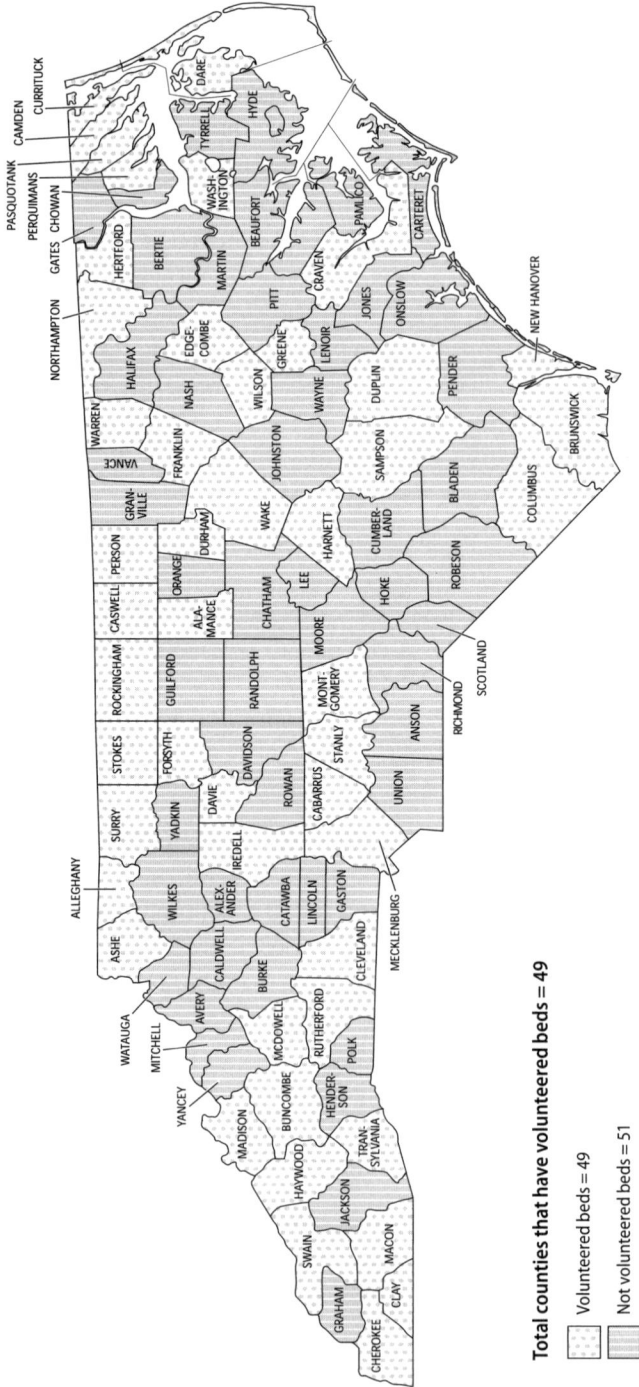

Total counties that have volunteered beds = 49

Volunteered beds = 49

Not volunteered beds = 51

Source: N.C. Sheriffs' Association

money in the Fund comes from two court costs effective August 1, 2011: (1) an $18 court cost for all district court convictions[20] and (2) a $50 cost specific to improper equipment violations.[21] As of June 30, 2012, the Fund had collected almost $19 million.[22]

Money in the Fund may be used for

- reimbursing counties for the costs of housing SMCP inmates, including their care, supervision, and transportation;
- reimbursing DAC for the costs of housing SMCP inmates when no space is available in the jails that have volunteered space to the program;
- paying the NCSA for administrative and operating expenses related to the program; and
- paying DAC for administrative and operating expenses related to the program.[23]

Ten percent of the receipts collected into the Fund are transferred on a monthly basis to the NCSA. One percent of the receipts collected into the Fund are transferred on a monthly basis into the General Fund to be allocated to DAC for administrative and operating expenses for the SMCP.[24]

SMCP "Safekeepers"

The JRA included a "safekeeper" provision, similar operationally to existing G.S. 162-39, for inmates housed under the SMCP. The new provision allows for the transfer of an SMCP inmate to DAC upon request and certification from the jail custodian to the clerk of superior court that the inmate (1) poses a security risk, (2) requires medical or mental health treatment that can best be provided by DAC, or (3) cannot be housed locally due to segregation requirements or noncompliance with jail standards and no other jail is available.[25] In response to the request, any superior or district court judge

---

20. G.S. 7A-304(a)(2b).

21. G.S. 7A-304(a)(4b). Money destined for the Statewide Misdemeanant Confinement Fund is exempt from the 10 percent collection assistance fee set out in G.S. 7A-321(d).

22. N.C. Sheriffs' Association, "Statewide Misdemeanant Confinement Program, Year-to-Date Reimbursement Summary" (June 30, 2012) (on file with the author).

23. G.S. 148-10.4(d).

24. G.S. 148-10.4(e).

25. G.S. 148-32.1(b3).

in the district in which the jail is located may transfer the inmate from the jail to prison. DAC is then reimbursed from the Fund for the cost of the misdemeanant's care. The jail custodian may use Form AOC-CR-623 to make a request for transfer under this provision. The court may use the same form to order the transfer. The transfer procedure set out in G.S. 148-32.1(b3) does not operate as a general exception to the SMCP—the transfer must be at the request of the custodian and for one of the reasons described above.

C. Confinement Rules Not Changed by the JRA
Special Probation (Split Sentences)

The JRA did not change the place-of-confinement rule for split sentences. The judge can, in his or her discretion, order a split sentence to be served in DAC or a designated local confinement facility or treatment facility. Noncontinuous periods of confinement (for example, "weekender" confinement) must be served in a local confinement facility or treatment facility; the judge may not order that noncontinuous periods be served in prison.[26]

Impaired Driving

The JRA did not change the baseline rule for where a DWI sentence should be served, set out in G.S. 20-176(c1). DWI inmates were excluded from the SMCP,[27] but impaired driving sentences were not excluded from the new rule for misdemeanor sentences in excess of 180 days. Taking G.S. 20-176(c1) and amended G.S. 15A-1352 into account, the complete rule for DWI sentences is as follows:

- DWI defendants who have no prior DWI convictions under G.S. 20-138.1 and who have never been previously imprisoned in a local confinement facility for a violation of G.S. Chapter 20 must be sentenced to the local jail. The rule, which applies "notwithstanding

---

26. G.S. 15A-1351(a).

27. The literal language of G.S. 15A-1352(e) and G.S. 148-32.1(b2) excludes only impaired driving sentences under G.S. 20-138.1 from the Statewide Misdemeanant Confinement Program. That language was probably intended to exclude all offenses sentenced under G.S. 20-179. *See supra* note 4 in Chapter 2.

any other provision of law," does not turn on the length of the sentence.[28]

- DWI defendants being sentenced for a subsequent conviction under G.S. 20-138.1 or who have previously been imprisoned in a local confinement facility for a violation of Chapter 20
  - must be sentenced to the jail if the sentence imposed is for 90 days or less, except as provided in G.S. 148-32.1(b).
  - may probably be sentenced to the local jail or to DAC, in the court's discretion, if the sentence imposed requires confinement of 91 to 180 days, although no statute addresses this category of DWI defendant directly.
  - must be sentenced to DAC if the sentence or sentences imposed require confinement for more than 180 days.[29]

Work Release for Certain Misdemeanants

The JRA did not amend G.S. 15A-1352(d), a statute that allows the court to order work release for consenting misdemeanants. Defendants sentenced under that law are exempt from the place-of-confinement rules described above to the extent that the law allows the court, notwithstanding any other provision of law, to commit the defendant to a specific prison facility or jail to facilitate the work release arrangement.

D. Sentence Reduction Credits

With more inmates serving longer sentences in the jail, sheriffs and jail administrators must be mindful of the governing regulations on sentence credits. DAC's regulations on credits must be distributed to and followed by local jail administrators.[30] In general, Structured Sentencing misdemeanants are eligible for earned time of up to 4 days per month. Impaired driving inmates are eligible for good time at the rate of one day of credit for each day in custody without a violation of inmate conduct rules, which essentially

---

28. G.S. 20-176(c1).

29. G.S. 15A-1352(a).

30. G.S. 148-13(e). STATE OF NORTH CAROLINA, DEP'T OF CORRECTION, DIV. OF PRISONS, POLICY & PROCEDURE MANUAL (2011), Chapter B (Sentence Credits) (2011), www.doc.state.nc.us/dop/policy_procedure_manual/b0100.pdf.

cuts the sentence in half. There are additional rules for medically and physically unfit inmates.

The sheriff may also institute his or her own program—independent of prison regulations—for awarding credit for certain work and educational programs for sentenced inmates in the jail. Under G.S. 162-58, a board of county commissioners, subject to approval by the sheriff, may issue rules and regulations for work "on projects to benefit units of State or local government" by convicted inmates. The work must be supervised by county employees or sheriff's office personnel. A sheriff or jail administrator may also allow a convicted misdemeanant to participate in a GED program or "any other education, rehabilitation, or training program"—a fairly broad authorization—under G.S. 162-59.1; no board action is required for those programs. An inmate is entitled to a sentence reduction of 4 days for each 30 days of work performed or each 30 days of classes attended—with the caveat that a misdemeanant's total sentence reduction by earned time and credit under G.S. 162-60 cannot exceed 4 days per month of incarceration.[31]

By statute, sentence reduction credits are not allowed for inmates serving sentences of special probation (split sentences).[32] As matter of DAC policy, no credits are awarded to inmates serving CRV periods.[33]

E. Correcting Place-of-Confinement Errors

Aside from typographical errors or discrepancies between the written judgment and the court's oral pronouncement about the place of confinement, an error related to the defendant's place of confinement is an error of law, not a clerical error.[34] Thus, when ambiguities or disagreements arise, they should be addressed like any other perceived legal error in a judgment: through the appeal process; through a motion for appropriate relief; or upon review in

---

31. G.S. 15A-1340.20(d).

32. G.S. 148-13(f).

33. *See supra* notes 114–15 in Chapter 2 and accompanying text.

34. *See* State v. Jarman, 140 N.C. App. 198, 202 (2000) (holding that errors are judicial, not clerical, when they involve "judicial reasoning or determination"). *See generally* Jessica Smith, *Trial Judge's Authority to* Sua Sponte *Correct Errors after Entry of Judgment in a Criminal Case*, ADMIN. OF JUSTICE BULLETIN No. 2003/02 (UNC Institute of Government, May 2003), www.sog.unc.edu/sites/www.sog.unc.edu/files/aoj200302.pdf.

response to notification from the custodian to the court, the State, and the defendant that the judgment appears to be in error.[35] The judgment should be carried out as ordered until it is corrected,[36] and any change to it should be made only after a proper proceeding in the defendant's presence.[37]

---

35. Hamilton v. Freeman, 147 N.C. App. 195, 200 (2001).

36. *Id.* at 204 ("It is well established that a judgment . . . must be honored unless the judgment is void. Where a court has authority to hear and determine the questions in dispute and has control over the parties to the controversy, a judgment issued by the court is not void, even if contrary to law. Such a judgment is voidable, but not void *ab initio*, and is binding until vacated or corrected.").

37. State v. Crumbley, 135 N.C. App. 59, 67 (1999) ("This substantive change in the sentence could only be made in the Defendant's presence, where he and/or his attorney would have an opportunity to be heard.").

Appendix A

Effective Dates of JRA Provisions

	Effective date	Applicability to DWI
Felony maximum sentences increased; all felons get post-release supervision (PRS)	Offenses committed on or after December 1, 2011	No
Class B1–E sex offender maximum sentences increased	Offenses committed on or after December 1, 2011	No
Advanced Supervised Release (ASR) created	Persons entering a plea or found guilty on or after January 1, 2012	No
Intermediate punishment redefined	Offenses committed on or after December 1, 2011	No
Community punishment redefined	Offenses committed on or after December 1, 2011	No
Community and intermediate probation conditions created	Offenses committed on or after December 1, 2011	No
Intensive supervision, residential program, and day-reporting centers repealed	Offenses committed on or after December 1, 2011	No
Delegated authority expanded (including probation officer "quick dips")	Offenses committed on or after December 1, 2011	No
Statutory absconding condition created	Offenses committed on or after December 1, 2011	Yes
Judges' probation revocation authority limited; confinement in response to violation (CRV, or "dunks") available	Probation violations occurring on or after December 1, 2011	Yes
G.S. 90-96 conditional discharge amended, made mandatory	Persons entering a plea or found guilty on or after January 1, 2012	No
Habitual felon law made a 4-class enhancement	Principal (substantive) felonies occurring on or after December 1, 2011	No

	Effective date	Applicability to DWI
Habitual breaking and entering status offense created	Principal (substantive) felonies occurring on or after December 1, 2011	No
Place-of-confinement rules amended; Statewide Misdemeanant Confinement Program (SMCP) created	Sentences imposed on or after January 1, 2012	No
Probation tolling repealed	Persons placed on probation on or after December 1, 2011	Yes
Post-release supervision (PRS) period tolled upon re-imprisonment	PRS violations occurring on or after July 16, 2012	Aggravated Level 1 only
Drug trafficking sentences increased; applicability of post-release supervision (PRS) to trafficking clarified	Offenses committed on or after December 1, 2012	No

Appendix B

N.C. Session Law 2011-62,
Amend Conditions of Probation

GENERAL ASSEMBLY OF NORTH CAROLINA
SESSION 2011

SESSION LAW 2011-62
HOUSE BILL 270

AN ACT TO AMEND THE LAW ESTABLISHING THE REGULAR AND SPECIAL CONDITIONS OF PROBATION AND TO REPEAL THE LAW TOLLING THE PROBATION PERIOD WHILE CRIMINAL CHARGES ARE PENDING THAT MIGHT RESULT IN REVOCATION PROCEEDINGS.

The General Assembly of North Carolina enacts:

SECTION 1. G.S. 15A-1343(b) reads as rewritten:
"(b)   Regular Conditions. – As regular conditions of probation, a defendant must:
(1)   Commit no criminal offense in any jurisdiction.
(2)   Remain ~~within the jurisdiction of the court~~accessible to the probation officer by making the defendant's whereabouts known to the officer and not leave the county of residence or the State of North Carolina unless granted written permission to leave by the court or his probation officer.
(3)   Report as directed by the court or his probation officer to the officer at reasonable times and places and in a reasonable manner, permit the officer to visit him at reasonable times, answer all reasonable inquiries by the officer and obtain prior approval from the officer for, and notify the officer of, any change in address or employment.
(4)   Satisfy child support and other family obligations as required by the court. If the court requires the payment of child support, the amount of the payments shall be determined as provided in G.S. 50-13.4(c).
(5)   Possess no firearm, explosive device or other deadly weapon listed in G.S. 14-269 without the written permission of the court.
(6)   Pay a supervision fee as specified in subsection (c1).
(7)   Remain gainfully and suitably employed or faithfully pursue a course of study or of vocational training that will equip him for suitable employment. A defendant pursuing a course of study or of vocational training shall abide by all of the rules of the institution providing the education or training, and the probation officer shall forward a copy of the probation judgment to that institution and request to be notified of any violations of institutional rules by the defendant.
(8)   Notify the probation officer if he fails to obtain or retain satisfactory employment.
(9)   Pay the costs of court, any fine ordered by the court, and make restitution or reparation as provided in subsection (d).
(10)   Pay the State of North Carolina for the costs of appointed counsel, public defender, or appellate defender to represent him in the case(s) for which he was placed on probation.
(11)   ~~At a time to be designated by his probation officer, visit with his probation officer a facility maintained by the Division of Prisons.~~
(12)   Attend and complete an abuser treatment program if (i) the court finds the defendant is responsible for acts of domestic violence and (ii) there is a program, approved by the Domestic Violence Commission, reasonably available to the defendant, unless the court finds that such would not be in the best interests of justice.
(13)   Submit at reasonable times to warrantless searches by a probation officer of the probationer's person and of the probationer's vehicle and premises while the probationer is present, for purposes directly related to the probation

H270-V-6

supervision, but the probationer may not be required to submit to any other search that would otherwise be unlawful. ~~Whenever the warrantless search consists of testing for the presence of illegal drugs, the probationer may also be required to reimburse the Department of Correction for the actual cost of drug screening and drug testing, if the results are positive.~~

(14) Submit to warrantless searches by a law enforcement officer of the probationer's person and of the probationer's vehicle, upon a reasonable suspicion that the probationer is engaged in criminal activity or is in possession of a firearm, explosive device, or other deadly weapon listed in G.S. 14-269 without written permission of the court.

(15) Not use, possess, or control any illegal drug or controlled substance unless it has been prescribed for him or her by a licensed physician and is in the original container with the prescription number affixed on it; not knowingly associate with any known or previously convicted users, possessors, or sellers of any such illegal drugs or controlled substances; and not knowingly be present at or frequent any place where such illegal drugs or controlled substances are sold, kept, or used.

<u>(16)</u> <u>Supply a breath, urine, or blood specimen for analysis of the possible presence of prohibited drugs or alcohol when instructed by the defendant's probation officer for purposes directly related to the probation supervision. If the results of the analysis are positive, the probationer may be required to reimburse the Department of Correction for the actual costs of drug or alcohol screening and testing.</u>

A defendant shall not pay costs associated with a substance abuse monitoring program or any other special condition of probation in lieu of, or prior to, the payments required by this subsection.

In addition to these regular conditions of probation, a defendant required to serve an active term of imprisonment as a condition of special probation pursuant to G.S. 15A-1344(e) or G.S. 15A-1351(a) shall, as additional regular conditions of probation, obey the rules and regulations of the Department of Correction governing the conduct of inmates while imprisoned and report to a probation officer in the State of North Carolina within 72 hours of his discharge from the active term of imprisonment.

Regular conditions of probation apply to each defendant placed on supervised probation unless the presiding judge specifically exempts the defendant from one or more of the conditions in open court and in the judgment of the court. It is not necessary for the presiding judge to state each regular condition of probation in open court, but the conditions must be set forth in the judgment of the court.

Defendants placed on unsupervised probation are subject to the provisions of this subsection, except that defendants placed on unsupervised probation are not subject to the regular conditions contained in subdivisions (2), (3), (6), (8), ~~(11),~~(13), (14), ~~and (15)~~(15), and (16) of this subsection."

SECTION 2. G.S. 15A-1343(b1) reads as rewritten:

"(b1) Special Conditions. – In addition to the regular conditions of probation specified in subsection (b), the court may, as a condition of probation, require that during the probation the defendant comply with one or more of the following special conditions:

(1) Undergo available medical or psychiatric treatment and remain in a specified institution if required for that purpose.

(2) Attend or reside in a facility providing rehabilitation, counseling, treatment, social skills, or employment training, instruction, recreation, or residence for persons on probation.

(2a) Repealed by Session Laws 2002, ch. 126, s. 17.18, effective August 15, 2002.

(2b) Participate in and successfully complete a Drug Treatment Court Program pursuant to Article 62 of Chapter 7A of the General Statutes.

(3) Submit to imprisonment required for special probation under G.S. 15A-1351(a) or G.S. 15A-1344(e).

(3a) Repealed by Session Laws 1997-57, s. 3.

(3b) Submit to intensive supervision and abide by the rules adopted by the Division of Community Corrections for that level of supervision.

(3c)   Remain at his or her residence. The court, in the sentencing order, may authorize the offender to leave the offender's residence for employment, counseling, a course of study, vocational training, or other specific purposes and may modify that authorization. The probation officer may authorize the offender to leave the offender's residence for specific purposes not authorized in the court order upon approval of the probation officer's supervisor. The offender shall be required to wear a device which permits the supervising agency to monitor the offender's compliance with the condition electronically and to pay a fee for the device as specified in subsection (c2) of this section.

(4)   Surrender his or her driver's license to the clerk of superior court, and not operate a motor vehicle for a period specified by the court.

(5)   Compensate the Department of Environment and Natural Resources or the North Carolina Wildlife Resources Commission, as the case may be, for the replacement costs of any marine and estuarine resources or any wildlife resources which were taken, injured, removed, harmfully altered, damaged or destroyed as a result of a criminal offense of which the defendant was convicted. If any investigation is required by officers or agents of the Department of Environment and Natural Resources or the Wildlife Resources Commission in determining the extent of the destruction of resources involved, the court may include compensation of the agency for investigative costs as a condition of probation. This subdivision does not apply in any case governed by G.S. 143-215.3(a)(7).

(6)   Perform community or reparation service under the supervision of the Division of Community Corrections and pay the fee required by G.S. 143B-262.4.

(7),   (8) Repealed by Session Laws 2009-372, s. 9(b), effective December 1, 2009, and applicable to offenses committed on or after that date.

(8a)   Purchase the least expensive annual statewide license or combination of licenses to hunt, trap, or fish listed in G.S. 113-270.2, 113-270.3, 113-270.5, 113-271, 113-272, and 113-272.2 that would be required to engage lawfully in the specific activity or activities in which the defendant was engaged and which constitute the basis of the offense or offenses of which he was convicted.

(9)   If the offense is one in which there is evidence of physical, mental or sexual abuse of a minor, the court should encourage the minor and the minor's parents or custodians to participate in rehabilitative treatment and may order the defendant to pay the cost of such treatment.

(9a)   Repealed by Session Laws 2004-186, s. 1.1, effective December 1, 2004, and applicable to offenses committed on or after that date.

(9b)   Any or all of the following conditions relating to street gangs as defined in G.S. 14-50.16(b):

    a.   Not knowingly associate with any known street gang members and not knowingly be present at or frequent any place or location where street gangs gather or where street gang activity is known to occur.

    b.   Not wear clothes, jewelry, signs, symbols, or any paraphernalia readily identifiable as associated with or used by a street gang.

    c.   Not initiate or participate in any contact with any individual who was or may be a witness against or victim of the defendant or the defendant's street gang.

(9c)   Participate in any Project Safe Neighborhood activities as directed by the probation officer.

(10)   Satisfy any other conditions determined by the court to be reasonably related to his rehabilitation."

SECTION 3. G.S. 15A-1344(g) is repealed.

SECTION 4. This act becomes effective December 1, 2011, and applies to persons placed on probation on or after that date.

In the General Assembly read three times and ratified this the 2nd day of May, 2011.

s/ Walter H. Dalton
President of the Senate

s/ Dale R. Folwell
Speaker Pro Tempore of the House of Representatives

s/ Beverly E. Perdue
Governor

Approved 5:25 p.m. this 3rd day of May, 2011

Appendix C

N.C. Session Law 2011-192, Justice Reinvestment Act

GENERAL ASSEMBLY OF NORTH CAROLINA
SESSION 2011

SESSION LAW 2011-192
HOUSE BILL 642

AN ACT TO IMPLEMENT CERTAIN RECOMMENDATIONS OF THE JUSTICE REINVESTMENT PROJECT AND TO PROVIDE THAT THE ACT SHALL BE ENTITLED "THE JUSTICE REINVESTMENT ACT OF 2011."

The General Assembly of North Carolina enacts:

PART I. STRENGTHEN PROBATION SUPERVISION

SECTION 1.(a) G.S. 15A-1340.11(2) reads as rewritten:

"(2)   Community punishment. – A sentence in a criminal case that does not include an active punishment or assignment to a drug treatment court, or special probation as defined in G.S. 15A-1351(a). punishment, an intermediate punishment, or any of the conditions of probation listed in subdivision (6) of this section.It may include any one or more of the conditions set forth in G.S. 15A-1343(a1)."

SECTION 1.(b) G.S. 15A-1340.11(6) reads as rewritten:

"(6)   Intermediate punishment. – A sentence in a criminal case that places an offender on supervised probation. probation and includes at least one It may include drug treatment court, special probation as defined in G.S. 15A-1351(a), and one or more of the following conditions:conditions set forth in G.S. 15A-1343(a1).

a.   Special probation as defined in G.S. 15A-1351(a).
b.   Assignment to a residential program.
c.   House arrest with electronic monitoring.
d.   Intensive supervision.
e.   Assignment to a day-reporting center.
f.   Assignment to a drug treatment court program."

SECTION 1.(c) G.S. 15A-1343 is amended by adding a new subsection to read:

"(a1)   Community and Intermediate Probation Conditions. – In addition to any conditions a court may be authorized to impose pursuant to G.S. 15A-1343(b1), the court may include any one or more of the following conditions as part of a community or intermediate punishment:

(1)   House arrest with electronic monitoring.
(2)   Perform community service.
(3)   Submission to a period or periods of confinement in a local confinement facility for a total of no more than six days per month during any three separate months during the period of probation. The six days per month confinement provided for in this subdivision may only be imposed as two-day or three-day consecutive periods.
(4)   Substance abuse assessment, monitoring, or treatment.
(5)   Participation in an educational or vocational skills development program, including an evidence-based program.
(6)   Submission to satellite-based monitoring, pursuant to Part 5 of Article 27A of Chapter 14 of the General Statutes, if the defendant is described by G.S. 14-208.40(a)(2)."

SECTION 1.(d) G.S. 15A-1343.2(e) reads as rewritten:

"(e)   Delegation to Probation Officer in Community Punishment. – Unless the presiding judge specifically finds in the judgment of the court that delegation is not appropriate, the Division of Community Corrections in the Department of Correction may require an offender sentenced to community punishment to:to do any of the following:

(1)   Perform up to 20 hours of community service, and pay the fee prescribed by law for this ~~supervision;~~supervision.
(2)   Report to the offender's probation officer on a frequency to be determined by the ~~officer; or~~officer.
(3)   Submit to substance abuse assessment, monitoring or treatment.
(4)   Submit to house arrest with electronic monitoring.
(5)   Submit to a period or periods of confinement in a local confinement facility for a total of no more than six days per month during any three separate months during the period of probation. The six days per month confinement provided for in this subdivision may only be imposed as two-day or three-day consecutive periods.
(6)   Submit to a curfew which requires the offender to remain in a specified place for a specified period each day and wear a device that permits the offender's compliance with the condition to be monitored electronically.
(7)   Participate in an educational or vocational skills development program, including an evidence-based program.

If the Division imposes any of the above requirements, then it may subsequently reduce or remove those same requirements.

The probation officer may exercise authority delegated to him or her by the court pursuant to subsection (e) of this section after administrative review and approval by a Chief Probation Officer. The offender may file a motion with the court to review the action taken by the probation officer. The offender shall be given notice of the right to seek such a court review. However, the offender shall have no right of review if he or she has signed a written waiver of rights as required by this subsection. The Division may exercise any authority delegated to it under this subsection only if it first determines that the offender has failed to comply with one or more of the conditions of probation imposed by the court or the offender is determined to be high risk based on the results of the risk assessment in G.S. 15A-1343.2, except that the condition at subdivision (5) of this subsection may not be imposed unless the Division determines that the offender failed to comply with one or more of the conditions imposed by the court. Nothing in this section shall be construed to limit the availability of the procedures authorized under G.S. 15A-1345.

~~If the probation officer exercises authority delegated to him or her by the court pursuant to this subsection, the offender may file a motion with the court to review the action taken by the probation officer. The offender shall be given notice of the right to seek such a court review. The Division may exercise any authority delegated to it under this subsection only if it first determines that the offender has failed to comply with one or more of the conditions of probation imposed by the court.~~

The Department shall adopt guidelines and procedures to implement the requirements of this section, which shall include a supervisor's approval prior to exercise of the delegation of authority authorized by this section. Prior to imposing confinement pursuant to subdivision (5) of this subsection, the probationer must first be presented with a violation report, with the alleged violations noted and advised of the right (i) to a hearing before the court on the alleged violation, with the right to present relevant oral and written evidence; (ii) to have counsel at the hearing, and that one will be appointed if the probationer is indigent; (iii) to request witnesses who have relevant information concerning the alleged violations; and (iv) to examine any witnesses or evidence. Upon the signing of a waiver of rights by the probationer, with both the probation officer and a supervisor signing as witnesses, the probationer may be confined for the period designated on the violation report."

SECTION 1.(e) G.S. 15A-1343.2(f) reads as rewritten:

"(f)   Delegation to Probation Officer in Intermediate Punishments. – Unless the presiding judge specifically finds in the judgment of the court that delegation is not appropriate, the Division of Community Corrections in the Department of Correction may require an offender sentenced to intermediate punishment ~~to:~~to do any of the following:
(1)   Perform up to 50 hours of community service, and pay the fee prescribed by law for this ~~supervision;~~supervision.
(2)   Submit to a curfew which requires the offender to remain in a specified place for a specified period each day and wear a device that permits the offender's compliance with the condition to be monitored ~~electronically;~~ electronically.

(3) Submit to substance abuse assessment, monitoring or ~~treatment;~~ treatment.

(4) Participate in an educational or vocational skills development ~~program.~~ program, including an evidence-based program.

(5) Submit to satellite-based monitoring pursuant to Part 5 of Article 27A of Chapter 14 of the General Statutes, if the defendant is described by G.S. 14-208.40(a)(2).

(6) Submit to a period or periods of confinement in a local confinement facility for a total of no more than six days per month during any three separate months during the period of probation. The six days per month confinement provided for in this subdivision may only be imposed as two-day or three-day consecutive periods.

(7) Submit to house arrest with electronic monitoring.

(8) Report to the offender's probation officer on a frequency to be determined by the officer.

If the Division imposes any of the above requirements, then it may subsequently reduce or remove those same requirements.

The probation officer may exercise authority delegated to him or her by the court pursuant to subsection (f) of this section after administrative review and approval by a Chief Probation Officer. The offender may file a motion with the court to review the action taken by the probation officer. The offender shall be given notice of the right to seek such a court review. However, the offender shall have no right of review if he or she has signed a written waiver of rights as required by this subsection. The Division may exercise any authority delegated to it under this subsection only if it first determines that the offender has failed to comply with one or more of the conditions of probation imposed by the court or the offender is determined to be high risk based on the results of the risk assessment in G.S. 15A-1343.2, except that the condition at subdivision (6) of this subsection may not be imposed unless the Division determines that the offender failed to comply with one or more of the conditions imposed by the court. Nothing in this section shall be construed to limit the availability of the procedures authorized under G.S. 15A-1345.

~~If the probation officer exercises authority delegated to him or her by the court pursuant to this subsection, the offender may file a motion with the court to review the action taken by the probation officer. The offender shall be given notice of the right to seek such a court review. The Division may exercise any authority delegated to it under this subsection only if it first determines that the offender has failed to comply with one or more of the conditions of probation imposed by the court.~~

The Department shall adopt guidelines and procedures to implement the requirements of this section, which shall include a supervisor's approval prior to exercise of the delegation of authority authorized by this section. Prior to imposing confinement pursuant to subdivision (6) of this subsection, the probationer must first be presented with a violation report, with the alleged violations noted and advised of the right (i) to a hearing before the court on the alleged violation, with the right to present relevant oral and written evidence; (ii) to have counsel at the hearing, and that one will be appointed if the probationer is indigent; (iii) to request witnesses who have relevant information concerning the alleged violations; and (iv) to examine any witnesses or evidence. Upon the signing of a waiver of rights by the probationer, with both the probation officer and a supervisor signing as witnesses, the probationer may be confined for the period designated on the violation report."

SECTION 1.(f) G.S. 15A-1343.2 is amended by adding a new subsection to read:

"(b1) Departmental Risk Assessment by Validated Instrument Required. – As part of the probation program developed by the Department of Correction pursuant to subsection (b) of this section, the Department of Correction shall use a validated instrument to assess each probationer for risk of reoffending and shall place a probationer in a supervision level based on the probationer's risk of reoffending and criminogenic needs."

SECTION 1.(g) G.S. 15A-1343(b1)(3b) is repealed.

SECTION 1.(h) G.S. 15A-1340.11(3) is repealed.

SECTION 1.(i) G.S. 15A-1340.11(5) is repealed.

SECTION 1.(j) G.S. 15A-1340.11(8) is repealed.

SECTION 1.(k) G.S. 15A-1343.2(c) reads as rewritten:

"(c) Probation Caseload Goals. – It is the goal of the General Assembly that, subject to the availability of funds, caseloads for probation officers supervising persons who are determined to be high or moderate risk of rearrest as determined by the Department's validated risk assessment should not exceed an average of 60 offenders per officer.~~sentenced to community punishment should not exceed an average of 90 offenders per officer, and caseloads for offenders sentenced to intermediate punishments should not exceed an average of 60 offenders per officer by July 1, 1998.~~"

SECTION 1.(l) This section becomes effective December 1, 2011, and applies to persons placed on probation based on offenses which occur on or after December 1, 2011; however, this section and the provisions of this act requiring the Department of Correction to adopt guidelines and procedures are effective when this act becomes law.

PART II. POST-RELEASE SUPERVISION CHANGES

SECTION 2.(a) G.S. 15A-1368.1 reads as rewritten:

"**§ 15A-1368.1. Applicability of Article 84A.**

This Article applies to all felons ~~in Class B1 through Class E~~ sentenced to an active punishment under Article 81B of this Chapter, but does not apply to felons in Class A and Class B1 sentenced to life imprisonment without parole. Prisoners subject to Articles 85 and 85A of this Chapter are excluded from this Article's coverage."

SECTION 2.(b) G.S. 15A-1368.2 reads as rewritten:

"**§ 15A-1368.2. Post-release supervision eligibility and procedure.**

(a) A prisoner to whom this Article applies shall be released from prison for post-release supervision on the date equivalent to his maximum imposed prison term less ~~nine months,~~ 12 months in the case of Class B1 through E felons and less nine months in the case of Class F through I felons, less any earned time awarded by the Department of Correction or the custodian of a local confinement facility under G.S. 15A-1340.13(d). If a prisoner has not been awarded any earned time, the prisoner shall be released for post-release supervision on the date equivalent to his maximum prison term less ~~nine months.~~12 months for Class B1 through E felons and less nine months for Class F through I felons.

(b) A prisoner shall not refuse post-release supervision.

(c) A supervisee's period of post-release supervision shall be for a period of ~~nine months,~~12 months in the case of Class B1 through E felons and nine months in the case of Class F through I felons, unless the offense is an offense for which registration is required pursuant to Article 27A of Chapter 14 of the General Statutes. For offenses subject to the registration requirement of Article 27A of Chapter 14 of the General Statutes, the period of post-release supervision is five years. The conditions of post-release supervision are as authorized in G.S. 15A-1368.5.

...."

SECTION 2.(c) G.S. 15A-1368.4(e) is amended by adding a new subdivision to read:

> "(7a) Not to abscond, by willfully avoiding supervision or by willfully making the supervisee's whereabouts unknown to the supervising probation officer."

SECTION 2.(d) G.S. 15A-1368.3(c) reads as rewritten:

"(c) Effect of Violation. – If the supervisee violates a condition, described in G.S. 15A-1368.4, at any time before the termination of the supervision period, the Commission may continue the supervisee on the existing supervision, with or without modifying the conditions, or if continuation or modification is not appropriate, may revoke post-release supervision as provided in G.S. 15A-1368.6 and reimprison the supervisee for a term consistent with the following requirements:

> (1) ~~The supervisee~~Supervisees who were convicted of an offense for which registration is required under Article 27A of Chapter 14 of the General Statutes and supervisees whose supervision is revoked for a violation of the required controlling condition under G.S. 15A-1368.4(b) or for absconding in violation of G.S. 15A-1368.4(e)(7a) will be returned to prison up to the time remaining on ~~his~~their maximum imposed ~~term.~~terms. All other supervisees will be returned to prison for three months and may be returned for three months on each of two subsequent violations, after which supervisees who were Class B1 through E felons may be returned to prison up to the time remaining on their maximum imposed terms.

(2)   The supervisee shall not receive any credit for days on post-release supervision against the maximum term of imprisonment imposed by the court under G.S. 15A-1340.13.

(3)   Pursuant to Article 19A of Chapter 15, the Department of Correction shall award a prisoner credit against any term of reimprisonment for all time spent in custody as a result of revocation proceedings under G.S. 15A-1368.6.

(4)   The prisoner is eligible to receive earned time credit against the maximum prison term as provided in G.S. 15A-1340.13(d) for time served in prison after the revocation."

SECTION 2.(e) G.S. 15A-1340.17(d) reads as rewritten:

"(d)   Maximum Sentences Specified for Class F through Class I Felonies. – Unless provided otherwise in a statute establishing a punishment for a specific crime, for each minimum term of imprisonment in the chart in subsection (c) of this section, expressed in months, the corresponding maximum term of imprisonment, also expressed in months, is as specified in the table below for Class F through Class I felonies. The first figure in each cell in the table is the minimum term and the second is the maximum term.

3-4	4-5	5-6	6-8	7-9	8-10	9-11	10-12
11-14	12-15	13-16	14-17	15-18	16-20	17-21	18-22
19-23	20-24	21-26	22-27	23-28	24-29	25-30	26-32
27-33	28-34	29-35	30-36	31-38	32-39	33-40	34-41
35-42	36-44	37-45	38-46	39-47	40-48	41-50	42-51
43-52	44-53	45-54	46-56	47-57	48-58	49-59	
3-13	4-14	5-15	6-17	7-18	8-19	9-20	10-21
11-23	12-24	13-25	14-26	15-27	16-29	17-30	18-31
19-32	20-33	21-35	22-36	23-37	24-38	25-39	26-41
27-42	28-43	29-44	30-45	31-47	32-48	33-49	34-50
35-51	36-53	37-54	38-55	39-56	40-57	41-59	42-60
43-61	44-62	45-63	46-65	47-66	48-67	49-68	

".

SECTION 2.(f) G.S. 15A-1340.17(e) reads as rewritten:

"(e)   Maximum Sentences Specified for Class B1 through Class E Felonies for Minimum Terms up to 339 Months. – Unless provided otherwise in a statute establishing a punishment for a specific crime, for each minimum term of imprisonment in the chart in subsection (c) of this section, expressed in months, the corresponding maximum term of imprisonment, also expressed in months, is as specified in the table below for Class B1 through Class E felonies. The first figure in each cell of the table is the minimum term and the second is the maximum term.

15-27	16-29	17-30	18-31	19-32	20-33	21-35	22-36
23-37	24-38	25-39	26-41	27-42	28-43	29-44	30-45
31-47	32-48	33-49	34-50	35-51	36-53	37-54	38-55
39-56	40-57	41-59	42-60	43-61	44-62	45-63	46-65
47-66	48-67	49-68	50-69	51-71	52-72	53-73	54-74
55-75	56-77	57-78	58-79	59-80	60-81	61-83	62-84
63-85	64-86	65-87	66-89	67-90	68-91	69-92	70-93
71-95	72-96	73-97	74-98	75-99	76-101	77-102	78-103
79-104	80-105	81-107	82-108	83-109	84-110	85-111	86-113
87-114	88-115	89-116	90-117	91-119	92-120	93-121	94-122
95-123	96-125	97-126	98-127	99-128	100-129	101-131	102-132
103-133	104-134	105-135	106-137	107-138	108-139	109-140	110-141
111-143	112-144	113-145	114-146	115-147	116-149	117-150	118-151
119-152	120-153	121-155	122-156	123-157	124-158	125-159	126-161
127-162	128-163	129-164	130-165	131-167	132-168	133-169	134-170
135-171	136-173	137-174	138-175	139-176	140-177	141-179	142-180
143-181	144-182	145-183	146-185	147-186	148-187	149-188	150-189
151-191	152-192	153-193	154-194	155-195	156-197	157-198	158-199
159-200	160-201	161-203	162-204	163-205	164-206	165-207	166-209
167-210	168-211	169-212	170-213	171-215	172-216	173-217	174-218
175-219	176-221	177-222	178-223	179-224	180-225	181-227	182-228
183-229	184-230	185-231	186-233	187-234	188-235	189-236	190-237
191-239	192-240	193-241	194-242	195-243	196-245	197-246	198-247

199-248	200-249	201-251	202-252	203-253	204-254	205-255	206-257
207-258	208-259	209-260	210-261	211-263	212-264	213-265	214-266
215-267	216-269	217-270	218-271	219-272	220-273	221-275	222-276
223-277	224-278	225-279	226-281	227-282	228-283	229-284	230-285
231-287	232-288	233-289	234-290	235-291	236-293	237-294	238-295
239-296	240-297	241-299	242-300	243-301	244-302	245-303	246-305
247-306	248-307	249-308	250-309	251-311	252-312	253-313	254-314
255-315	256-317	257-318	258-319	259-320	260-321	261-323	262-324
263-325	264-326	265-327	266-329	267-330	268-331	269-332	270-333
271-335	272-336	273-337	274-338	275-339	276-341	277-342	278-343
279-344	280-345	281-347	282-348	283-349	284-350	285-351	286-353
287-354	288-355	289-356	290-357	291-359	292-360	293-361	294-362
295-363	296-365	297-366	298-367	299-368	300-369	301-371	302-372
303-373	304-374	305-375	306-377	307-378	308-379	309-380	310-381
311-383	312-384	313-385	314-386	315-387	316-389	317-390	318-391
319-392	320-393	321-395	322-396	323-397	324-398	325-399	326-401
327-402	328-403	329-404	330-405	331-407	332-408	333-409	334-410
335-411	336-413	337-414	338-415	339-416			
15-30	16-32	17-33	18-34	19-35	20-36	21-38	22-39
23-40	24-41	25-42	26-44	27-45	28-46	29-47	30-48
31-50	32-51	33-52	34-53	35-54	36-56	37-57	38-58
39-59	40-60	41-62	42-63	43-64	44-65	45-66	46-68
47-69	48-70	49-71	50-72	51-74	52-75	53-76	54-77
55-78	56-80	57-81	58-82	59-83	60-84	61-86	62-87
63-88	64-89	65-90	66-91	67-93	68-94	69-95	70-96
71-98	72-99	73-100	74-101	75-102	76-104	77-105	78-106
79-107	80-108	81-110	82-111	83-112	84-113	85-114	86-115
87-117	88-118	89-119	90-120	91-122	92-123	93-124	94-125
95-126	96-128	97-129	98-130	99-131	100-132	101-134	102-135
103-136	104-137	105-138	106-140	107-141	108-142	109-143	110-144
111-146	112-147	113-148	114-149	115-150	116-152	117-153	118-154
119-155	120-156	121-158	122-159	123-160	124-161	125-162	126-164
127-165	128-166	129-167	130-168	131-170	132-171	133-172	134-173
135-174	136-176	137-177	138-178	139-179	140-180	141-182	142-183
143-184	144-185	145-186	146-188	147-189	148-190	149-191	150-192
151-194	152-195	153-196	154-197	155-198	156-200	157-201	158-202
159-203	160-204	161-206	162-207	163-208	164-209	165-210	166-212
167-213	168-214	169-215	170-216	171-218	172-219	173-220	174-221
175-222	176-224	177-225	178-226	179-227	180-228	181-230	182-231
183-232	184-233	185-234	186-236	187-237	188-238	189-239	190-240
191-242	192-243	193-244	194-245	195-246	196-248	197-249	198-250
199-251	200-252	201-254	202-255	203-256	204-257	205-258	206-260
207-261	208-262	209-263	210-264	211-266	212-267	213-268	214-269
215-270	216-271	217-273	218-274	219-275	220-276	221-278	222-279
223-280	224-281	225-282	226-284	227-285	228-286	229-287	230-288
231-290	232-291	233-292	234-293	235-294	236-296	237-297	238-298
239-299	240-300	241-302	242-303	243-304	244-305	245-306	246-308
247-309	248-310	249-311	250-312	251-314	252-315	253-316	254-317
255-318	256-320	257-321	258-322	259-323	260-324	261-326	262-327
263-328	264-329	265-330	266-332	267-333	268-334	269-335	270-336
271-338	272-339	273-340	274-341	275-342	276-344	277-345	278-346
279-347	280-348	281-350	282-351	283-352	284-353	285-354	286-356
287-357	288-358	289-359	290-360	291-362	292-363	293-364	294-365
295-366	296-368	297-369	298-370	299-371	300-372	301-374	302-375
303-376	304-377	305-378	306-380	307-381	308-382	309-383	310-384
311-386	312-387	313-388	314-389	315-390	316-392	317-393	318-394
319-395	320-396	321-398	322-399	323-400	324-401	325-402	326-404
327-405	328-408	329-407	330-408	331-410	332-411	333-412	334-413
335-414	336-416	337-417	338-418	339-419".			

SECTION 2.(g) G.S. 15A-1340.17(e1) reads as rewritten:

"(e1) Maximum Sentences Specified for Class B1 through Class E Felonies for Minimum Terms of 340 Months or More. – Unless provided otherwise in a statute establishing a punishment for a specific crime, when the minimum sentence is 340 months or more, the corresponding maximum term of imprisonment shall be equal to the sum of the minimum term of imprisonment and twenty percent (20%) of the minimum term of imprisonment, rounded to the next highest month, plus ~~nine~~ 12 additional months."

SECTION 2.(h) G.S. 15A-1368(a)(5) reads as rewritten:

"(5) Maximum imposed term. – The maximum term of imprisonment imposed on an individual prisoner by a court judgment, as described in G.S. 15A-1340.13(c). When a prisoner is serving consecutive prison terms, the maximum imposed term, for purposes of this Article, is the sum of all maximum terms imposed in the court judgment or judgments, less ~~nine~~ 12 months for each of the second and subsequent sentences imposed for Class B through Class E ~~felonies.~~ felonies and less nine months for each of the second and subsequent sentences imposed for Class F through Class I felonies."

SECTION 2.(i) G.S. 15A-1354(b)(1) reads as rewritten:

"(1) The maximum prison sentence consists of the total of the maximum terms of the consecutive sentences, less ~~nine~~ 12 months for each of the second and subsequent sentences imposed for Class B through Class E ~~felonies;~~ felonies and less nine months for each of the second and subsequent sentences imposed for Class F through Class I felonies; and"

SECTION 2.(j) This section becomes effective December 1, 2011, and applies to offenses committed on or after that date.

PART III. STATUS OFFENSE OF HABITUAL BREAKING AND ENTERING

SECTION 3.(a) Chapter 14 of the General Statutes is amended by adding a new Article to read:

"Article 2D.
"Habitual Breaking and Entering Status Offense.

"§ 14-7.25. Definitions.

The following definitions apply in this Article:

(1) "Breaking and entering." – The term means any of the following felony offenses:
  a. First degree burglary (G.S. 14-51).
  b. Second degree burglary (G.S. 14-51).
  c. Breaking out of dwelling house burglary (G.S. 14-53).
  d. Breaking or entering buildings generally (G.S. 14-54(a)).
  e. Breaking or entering a building that is a place of religious worship (G.S. 14-54.1).
  f. Any repealed or superseded offense substantially equivalent to any of the offenses in sub-subdivision a., b., c., d., or e. of this subdivision.
  g. Any offense committed in another jurisdiction substantially similar to any of the offenses in sub-subdivision a., b., c., d., or e. of this subdivision.
(2) "Convicted." – The person has been adjudged guilty of or has entered a plea of guilty or no contest to the offense of breaking and entering.
(3) "Status offender." – A person who is a habitual breaking and entering status offender as described in G.S. 14-7.26.

"§ 14-7.26. Habitual breaking and entering status offender.

Any person who has been convicted of or pled guilty to one or more prior felony offenses of breaking and entering in any federal court or state court in the United States, or combination thereof, is guilty of the status offense of habitual breaking and entering and may be charged with that status offense pursuant to this Article.

This Article does not apply to a second felony offense of breaking and entering unless it is committed after the conviction of the first felony offense of breaking and entering. For purposes of this Article, felony offenses of breaking and entering committed before the person is 18 years of age shall not constitute more than one felony of breaking and entering. Any felony to which a pardon has been extended shall not, for the purposes of this Article, constitute a felony offense of breaking and entering.

"§ 14-7.27. Punishment.

When any person is charged with a felony offense of breaking and entering and is also charged with being a status offender as defined in G.S. 14-7.26, the person must, upon conviction, be sentenced and punished as a status offender as provided by this Article.

"§ 14-7.28. Charge of habitual breaking and entering status offender.

(a)   The district attorney, in his or her discretion, may charge a person with the status offense of habitual breaking and entering pursuant to this Article. To sustain a conviction of a person as a status offender, the person must be charged separately for the felony offense of breaking and entering and for the habitual breaking and entering status offense. The indictment charging the defendant as a status offender shall be separate from the indictment charging the person with the principal felony offense of breaking and entering.

(b)   An indictment that charges a person with being a status offender must set forth the date that the prior felony offense of breaking and entering was committed, the name of the state or other sovereign against whom the felony offense of breaking and entering was committed, the dates that the plea of guilty was entered into or conviction returned in the felony offense of breaking and entering, and the identity of the court in which the plea or conviction took place. No defendant charged with being a status offender in a bill of indictment shall be required to go to trial on the charge within 20 days of the finding of a true bill by the grand jury; provided, the defendant may waive this 20-day period.

"§ 14-7.29. Evidence of prior convictions of breaking and entering.

In all cases in which a person is charged under the provisions of this Article with being a status offender, the record of prior conviction of the felony offense of breaking and entering shall be admissible in evidence, but only for the purpose of proving that the person has been convicted of a former felony offense of breaking and entering. A prior conviction may be proved by stipulation of the parties or by the original or a certified copy of the court record of the prior conviction. The original or certified copy of the court record, bearing the same name as that by which the defendant is charged, shall be prima facie evidence that the defendant named therein is the same as the defendant before the court and shall be prima facie evidence of the facts set out therein.

"§ 14-7.30. Verdict and judgment.

(a)   When an indictment charges a person with a felony offense of breaking and entering as provided by this Article and an indictment also charges that the person is a status offender, the defendant shall be tried for the principal offense of breaking and entering as provided by law. The indictment that the person is a status offender shall not be revealed to the jury unless the jury shall find that the defendant is guilty of the principal felony offense of breaking and entering with which the defendant is charged.

(b)   If the jury finds the defendant guilty of the felony offense of breaking and entering, the bill of indictment charging the defendant as a status offender may be presented to the same jury. Except that the same jury may be used, the proceedings shall be as if the issue of status offender were a principal charge.

(c)   If the jury finds that the defendant is a status offender, the trial judge shall enter judgment according to the provisions of this Article. If the jury finds that the defendant is not a status offender, the trial judge shall pronounce judgment on the principal felony offense of breaking and entering as provided by law.

"§ 14-7.31. Sentencing of status offenders.

(a)   When a status offender as defined in this Article commits a felony offense of breaking and entering under the laws of the State of North Carolina, the status offender must, upon conviction or plea of guilty under indictment as provided in this Article, be sentenced as a Class E felon.

(b)   In determining the prior record level, any conviction used to establish a person's status as a status offender shall not be used. Sentences imposed under this Article shall run consecutively with and shall commence at the expiration of any sentence being served by the person sentenced under this section.

(c)   A conviction as a status offender under this Article shall not constitute commission of a felony for the purpose of either Article 2A or Article 2B of Chapter 14 of the General Statutes."

SECTION 3.(b) G.S. 14-7.1 reads as rewritten:

"§ 14-7.1. Persons defined as habitual felons.

Any person who has been convicted of or pled guilty to three felony offenses in any federal court or state court in the United States or combination thereof is declared to be an habitual felon. felon and may be charged as a status offender pursuant to this Article. For the purpose of this Article, a felony offense is defined as an offense which is a felony under the laws of the State or other sovereign wherein a plea of guilty was entered or a conviction was returned regardless of the sentence actually imposed. Provided, however, that federal offenses relating to the manufacture, possession, sale and kindred offenses involving intoxicating liquors shall not be considered felonies for the purposes of this Article. For the purposes of this Article, felonies committed before a person attains the age of 18 years shall not constitute more than one felony. The commission of a second felony shall not fall within the purview of this Article unless it is committed after the conviction of or plea of guilty to the first felony. The commission of a third felony shall not fall within the purview of this Article unless it is committed after the conviction of or plea of guilty to the second felony. Pleas of guilty to or convictions of felony offenses prior to July 6, 1967, shall not be felony offenses within the meaning of this Article. Any felony offense to which a pardon has been extended shall not for the purpose of this Article constitute a felony. The burden of proving such pardon shall rest with the defendant and the State shall not be required to disprove a pardon."

SECTION 3.(c) G.S. 14-7.3 reads as rewritten:

"§ 14-7.3. Charge of habitual felon.

The district attorney, in his or her discretion, may charge a person as an habitual felon pursuant to this Article. An indictment which charges a person who is an habitual felon within the meaning of G.S. 14-7.1 with the commission of any felony under the laws of the State of North Carolina must, in order to sustain a conviction of habitual felon, also charge that said person is an habitual felon. The indictment charging the defendant as an habitual felon shall be separate from the indictment charging him with the principal felony. An indictment which charges a person with being an habitual felon must set forth the date that prior felony offenses were committed, the name of the state or other sovereign against whom said felony offenses were committed, the dates that pleas of guilty were entered to or convictions returned in said felony offenses, and the identity of the court wherein said pleas or convictions took place. No defendant charged with being an habitual felon in a bill of indictment shall be required to go to trial on said charge within 20 days of the finding of a true bill by the grand jury; provided, the defendant may waive this 20-day period."

SECTION 3.(d) G.S. 14-7.6 reads as rewritten:

"§ 14-7.6. Sentencing of habitual felons.

When an habitual felon as defined in this Article commits any felony under the laws of the State of North Carolina, the felon must, upon conviction or plea of guilty under indictment as provided in this Article (except where the felon has been sentenced as a Class A, B1, or B2 felon) be sentenced as a Class C felon. at a felony class level that is four classes higher than the principal felony for which the person was convicted; but under no circumstances shall an habitual felon be sentenced at a level higher than a Class C felony. In determining the prior record level, convictions used to establish a person's status as an habitual felon shall not be used. Sentences imposed under this Article shall run consecutively with and shall commence at the expiration of any sentence being served by the person sentenced under this section."

SECTION 3.(e) This section becomes effective December 1, 2011, and applies to any offense that occurs on or after that date and that is the principal felony offense for a charge of either the status offenses of habitual breaking and entering or habitual felon. Prosecutions for offenses committed before the effective date of this act are not abated or affected by this act, and the statutes that would be applicable but for this act remain applicable to those prosecutions.

PART IV. LIMIT TIME/CERTAIN VIOLATIONS OF PROBATION

SECTION 4.(a) G.S. 15A-1343(b) is amended by adding a new subdivision to read:

"(3a) Not to abscond, by willfully avoiding supervision or by willfully making the defendant's whereabouts unknown to the supervising probation officer."

SECTION 4.(b) G.S. 15A-1344(a) reads as rewritten:

"(a) Authority to Alter or Revoke. – Except as provided in subsection (a1) or (b), probation may be reduced, terminated, continued, extended, modified, or revoked by any judge entitled to sit in the court which imposed probation and who is resident or presiding in the district court district as defined in G.S. 7A-133 or superior court district or set of districts as defined in G.S. 7A-41.1, as the case may be, where the sentence of probation was imposed, where the probationer violates probation, or where the probationer resides. Upon a finding that an offender sentenced to community punishment under Article 81B has violated one or more conditions of probation, the court's authority to modify the probation judgment includes the authority to require the offender to comply with conditions of probation that would otherwise make the sentence an intermediate punishment. The court may only revoke probation for a violation of a condition of probation under G.S. 15A-1343(b)(1) or G.S. 15A-1343(b)(3a), except as provided in G.S. 15A-1344(d2). Imprisonment may be imposed pursuant to G.S. 15A-1344(d2) for a violation of a requirement other than G.S. 15A-1343(b)(1) or G.S. 15A-1343(b)(3a). The district attorney of the prosecutorial district as defined in G.S. 7A-60 in which probation was imposed must be given reasonable notice of any hearing to affect probation substantially."

      SECTION 4.(c) G.S. 15A-1344 is amended by adding a new subsection to read:

"(d2)   Confinement in Response to Violation. – When a defendant has violated a condition of probation other than G.S. 15A-1343(b)(1) or G.S. 15A-1343(b)(3a), the court may impose a 90-day period of confinement for a defendant under supervision for a felony conviction or a period of confinement of up to 90 days for a defendant under supervision for a misdemeanor conviction. The court may not revoke probation unless the defendant has previously received a total of two periods of confinement under this subsection. A defendant may receive only two periods of confinement under this subsection. If the time remaining on the defendant's maximum imposed sentence is less than 90 days, then the term of confinement is for the remaining period of the sentence. Confinement under this section shall be credited pursuant to G.S. 15-196.1."

      SECTION 4.(d) This section is effective December 1, 2011, and applies to probation violations occurring on or after that date.

PART V. DIVERSION PROGRAM/FELONY DRUG POSSESSION

      SECTION 5.(a) G.S. 90-96 reads as rewritten:

"**§ 90-96. Conditional discharge for first offense.**

    (a)   Whenever any person who has not previously been convicted of (i) any felony offense under any state or federal laws; (ii) any offense under this Article Article; or (iii) an offense under any statute of the United States or any state relating to those substances included in Article 5 or 5A of Chapter 90 or to that paraphernalia included in Article 5B of Chapter 90 90 of the General Statutes pleads guilty to or is found guilty of (i) a misdemeanor under this Article by possessing a controlled substance included within Schedules II I through VI of this Article or by possessing drug paraphernalia as prohibited by G.S. 90 113.22, or (ii) a felony under G.S. 90-95(a)(3), G.S. 90 95(a)(3) by possessing less than one gram of cocaine, the court may, shall, without entering a judgment of guilt and with the consent of such person, defer further proceedings and place him on probation upon such reasonable terms and conditions as it may require. Notwithstanding the provisions of G.S. 15A 1342(c) or any other statute or law, probation may be imposed under this section for an offense under this Article for which the prescribed punishment includes only a fine. To fulfill the terms and conditions of probation the court may allow the defendant to participate in a drug education program approved for this purpose by the Department of Health and Human Services. Services or in the Treatment for Effective Community Supervision Program under Article 6B of Chapter 143B of the General Statutes. Upon violation of a term or condition, the court may enter an adjudication of guilt and proceed as otherwise provided. Upon fulfillment of the terms and conditions, the court shall discharge such person and dismiss the proceedings against him. Discharge and dismissal under this section shall be without court adjudication of guilt and shall not be deemed a conviction for purposes of this section or for purposes of disqualifications or disabilities imposed by law upon conviction of a crime including the additional penalties imposed for second or subsequent convictions under this Article. Discharge and dismissal under this section or G.S. 90 113.14 may occur only once with respect to any person. Disposition of a case to determine discharge and dismissal under this section at the district court division of the General Court of Justice shall be final for the purpose of appeal. Prior to taking any action to discharge and dismiss under this section the court shall make a finding that the defendant has no record of previous convictions under the "North Carolina Controlled Substances Act", Article 5, Chapter 90, the

~~"North Carolina Toxic Vapors Act", Article 5A, Chapter 90, or the "Drug Paraphernalia Act",~~
~~Article 5B, Chapter 90.~~as provided in this subsection.

(a1)   Upon the first conviction only of any offense ~~included in G.S. 90-95(a)(3) or~~
~~G.S. 90-113.22 and subject to the provisions of this subsection (a1),~~ which qualifies under the
provisions of subsection (a) of this section, and the provisions of this subsection, the court may
place defendant on probation under this section for an offense under this Article including an
offense for which the prescribed punishment includes only a fine. The probation, if imposed,
shall be for not less than one year and shall contain a minimum condition that the defendant
who was found guilty or pleads guilty enroll in and successfully complete, within 150 days of
the date of the imposition of said probation, the program of instruction at the drug education
school approved by the Department of Health and Human Services pursuant to G.S. 90 96.01.
The court may impose probation that does not contain a condition that defendant successfully
complete the program of instruction at a drug education school if:

(1)   There is no drug education school within a reasonable distance of the
defendant's residence; or

(2)   There are specific, extenuating circumstances which make it likely that
defendant will not benefit from the program of instruction.

The court shall enter such specific findings in the record; provided that in the case of
subdivision (2) above, such findings shall include the specific, extenuating circumstances
which make it likely that the defendant will not benefit from the program of instruction.

Upon fulfillment of the terms and conditions of the probation, the court shall discharge such
person and dismiss the proceedings against the person.

For the purposes of determining whether the conviction is a first conviction or whether a
person has already had discharge and dismissal, no prior offense occurring more than seven
years before the date of the current offense shall be considered. In addition, convictions for
violations of a provision of G.S. 90-95(a)(1) or 90-95(a)(2) or 90-95(a)(3), or 90-113.10, or
90-113.11, or 90-113.12, or 90-113.22 shall be considered previous convictions.

Failure to complete successfully an approved program of instruction at a drug education
school shall constitute grounds to revoke probation pursuant to this subsection and deny
application for expunction of all recordation of defendant's arrest, indictment, or information,
trial, finding of guilty, and dismissal and discharge pursuant to G.S. 15A-145.2. For purposes
of this subsection, the phrase "failure to complete successfully the prescribed program of
instruction at a drug education school" includes failure to attend scheduled classes without a
valid excuse, failure to complete the course within 150 days of imposition of probation, willful
failure to pay the required fee for the course as provided in G.S. 90-96.01(b), or any other
manner in which the person fails to complete the course successfully. The instructor of the
course to which a person is assigned shall report any failure of a person to complete
successfully the program of instruction to the court which imposed probation. Upon receipt of
the instructor's report that the person failed to complete the program successfully, the court
shall revoke probation, shall not discharge such person, shall not dismiss the proceedings
against the person, and shall deny application for expunction of all recordation of defendant's
arrest, indictment, or information, trial, finding of guilty, and dismissal and discharge pursuant
to G.S. 15A-145.2. A person may obtain a hearing before the court of original jurisdiction prior
to revocation of probation or denial of application for expunction.

This subsection is supplemental and in addition to existing law and shall not be construed
so as to repeal any existing provision contained in the General Statutes of North Carolina.

(b)   Upon the discharge of such person, and dismissal of the proceedings against the
person under subsection (a) or (a1) of this section, such person, if he or she was not over 21
years of age at the time of the offense, may be eligible to apply for expunction of certain
records relating to the offense pursuant to G.S. 15A-145.2(a).

(c)   Repealed by Session Laws 2009-510, s. 8(b), effective October 1, 2010.

(d)   Whenever any person is charged with a misdemeanor under this Article by
possessing a controlled substance included within Schedules ~~II~~-I through VI of this Article or a
felony under ~~G.S. 90-95(a)(3) by possessing less than one gram of cocaine,~~ G.S. 90-95(a)(3),
upon dismissal by the State of the charges against such person, upon entry of a nolle prosequi,
or upon a finding of not guilty or other adjudication of innocence, the person may be eligible to
apply for expunction of certain records relating to the offense pursuant to G.S. 15A-145.2(b).

(e)   Whenever any person who has not previously been convicted of (i) any felony
offense under any state or federal laws; (ii) any offense under this Article; or (iii) an offense

under any statute of the United States or any state relating to ~~Whenever any person who has not previously been convicted of an offense under this Article or under any statute of the United States or any state relating to~~ controlled substances included in any schedule of this Article or to that paraphernalia included in Article 5B of Chapter 90 of the General Statutes pleads guilty to or has been found guilty of (i) a misdemeanor under this Article by possessing a controlled substance included within Schedules ~~II~~ I through VI of this Article, or by possessing drug paraphernalia as prohibited by G.S. 90-113.22 or (ii) a felony under ~~G.S. 90-95(a)(3) by possessing less than one gram of cocaine,~~ G.S. 90-95(a)(3), the person may be eligible to apply for cancellation of the judgment and expunction of certain records related to the offense pursuant to G.S. 15A-145.2(c).
...."

SECTION 5.(b) G.S. 15A-145.2 reads as rewritten:
"**§ 15A-145.2. Expunction of records for first offenders not over 21 years of age at the time of the offense of certain drug offenses.**
...
(b)   Whenever any person is charged with a misdemeanor under Article 5 of Chapter 90 of the General Statutes by possessing a controlled substance included within Schedules ~~II~~ I through VI of Article 5 of Chapter 90 of the General Statutes or a felony under ~~G.S. 90-95(a)(3) by possessing less than one gram of cocaine,~~ G.S. 90-95(a)(3), upon dismissal by the State of the charges against the person, upon entry of a nolle prosequi, or upon a finding of not guilty or other adjudication of innocence, such person may apply to the court for an order to expunge from all official records all recordation relating to his or her arrest, indictment or information, or trial. If the court determines, after hearing, that such person was not over 21 years of age at the time the offense for which the person was charged occurred, it shall enter such order. The clerk shall notify State and local agencies of the court's order as provided in G.S. 15A-150. No person as to whom such order has been entered shall be held thereafter under any provision of any law to be guilty of perjury or otherwise giving a false statement by reason of the person's failures to recite or acknowledge such arrest, or indictment or information, or trial in response to any inquiry made of him or her for any purpose.
(c)   Whenever any person who has not previously been convicted of (i) any felony offense under any state or federal laws; (ii) any offense under Chapter 90 of the General Statutes; or (iii) an offense under any statute of the United States or any state relating to controlled substances included in any schedule of Chapter 90 of the General Statutes or to that paraphernalia included in Article 5B of Chapter 90 of the General Statutes, pleads guilty to or has been found guilty of (i) a misdemeanor under this Article by possessing a controlled substance included within Schedules I through VI of Chapter 90, or by possessing drug paraphernalia as prohibited by G.S. 90-113.22 or (ii) a felony under G.S. 90-95(a)(3), ~~Whenever any person who has not previously been convicted of an offense under Article 5 of Chapter 90 of the General Statutes or under any statute of the United States or any state relating to controlled substances included in any schedule of Article 5 of Chapter 90 of the General Statutes or to that paraphernalia included in Article 5B of Chapter 90 of the General Statutes pleads guilty to or has been found guilty of (i) a misdemeanor under Article 5 of Chapter 90 of the General Statutes by possessing a controlled substance included within Schedules through VI of Article 5 of Chapter 90 of the General Statutes or by possessing drug paraphernalia as prohibited by G.S. 90-113.22 or (ii) a felony under~~ the court may, upon application of the person not sooner than 12 months after conviction, order cancellation of the judgment of conviction and expunction of the records of the person's arrest, indictment or information, trial, and conviction. A conviction in which the judgment of conviction has been canceled and the records expunged pursuant to this subsection shall not be thereafter deemed a conviction for purposes of this subsection or for purposes of disqualifications or liabilities imposed by law upon conviction of a crime, including the additional penalties imposed for second or subsequent convictions of Article 5 of Chapter 90 of the General Statutes. Cancellation and expunction under this subsection may occur only once with respect to any person. Disposition of a case under this subsection at the district court division of the General Court of Justice shall be final for the purpose of appeal.
The granting of an application filed under this subsection shall cause the issue of an order to expunge from all official records, other than the confidential files retained under G.S. 15A-151, all recordation relating to the petitioner's arrest, indictment or information, trial, finding of

guilty, judgment of conviction, cancellation of the judgment, and expunction of records pursuant to this subsection.

The judge to whom the petition is presented is authorized to call upon a probation officer for additional investigation or verification of the petitioner's conduct since conviction. If the court determines that the petitioner was convicted of (i) a misdemeanor under Article 5 of Chapter 90 of the General Statutes for possessing a controlled substance included within Schedules II-I through VI of Article 5 of Chapter 90 of the General Statutes or for possessing drug paraphernalia as prohibited in G.S. 90-113.22 or (ii) a felony under G.S. 90-95(a)(3) for possession of less than one gram of cocaine, G.S. 90-95(a)(3), that the petitioner has no disqualifying previous convictions as set forth in this subsection, that the petitioner was not over 21 years of age at the time of the offense, that the petitioner has been of good behavior since his or her conviction, that the petitioner has successfully completed a drug education program approved for this purpose by the Department of Health and Human Services, and that the petitioner has not been convicted of a felony or misdemeanor other than a traffic violation under the laws of this State at any time prior to or since the conviction for the offense in question, it shall enter an order of expunction of the petitioner's court record. The effect of such order shall be to restore the petitioner in the contemplation of the law to the status the petitioner occupied before arrest or indictment or information or conviction. No person as to whom such order was entered shall be held thereafter under any provision of any law to be guilty of perjury or otherwise giving a false statement by reason of the person's failures to recite or acknowledge such arrest, or indictment or information, or conviction, or trial in response to any inquiry made of him or her for any purpose. The judge may waive the condition that the petitioner attend the drug education school if the judge makes a specific finding that there was no drug education school within a reasonable distance of the defendant's residence or that there were specific extenuating circumstances which made it likely that the petitioner would not benefit from the program of instruction.

The court shall also order all law enforcement agencies, the Department of Correction, the Division of Motor Vehicles, and any other State or local agencies identified by the petitioner as bearing records of the conviction and records relating thereto to expunge their records of the conviction. The clerk shall notify State and local agencies of the court's order as provided in G.S. 15A-150."

SECTION 5.(c) Article 81B of Chapter 15A of the General Statutes is amended by adding a new section to read:

"**§ 15A-1340.18. Advanced supervised release.**

    (a)   Definitions. – For the purposes of this section, the following definitions apply:

        (1)   "Advanced supervised release" or "ASR" means release from prison and placement on post-release supervision under this section if an eligible defendant is sentenced to active time.

        (2)   "Eligible defendant" means a defendant convicted and sentenced based upon any of the following felony classes and prior record levels:

            a.   Class D, Prior Record Level I-III.

            b.   Class E, Prior Record Level I-IV.

            c.   Class F, Prior Record Level I-V.

            d.   Class G, Prior Record Level I-VI.

            e.   Class H, Prior Record Level I-VI.

        (3)   "Risk reduction incentive" is a sentencing condition which, upon successful completion during incarceration, results in a prisoner being placed on ASR.

    (b)   The Department of Correction is authorized to create risk reduction incentives consisting of treatment, education, and rehabilitative programs. The incentives shall be designed to reduce the likelihood that the prisoner who receives the incentive will reoffend.

    (c)   The court, in its discretion and without objection from the prosecutor, may include a risk reduction incentive or incentives in sentencing an eligible defendant to an active sentence.

    (d)   The court shall impose a sentence calculated pursuant to Article 81B of the General Statutes. The ASR date shall be the shortest mitigated sentence for the offense at the offender's prior record level. If the court utilizes the mitigated range in sentencing the defendant, then the ASR date shall be eighty percent (80%) of the minimum sentence imposed.

    (e)   The defendant shall be notified at sentencing that if the defendant completes the risk reduction incentives as identified by the Department, then he or she will be released on the ASR date. If the Department determines that the defendant is unable to complete the incentives by the ASR date, through no fault of the defendant, then the defendant shall be released at the ASR date.

(f)   Termination from the risk reduction incentive program shall result in the nullification of the ASR date, and the defendant's release date shall be calculated based upon the adjudged sentence. A prisoner who has completed the risk reduction incentives prior to the ASR date may have the ASR date nullified due to noncompliance with Department rules or regulations.

(g)   A defendant released on the ASR date is subject to post-release supervision under this Article. Notwithstanding the provisions in G.S. 15A-1368.3(c), if the defendant has been returned to prison for three, three-month periods of confinement, a subsequent violation shall result in the defendant returning to prison to serve the time remaining on the maximum imposed term, and is ineligible for further post-release supervision regardless of the amount of time remaining to be served.

(h)   The Department shall adopt policies and procedures for the assessment to occur at diagnostic processing, for documentation of the inmate's progress, and for termination from the incentive program due to a lack of progress or a pattern of noncompliance in the program or with other Department rules or regulations."

SECTION 5.(d) G.S. 15A-1340.13(d) reads as rewritten:

"(d)   Service of Minimum Required; Earned Time Authorization. – An offender sentenced to an active punishment shall serve the minimum term ~~imposed.~~ imposed, except as provided in G.S. 15A-1340.18. The maximum term may be reduced to, but not below, the minimum term by earned time credits awarded to an offender by the Department of Correction or the custodian of the local confinement facility, pursuant to rules adopted in accordance with law."

SECTION 5.(e) This section becomes effective January 1, 2012, and applies to persons entering a plea or who are found guilty of an offense on or after that date.

PART VI. REFOCUS CRIMINAL JUSTICE PARTNERSHIP PROGRAM

SECTION 6.(a) Article 6A of Chapter 143B of the General Statutes is repealed.

SECTION 6.(b) Chapter 143B of the General Statutes is amended by adding a new Article to read:

"Article 6B.

"Treatment for Effective Community Supervision Program.

"§ 143B-274.1. Short title.

This Article is the "Treatment for Effective Community Supervision Act of 2011" and may be cited by that name.

"§ 143B-274.2. Legislative policy.

The policy of the General Assembly with respect to the Treatment for Effective Community Supervision Program is to support the use of evidence-based practices to reduce recidivism and to promote coordination between State and community-based corrections programs.

"§ 143B-274.3. Definitions.

The following definitions apply in this Article:

(1)   Certified and licensed. – North Carolina Substance Abuse Professional Practice Board certified or licensed substance abuse professionals or Department of Health and Human Services licensed agencies.

(2)   Department. – The Department of Correction.

(3)   Division. – The Department of Correction, Division of Community Corrections.

(4)   Eligible entity. – A local or regional government, a nongovernmental entity, or collaborative partnership that demonstrates capacity to provide services that address the criminogenic needs of offenders.

(5)   Program. – A community-based corrections program.

(6)   Secretary. – The Secretary of the Department of Correction.

(7)   State Board. – The State Community Corrections Advisory Board.

"§ 143B-274.4. Goals of community-based corrections programs funded under this Article.

The goals of community-based programs funded under this Article are to reduce recidivism and to reduce the rate of probation and post-release supervision revocations from the rate in the 2009-2010 fiscal year.

"**§ 143B-274.5. Eligible population.**

    (a)   An eligible offender is an adult offender who was convicted of a misdemeanor or a felony offense or is sentenced under the conditional discharge program as defined in G.S. 90-96 and meets any one of the following criteria:

    (1)   Received a nonincarcerative sentence of a community punishment.

    (2)   Received a nonincarcerative sentence of an intermediate punishment.

    (3)   Is serving a term of parole or post-release supervision after serving an active sentence of imprisonment.

    (b)   The priority populations for programs funded under this Article shall be as follows:

    (1)   Offenders convicted of a felony or offenders sentenced under G.S. 90-96 conditional discharge for a felony offense.

    (2)   Offenders identified by the Department of Correction using a validated risk assessment instrument to have a high likelihood of reoffending and a moderate to high need for substance abuse treatment.

"**§ 143B-274.6. Duties of Department of Correction.**

    (a)   In addition to those otherwise provided by law, the Department of Correction shall have the following duties:

    (1)   To enter into contractual agreements with eligible entities for the operation of community-based corrections programs and monitor compliance with those agreements.

    (2)   To develop the minimum program standards, policies, and rules for community-based corrections programs and to consult with the Department of Health and Human Services on those standards, policies, and rules that are applicable to licensed and credentialed substance abuse services.

    (3)   To monitor, oversee, and evaluate contracted service providers.

    (4)   To act as an information clearinghouse regarding community-based corrections programs.

    (5)   To collaborate with the Department of Health and Human Services on focusing treatment resources on high-risk and moderate to high need offenders on probation, parole, and post-release supervision.

    (b)   The Department of Correction, Division of Community Corrections, shall develop and publish a recidivism reduction plan for the State that accomplishes the following:

    (1)   Articulates a goal of reducing revocations among people on probation and post-release supervision by twenty percent (20%) from the rate in the 2009-2010 fiscal year.

    (2)   Identifies the number of people on probation and post-release supervision in each county that are in the priority population and have a likely need for substance abuse and/or mental health treatment, employment, education, and/or housing.

    (3)   Identifies the program models that research has shown to be effective at reducing recidivism for the target population and ranks those programs based on their cost-effectiveness.

    (4)   Propose a plan to fund the provision of the most cost-effective programs and services across the State. The plan shall describe the number and types of programs and/or services to be funded in each region of the State and how that program capacity compares with the needs of the target population in that region.

    (c)   The Department of Correction shall report by March 1 of each year to the Chairs of the Senate and House of Representatives Appropriations Committees, the Senate and House of Representatives Appropriations Subcommittees on Justice and Public Safety, and the Joint Legislative Corrections, Crime Control, and Juvenile Justice Oversight Committee on the status of the Treatment for Effective Community Supervision Program. The report shall include the following information:

    (1)   The dollar amount and purpose of funds provided on a contractual basis to service providers for the previous fiscal year.

    (2)   An analysis of offender participation data received, including the following:

        a.   The number of people on probation and post-release supervision that are in the priority population that received services.

       b.   The number of people on probation and post-release supervision that are in the priority population that did not receive services.
       c.   The number of people on probation and post-release supervision outside of the priority population that received services.
       d.   The type of services provided to these populations.
       e.   The rate of revocations and successful completions for people who received services.
       f.   Other measures as determined appropriate.
   (3)   The dollar amount needed to provide additional services to meet the needs of the priority population in the upcoming budget year.
   (4)   Details of personnel, travel, contractual, operating, and equipment expenditures for each program type.

"§ 143B-274.7. Contract for services.
   (a)   The Department of Correction shall contract with service providers through a competitive procurement process to provide community-based services to offenders on probation, parole, or post-release supervision.
   (b)   Contracts for substance abuse treatment services shall be awarded to certified or licensed substance abuse professionals and appropriately licensed agencies to provide services and use practices that have a demonstrated evidence base.
   (c)   The Department of Correction, in partnership with the Department of Health and Human Services, shall develop standard service definitions and performance measures for substance abuse and aftercare support services for inclusion in the contracts.
   (d)   The percentage of funds received by a service provider that may be used for administrative purposes is up to fifteen percent (15%).

"§ 143B-274.8. State Community Corrections Advisory Board.
   (a)   The State Board shall act as an advisory body to the Secretary with regard to this Article. The State Board shall consist of 23 members as follows, to be appointed as provided in subsection (b) of this section:
   (1)   A member of the Senate.
   (2)   A member of the House of Representatives.
   (3)   A judge of the superior court.
   (4)   A judge of the district court.
   (5)   A district attorney.
   (6)   A criminal defense attorney.
   (7)   A county sheriff.
   (8)   A chief of a city police department.
   (9)   Two county commissioners, one from a predominantly urban county and one from a predominantly rural county.
   (10)   A representative of an existing community-based corrections program.
   (11)   A member of the public who has been the victim of a crime.
   (12)   Two rehabilitated ex-offenders.
   (13)   A member of the business community.
   (14)   Three members of the general public, one of whom is a person recovering from chemical dependency or who is a previous consumer of substance abuse treatment services.
   (15)   A victim service provider.
   (16)   A member selected from each of the following service areas: mental health, substance abuse, and employment and training.
   (17)   A clerk of superior court.
   (b)   The membership of the State Board shall be selected as follows:
   (1)   The Governor shall appoint the following members: the county sheriff, the chief of a city police department, the member of the public who has been the victim of a crime, a rehabilitated ex-offender, and the members selected from each of the service areas.
   (2)   The Lieutenant Governor shall appoint the following members: the member of the business community, one member of the general public who is a person recovering from chemical dependency or who is a previous consumer of substance abuse treatment services, and the victim service provider.

(3)   The Chief Justice of the North Carolina Supreme Court shall appoint the following members: the superior court judge, the district court judge, the district attorney, the clerk of superior court, the criminal defense attorney, and the representative of an existing community-based corrections program.

(4)   The President Pro Tempore of the Senate shall appoint the following members: the member of the Senate, the county commissioner from a predominantly urban county, and one member of the general public.

(5)   The Speaker of the House of Representatives shall appoint the following members: the member of the House of Representatives, the county commissioner from a predominantly rural county, and one member of the general public.

In appointing the members of the State Board, the appointing authorities shall make every effort to ensure fair geographic representation of the State Board membership and to ensure that minority persons and women are fairly represented.

(c)   The initial members shall serve staggered terms; one-third shall be appointed for a term of one year, one-third shall be appointed for a term of two years, and one-third shall be appointed for a term of three years. The members identified in subdivisions (1) through (7) of subsection (a) of this section shall be appointed initially for a term of one year. The members identified in subdivisions (8) through (13) in subsection (a) of this section shall be appointed initially for a term of two years. The members identified in subdivisions (14) through (16) of subsection (a) of this section shall each be appointed for a term of three years. The additional member identified in subdivision (17) in subsection (a) of this section shall be appointed initially for a term of three years.

At the end of their respective terms of office their successors shall be appointed for terms of three years. A vacancy occurring before the expiration of the term of office shall be filled in the same manner as original appointments for the remainder of the term. Members may be reappointed without limitation.

(d)   Each appointing authority shall have the power to remove a member it appointed from the State Board for misfeasance, malfeasance, or nonfeasance.

(e)   The members of the State Board shall, within 30 days after the last initial appointment is made, meet and elect one member as Chair and one member as Vice-Chair.

(f)   The State Board shall meet at least quarterly and may also hold special meetings at the call of the Chair. For purposes of transacting business, a majority of the membership shall constitute a quorum.

(g)   Any member who has an interest in a governmental agency or unit or private nonprofit agency which is applying for a Treatment for Effective Community Supervision Program contract or which has received a contract and which is the subject of an inquiry or vote by a contract oversight committee, shall publicly disclose that interest on the record and shall take no part in discussion or have any vote in regard to any matter directly affecting that particular grant applicant or grantee. "Interest" in a grant applicant or grantee means a formal and direct connection to the entity, including, but not limited to, employment, partnership, serving as an elected official, board member, director, officer, or trustee, or being an immediate family member of someone who has such a connection to the grant applicant or grantee.

(h)   The members of the State Board shall serve without compensation but shall be reimbursed for necessary travel and subsistence expenses.

"**§ 143B-274.9. State Community Corrections Advisory Board; powers and duties.**

(a)   The State Community Corrections Advisory Board, as defined under this Article, has the following duties and responsibilities:

(1)   To review the criteria for monitoring and evaluating community-based corrections programs.

(2)   To recommend community-based corrections program priorities.

(3)   To review the minimum program standards, policies, and rules for community-based corrections programs.

(4)   To review the evaluation of programs funded by this Article.

"**§ 143B-274.10. North Carolina Sentencing and Policy Advisory Commission report.**

The North Carolina Sentencing and Policy Advisory Commission shall report by April 30 of each even-numbered year to the General Assembly and the Governor on recidivism rates for offenders on probation, parole, and post-release supervision participating in programming funded through this Article according to risk level.

"§ 143B-274.11. Program types eligible for funding; community-based corrections programs.
Based on the prioritized populations in G.S. 143B-274.5(b), program types eligible for funding may include, but are not limited to, the following:

(1)   Substance abuse treatment services, to include co-occurring substance abuse and mental health disorder services, residential, intensive outpatient, outpatient, peer support, and relapse prevention.

(2)   Cognitive behavioral programming and other evidence-based programming deemed to be the most cost-effective method to reduce criminogenic needs identified by the risk/needs assessment."

SECTION 6.(c) This section becomes effective July 1, 2011. The Department of Correction may enter into contracts under this section with current program providers in the Criminal Justice Partnership Program on a sole-source basis during the 2011-2012 fiscal year.

PART VII. MOST MISDEMEANANTS TO SERVE SENTENCES IN JAIL
SECTION 7.(a) G.S. 148-32.1 is amended by adding a new subsection to read:
"(b1)   It is the intent of the General Assembly to authorize the Department of Correction to enter into voluntary agreements with counties to provide housing for misdemeanants serving periods of confinement of more than 90 days and up to 180 days, except for those serving a sentence for an impaired driving offense. It is further the intent of the General Assembly that the Department of Correction, in conjunction with the North Carolina Sheriffs' Association, Inc., establish a program for housing misdemeanants serving periods of confinement of more than 90 days and up to 180 days, except for those serving sentences for an impaired driving offense. It is also the intent of the General Assembly that the Department of Correction contract with the North Carolina Sheriffs' Association, Inc., to provide a service that identifies space in local confinement facilities that is available for housing these misdemeanants.

The General Assembly intends that the cost of housing and caring for these misdemeanants, including, but not limited to, care, supervision, transportation, medical, and any other related costs, be covered by State funds and not be imposed as a local cost. Therefore, the General Assembly intends that the funds in the Statewide Misdemeanant Confinement Fund established in G.S. 148-10.4 be used to provide funding to cover the costs of managing a system for providing that housing of misdemeanants in local confinement facilities as well as reimbursing the counties for housing and related expenses for those misdemeanants."

SECTION 7.(b) G.S. 15A-1352 reads as rewritten:
"§ 15A-1352. Commitment to Department of Correction or local confinement facility.

(a)   A person sentenced to imprisonment for a misdemeanor under this Article or for nonpayment of a fine under Article 84 of this Chapter shall be committed for the term designated by the court to the custody of the Department of Correction or to a local confinement facility. If the sentence imposed for a misdemeanor is for a period of 90 days or less, the commitment must be to a facility other than one maintained by the Department of Correction, except as provided in G.S. 148-32.1(b). If the sentence or sentences imposed require confinement for more than 180 days, the commitment must be to the custody of the Department of Correction.

If a person is sentenced to imprisonment for a misdemeanor under this Article or for nonpayment of a fine under Article 84 of this Chapter, the sentencing judge shall make a finding of fact as to whether the person would be suitable for placement in a county satellite jail/work release unit operated pursuant to G.S. 153A-230.3. If the sentencing judge makes a finding of fact that the person would be suitable for placement in a county satellite jail/work release unit and the person meets the requirements listed in G.S. 153A-230.3(a)(1), then the custodian of the local confinement facility may transfer the misdemeanant to a county satellite jail/work release unit.

(b)   A person sentenced to imprisonment for a felony under this Article shall be committed for the term designated by the court to the custody of the Department of Correction; except that, upon request of the sheriff or the board of commissioners of a county, the presiding judge may, in his discretion, sentence the person to a local confinement facility in that county. Correction.

(c)   A person sentenced to imprisonment for nonpayment of a fine under Article 84, Fines, shall be committed for the term designated by the court:

(1)   To the custody of the Department of Correction if the person was fined for conviction of a felony;

(2)   To the custody of the Department of Correction or to a local confinement facility if the person was fined for conviction of a misdemeanor, provided that (i) if the sentence imposed is for a period of 90 days or less, the commitment shall be to a facility other than one maintained by the Department of Correction, except as provided in ~~G.S. 148-32.1(b).~~ G.S. 148-32.1(b) and (ii) if the sentence or sentences imposed require confinement for more than 180 days, the commitment must be to the custody of the Department of Correction.

..."

SECTION 7.(c) G.S. 15A-1352 is amended by adding a new subsection to read:

"(e)   A person sentenced for a misdemeanor who has a sentence imposed that requires confinement for a period of more than 90 days and up to 180 days, except for those serving sentences for an impaired driving offense under G.S. 20-138.1 under this Article or for nonpayment of a fine under Article 84 of this Chapter, shall be committed for the term designated by the court to confinement pursuant to the Statewide Misdemeanant Confinement Program established by G.S. 148-32.1."

SECTION 7.(d) G.S. 148-32.1(b) reads as rewritten:

"(b)   In the event that the custodian of the local confinement facility certifies in writing to the clerk of the superior court in the county in which ~~said~~ the local confinement facility is located that the local confinement facility is filled to capacity, or that the facility cannot reasonably accommodate any more prisoners due to segregation requirements for particular prisoners, or that the custodian anticipates, in light of local experiences, an influx of temporary prisoners at that time, or if the local confinement facility does not meet the minimum standards published pursuant to G.S. 153A-221, any judge of the district court in the district court district as defined in G.S. 7A-133 where the facility is located, or any superior court judge who has jurisdiction pursuant to G.S. 7A-47.1 or G.S. 7A-48 in a district or set of districts as defined in G.S. 7A-41.1 where the facility is located may order that ~~the~~ a prisoner not housed pursuant to the Statewide Misdemeanant Confinement Program established in subsection (b2) of this section be transferred to any other qualified local confinement facility within that district or within another such district where space is available, including a satellite jail unit operated pursuant to G.S. 153A-230.3 if the prisoner is a non-violent misdemeanant, which local facility shall accept the transferred ~~prisoner, if the prison population has exceeded a manageable level as provided for in G.S. 148-4.1(a). If no such local confinement facility is available, then any such judge may order the prisoner transferred to such camp or facility as the proper authorities of the Department of Correction shall designate, notwithstanding that the term of imprisonment of the prisoner is 90 days or less. In no event, however, shall a prisoner whose term of imprisonment is less than 30 days be assigned or ordered transferred to any such camp or facility.~~prisoner.

If no other local confinement facility is available and the reason for the requested transfer is that the local confinement facility that would be required to house the prisoner cannot reasonably accommodate any more prisoners due to segregation requirements for particular prisoners or the local facility does not meet the minimum standards published pursuant to G.S. 153A-221, then the judge may order that a prisoner not housed pursuant to the Statewide Misdemeanant Confinement Program established in subsection (b2) of this section be transferred to a facility operated by the Department of Correction as designated by the Department of Correction. In no event, however, shall a prisoner whose term of imprisonment is less than 30 days be assigned or ordered transferred to a facility operated by the Department of Correction."

SECTION 7.(e) G.S. 148-32.1 is amended by adding a new subsection to read:

"(b2)   The Statewide Misdemeanant Confinement Program is established. The Program shall provide for the housing of misdemeanants from all counties serving sentences imposed for a period of more than 90 days and up to 180 days, except for those serving sentences for an impaired driving offense under G.S. 20-138.1. Those misdemeanants shall be confined in local confinement facilities except as provided in subsections (b3) and (b4) of this section. The Program shall address methods for the placement and transportation of inmates and reimbursement to counties for the housing of those inmates. Any county that voluntarily agrees to house misdemeanants from that county or from other counties pursuant to the Program may enter into a written agreement with the Department of Correction to do so.

This Program shall only operate as long as sufficient State funds are available through the Statewide Misdemeanant Confinement Fund established in G.S. 148-10.4(c). "

SECTION 7.(f) The North Carolina Sheriffs' Association, Inc., in consultation with the Department of Correction, shall develop the Statewide Misdemeanant Confinement Program established in G.S. 148-32.1, as enacted in subsection (e) of this section, by September 1, 2011.

Notwithstanding any other provision of law, no later than November 1, 2011, the Secretary of Correction shall contract with the North Carolina Sheriffs' Association, Inc., to implement the Program. The contract terms shall include all of the following:

(1)   A provision that the Program shall be operated on a statewide basis no later than January 1, 2012, but may be phased in beginning at an earlier date.

(2)   A provision addressing the method of payment to the North Carolina Sheriffs' Association, Inc., for the costs of administering the Program.

(3)   A provision authorizing reimbursement by the North Carolina Sheriffs' Association, Inc., to counties or to the Department of Correction, as appropriate, for all expenses incurred on behalf of those misdemeanants.

SECTION 7.(g) G.S. 148-32.1 is amended by adding new subsections to read:

"(b3) The custodian of a local confinement facility may request a judicial order to transfer a misdemeanant housed pursuant to the Statewide Misdemeanant Confinement Program to a facility operated by the Department of Correction by certifying in writing to the clerk of the superior court in the county in which the local confinement facility is located that:

(1)   The misdemeanant poses a security risk because the misdemeanant:

a.   Poses a serious escape risk;

b.   Exhibits violently aggressive behavior that cannot be contained and warrants a higher level of supervision;

c.   Needs to be protected from other inmates, and the county jail facility cannot provide such protection;

d.   Is a female or a person 18 years of age or younger, and the county jail facility does not have adequate housing for such prisoners;

e.   Is in custody at a time when a fire or other catastrophic event has caused the county jail facility to cease or curtail operations; or

f.   Otherwise poses an imminent danger to the staff of the county jail facility or to other prisoners in the facility.

(2)   The misdemeanant requires medical or mental health treatment that the county decides can best be provided by the Department of Correction.

(3)   The local confinement facility that would be required to house the prisoner (i) cannot reasonably accommodate any more prisoners due to segregation requirements for particular prisoners, or the local facility does not meet the minimum standards published pursuant to G.S. 153A-221, and (ii) no other local confinement facility is available.

Upon receiving such request and certification in writing, any superior or district court judge for the district in which the local confinement facility is located may, after ascertaining that the request meets the criteria set forth in subdivision (1), (2), or (3) of this subsection, order the misdemeanant transferred to a unit of the State prison system designated by the Secretary of Correction or the Secretary's authorized representative. The Department of Correction shall be reimbursed from the Statewide Misdemeanant Confinement Fund for the costs of housing the misdemeanant, including the care, supervision, and transportation of the misdemeanant.

(b4) A misdemeanant housed under the Statewide Misdemeanant Confinement Program established pursuant to subsection (b2) of this section may be transferred to a facility operated by the Department of Correction if the North Carolina Sheriffs' Association, Inc., determines that the local confinement facilities available for housing misdemeanants under the Program are filled to capacity. The Department of Correction shall be reimbursed from the Statewide Misdemeanant Confinement Fund for the costs of housing the misdemeanant, including the care, supervision, and transportation of the misdemeanant."

SECTION 7.(h) Article 1 of Chapter 148 of the General Statutes is amended by adding a new section to read:

"**§ 148-10.4. Statewide Misdemeanant Confinement Fund.**

(a) Definitions. – The following definitions apply in this section:
  (1) Department. – Department of Correction.
  (2) Fund. – The Statewide Misdemeanant Confinement Fund established by this section.
  (3) Program. – Statewide Misdemeanant Confinement Program established under G.S. 148-32.1(b3).
  (4) Sheriffs' Association. – North Carolina Sheriffs' Association, Inc.
(b) Intent and Purpose. – It is the intent of the General Assembly that the funds in the Fund established by this section be used to reimburse local governments for expenses incurred for housing misdemeanants under the Program, and other related expenses; and to cover administrative costs incurred by the Sheriffs' Association for services provided by it regarding the housing of these misdemeanants.
(c) Statewide Misdemeanant Confinement Fund established. – There is created within the Department of Correction a special nonreverting fund called the Statewide Misdemeanant Confinement Fund.
(d) Fund Uses. – Moneys in the Fund may be used for the following:
  (1) Reimbursements by the Sheriffs' Association to counties for the costs of housing misdemeanants under the Program, including the care, supervision, and transportation of those misdemeanants.
  (2) Reimbursements to the Department of Correction for the cost of housing misdemeanants transferred to the Department pursuant to G.S. 148-32.1(b3), including the care, supervision, and transportation of those misdemeanants.
  (3) To pay the Sheriffs' Association for administrative and operating expenses pursuant to subsection (e) of this section.
  (4) To pay the Department of Correction for administrative and operating expenses pursuant to subsection (e) of this section.
(e) Operating and Administrative Expenses. – Ten percent (10%) of the monthly receipts collected and credited to the Statewide Misdemeanant Confinement Fund shall be transferred on a monthly basis to the Sheriffs' Association to be used to support the Program and for administrative and operating expenses of the Association and its staff. One percent (1%) of the monthly receipts collected and credited to the Statewide Misdemeanant Confinement Fund shall be transferred on a monthly basis to the General Fund to be allocated to the Department of Correction for its administrative and operating expenses for the Program."

  SECTION 7.(i) The North Carolina Sheriffs' Association, Inc., shall report to the Joint Legislative Corrections, Crime Control, and Juvenile Justice Oversight Committee by October 1, 2011, on the implementation of this Part, and shall report thereafter as requested by the Committee. The report shall include relevant information collected monthly by the North Carolina Sheriffs' Association, Inc., regarding the jail capacity and population in each county.

  SECTION 7.(j) The General Assembly finds that while the Program developed pursuant to G.S. 148-32.1(b2), as enacted by subsection (e) of this section, shall be available statewide on January 1, 2012, it may be available to some counties at an earlier date. Therefore, notwithstanding any other provision of law, a misdemeanant, who has a sentence imposed of more than 90 days and up to 180 days prior to January 1, 2012, excluding those serving sentences for an impaired driving offense under G.S. 20-138.1, may be transferred or reassigned to a local confinement facility designated by the North Carolina Sheriffs' Association, Inc., as provided by the Program developed pursuant to G.S. 148-32.1(b2).

  SECTION 7.(k) Of the funds appropriated to the Department of Correction for the 2011-2012 fiscal year, the Department shall transfer the sum of three hundred thousand dollars ($300,000) to the North Carolina Sheriffs' Association, Inc., for expenses related to initiating the provisions of this Part.

  SECTION 7.(l) If there is not adequate capacity in the Statewide Misdemeanant Confinement program, such that the Department of Correction must continue to house prisoners serving more than 90 days and up to 180 days pursuant to G.S. 148-32.1(b4), then the Department of Correction is authorized to use funds received from the Statewide Misdemeanant Confinement Fund to operate facilities previously identified for closure and for diagnostic staff positions.

  SECTION 7.(m) If House Bill 200, 2011 Regular Session, becomes law, then that act is amended by deleting subsection (a) of Section 31.26 of that act.

SECTION 7.(n) If House Bill 200, 2011 Regular Session, becomes law, then section 31.26 of that act is amended by adding a new subsection to read:

"**SECTION 31.26.(g)** This section becomes effective August 1, 2011."

SECTION 7.(o) If House Bill 200, 2011 Regular Session, becomes law, then that act is amended by adding a new section to read:

"**SECTION 31.23B.** G.S. 15A-932 is amended by adding a new subsection to read:

'(d1) If the proceeding was dismissed pursuant to subdivision (2) of subsection (a) of this section and charged only offenses for which written appearance, waiver of trial or hearing, and plea of guilty or admission of responsibility are permitted pursuant to G.S. 7A-148(a), and the defendant later tenders to the court that waiver and payment in full of all applicable fines, costs, and fees, the clerk shall accept said waiver and payment without need for a written reinstatement from the prosecutor. Upon disposition of the case pursuant to this subsection, the clerk shall recall any outstanding criminal process in the case pursuant to G.S. 15A-301(g)(2)b.'"

SECTION 7.(p) If House Bill 200, 2011 Regular Session, becomes law, then Section 31.26 of that act is amended by adding a new subsection to read:

"**SECTION 31.26.(f1)** G.S. 7A-321(d) is amended by adding a new subdivision to read:

'(d) The court shall retain a collection assistance fee in the amount of ten percent (10%) of any cost or fee collected by the Department pursuant to this Article or Chapter 20 of the General Statutes and remitted to an agency of the State or any of its political subdivisions, other than a cost or fee listed in this subsection. The court shall remit the collection assistance fee to the State Treasurer for the support of the General Court of Justice.

The collection assistance fee shall not be retained from the following:

...

(3) Costs and fees designated by law for remission to the Statewide Misdemeanant Confinement Fund.'"

SECTION 7.(q) G.S. 148-32.1(b2), as enacted by subsection (e) of this section, and subsections (a), (h), (i), (j), (k), (l), (m), (n), (o), (p), and (q) of this section become effective July 1, 2011. The remainder of this section becomes effective January 1, 2012, and applies to sentences imposed on or after that date.

PART VIII. ANNUAL REPORT AND SENTENCING COMMISSION DUTIES

SECTION 8.(a) Article 4 of Chapter 164 of the General Statutes is amended by adding a new section to read:

"**§ 164-50. Annual report on implementation of Justice Reinvestment Project.**

The Judicial Department, through the North Carolina Sentencing and Policy Advisory Commission, and the Department of Correction shall jointly conduct ongoing evaluations regarding the implementation of the Justice Reinvestment Act of 2011. The Commission shall present the first evaluation report to the Joint Legislative Correction, Crime Control, and Juvenile Justice Oversight Committee and to the Chairs of the Senate and House of Representatives Appropriations Subcommittees on Justice and Public Safety by April 15, 2012, and future reports shall be made annually by April 15 of each year."

SECTION 8.(b) G.S. 164-44(a) reads as rewritten:

"(a) The Commission shall have the secondary duty of collecting, developing, and maintaining statistical data relating to sentencing, corrections, and juvenile justice so that the primary duties of the Commission will be formulated using data that is valid, accurate, and relevant to this State. All State agencies shall provide data as it is requested by the Commission. For the purposes of G.S. 114-19.1, the Commission shall be considered to be engaged in the administration of criminal justice. All meetings of the Commission shall be open to the public and the information presented to the Commission shall be available to any State agency or member of the General Assembly."

PART IX. TITLE

SECTION 9. This act shall be known as "The Justice Reinvestment Act of 2011."

PART X. EFFECTIVE DATE
SECTION 10. Except as otherwise provided in this act, this act is effective when it becomes law. Prosecutions for offenses committed before the effective date of this act are not abated or affected by this act, and the statutes that would be applicable but for this act remain applicable to those prosecutions.

In the General Assembly read three times and ratified this the 16th day of June, 2011.

s/ Walter H. Dalton
President of the Senate

s/ Thom Tillis
Speaker of the House of Representatives

s/ Beverly E. Perdue
Governor

Approved 10:40 a.m. this 23rd day of June, 2011

Appendix D

N.C. Session Law 2011-307, Sex Offender Supervision/ Forensic Amendments

GENERAL ASSEMBLY OF NORTH CAROLINA
SESSION 2011

SESSION LAW 2011-307
SENATE BILL 684

AN ACT TO CLARIFY AND AMEND THE LAW PROVIDING FOR A FIVE-YEAR PERIOD OF POST-RELEASE SUPERVISION FOR SEX OFFENDERS BY INCREASING THE MAXIMUM SENTENCE FOR SEX OFFENDERS AND PROVIDING FOR THEIR RELEASE ON POST-RELEASE SUPERVISION WITH FIVE YEARS REMAINING ON THEIR SENTENCES AND TO PROVIDE THAT WILLFUL REFUSAL TO ACCEPT OR COMPLY WITH THE TERMS OF POST-RELEASE SUPERVISION IS PUNISHABLE AS CONTEMPT OF COURT, AND TO AMEND THE FORENSIC SCIENCES ACT.

The General Assembly of North Carolina enacts:

    SECTION 1. G.S. 15A-1340.17 is amended by adding a new subsection to read:
    "(f)   Maximum Sentences Specified for Class B1 Through Class E Sex Offenses. – Unless provided otherwise in a statute establishing a punishment for a specific crime, for offenders sentenced for a Class B1 through E felony that is a reportable conviction subject to the registration requirement of Article 27A of Chapter 14 of the General Statutes, the maximum term of imprisonment shall be equal to the sum of the minimum term of imprisonment and twenty percent (20%) of the minimum term of imprisonment, rounded to the next highest month, plus 60 additional months."
    SECTION 2. G.S. 15A-1368.2(a) reads as rewritten:
    "(a)   A Except as otherwise provided in this subsection, a prisoner to whom this Article applies shall be released from prison for post-release supervision on the date equivalent to his maximum imposed prison term less nine months, less any earned time awarded by the Department of Correction or the custodian of a local confinement facility under G.S. 15A-1340.13(d). A prisoner whose maximum sentence is established pursuant to G.S. 15A-1340.17(f) shall be released from prison for post-release supervision on the date equivalent to his or her maximum imposed prison term less 60 months, less any earned time awarded by the Department of Correction or the custodian of a local confinement facility under G.S. 15A-1340.13(d). If a prisoner has not been awarded any earned time, the prisoner shall be released for post-release supervision on the date equivalent to his maximum prison term less nine months."
    SECTION 3. G.S. 15A-1354(b) reads as rewritten:
    "(b)   Effect of Consecutive Terms. – In determining the effect of consecutive sentences imposed under authority of this Article and the manner in which they will be served, the Department of Correction must treat the defendant as though he has been committed for a single term with the following incidents:
        (1)   The maximum prison sentence consists of the total of the maximum terms of the consecutive sentences, less nine months for each of the second and subsequent sentences imposed for Class B through Class E felonies; felonies, or less 60 months for each second or subsequent Class B1 through E felony for which the sentence was established pursuant to G.S. 15A-1340.17(f); and
        (2)   The minimum term consists of the total of the minimum terms of the consecutive sentences."
    SECTION 4. G.S. 15A-1368(a)(5) reads as rewritten:
    "(5)   Maximum imposed term. – The maximum term of imprisonment imposed on an individual prisoner by a court judgment, as described in G.S. 15A-1340.13(c). When a prisoner is serving consecutive prison terms, the maximum imposed term, for purposes of this Article, is the sum of all

S684-V-5

maximum terms imposed in the court judgment or judgments, less nine months for each of the second and subsequent sentences imposed for Class B through Class E ~~felonies.~~ felonies, or less 60 months for each second or subsequent Class B1 through E felony for which the sentence was established pursuant to G.S. 15A-1340.17(f)."

SECTION 5. G.S. 15A-1368.2(b) reads as rewritten:

"(b)   A prisoner shall not refuse post-release supervision. Willful refusal to accept post-release supervision or to comply with the terms of post-release supervision by a prisoner whose offense requiring post-release supervision is a reportable conviction subject to the registration requirement of Article 27A of Chapter 14 of the General Statutes, is punishable as contempt of court under G.S. 5A-11 and may result in imprisonment under G.S. 5A-12. Furthermore, any period of time during which a prisoner whose offense requiring post-release supervision is a reportable conviction subject to the registration requirement of Article 27A of Chapter 14 of the General Statutes is not in fact released pursuant to subsection (a) of this section due to the prisoner's resistance to that release shall toll the running of the period of supervised release imposed by subsection (c) of this section. For purposes of this subsection and the provisions of G.S. 5A-11, "willful refusal to accept post-release supervision or to comply with the terms of post-release supervision" includes, but is not limited to, knowingly violating the terms of post-release supervision in order to be returned to prison to serve out the remainder of the prisoner's sentence. Notwithstanding any other provision of law, a prisoner punished for the offense of contempt of court under this subsection is not eligible for credit for time served against the sentence for which the prisoner is subject to post-release supervision. Punishment by contempt for willful refusal to accept post-release supervision or to comply with the terms of post-release supervision does not preclude the application of any other sanction provided by law for the same conduct."

SECTION 6. G.S. 5A-11(a) reads as rewritten:

"(a)   Except as provided in subsection (b), each of the following is criminal contempt:

(1)   Willful behavior committed during the sitting of a court and directly tending to interrupt its proceedings.

(2)   Willful behavior committed during the sitting of a court in its immediate view and presence and directly tending to impair the respect due its authority.

(3)   Willful disobedience of, resistance to, or interference with a court's lawful process, order, directive, or instruction or its execution.

(4)   Willful refusal to be sworn or affirmed as a witness, or, when so sworn or affirmed, willful refusal to answer any legal and proper question when the refusal is not legally justified.

(5)   Willful publication of a report of the proceedings in a court that is grossly inaccurate and presents a clear and present danger of imminent and serious threat to the administration of justice, made with knowledge that it was false or with reckless disregard of whether it was false. No person, however, may be punished for publishing a truthful report of proceedings in a court.

(6)   Willful or grossly negligent failure by an officer of the court to perform his duties in an official transaction.

(7)   Willful or grossly negligent failure to comply with schedules and practices of the court resulting in substantial interference with the business of the court.

(8)   Willful refusal to testify or produce other information upon the order of a judge acting pursuant to Article 61 of Chapter 15A, Granting of Immunity to Witnesses.

(9)   Willful communication with a juror in an improper attempt to influence his deliberations.

(9a)   Willful refusal by a defendant to comply with a condition of probation.

(9b)   Willful refusal to accept post-release supervision or to comply with the terms of post-release supervision by a prisoner whose offense requiring post-release supervision is a reportable conviction subject to the registration requirement of Article 27A of Chapter 14 of the General Statutes. For purposes of this subdivision, "willful refusal to accept post-release supervision or to comply with the terms of post-release supervision" includes, but is not limited to, knowingly violating the terms of post-release supervision in order to be returned to prison to serve out the remainder of the supervisee's sentence.

(10) Any other act or omission specified elsewhere in the General Statutes of North Carolina as grounds for criminal contempt.

The grounds for criminal contempt specified here are exclusive, regardless of any other grounds for criminal contempt which existed at common law."

SECTION 7. G.S. 143B-266(a) reads as rewritten:

"(a) There is hereby created a Post-Release Supervision and Parole Commission of the Department of Correction with the authority to grant paroles, including both regular and temporary paroles, to persons held by virtue of any final order or judgment of any court of this State as provided in Chapter 148 of the General Statutes and laws of the State of North Carolina, except that persons sentenced under Article 81B of Chapter 15A of the General Statutes are not eligible for parole but may be conditionally released into the custody and control of United States Immigration and Customs Enforcement pursuant to G.S. 148-64.1. The Commission shall also have authority to revoke, terminate, and suspend paroles of such persons (including persons placed on parole on or before the effective date of the Executive Organization Act of 1973) and to assist the Governor in exercising his authority in granting reprieves, commutations, and pardons, and shall perform such other services as may be required by the Governor in exercising his powers of executive clemency. The Commission shall also have authority to revoke and terminate persons on post-release supervision, as provided in Article 84A of Chapter 15A of the General Statutes. The Commission shall also have the authority to punish for criminal contempt for willful refusal to accept post-release supervision or to comply with the terms of post-release supervision by a prisoner whose offense requiring post-release supervision is a reportable conviction subject to the registration requirement of Article 27A of Chapter 14 of the General Statutes. Any contempt proceeding conducted by the Commission shall be in accordance with G.S. 5A-15 as if the Commission were a judicial official."

SECTION 8. Section 4 of S.L. 2011-19 reads as rewritten:

"**SECTION 4.** Forensic science professionals at the State Crime Laboratory shall be required to obtain individual certification consistent with international and ISO standards as soon as practicable, but no later than June 1, 2012, within 18 months of the date the analyst becomes eligible to seek certification according to the standards of the certifying entity or by June 1, 2012, whichever occurs later, unless no certification is available. All such forensic science professionals shall have access to the certification process."

SECTION 9. Section 11 of S.L. 2011-19 reads as rewritten:

"**SECTION 11.** Sections 1 through 5 and 7Sections 9 through 11 are effective when this act becomes law, and Section 6 becomes effective July 1, 2011. Sections 7 and 8 of this act are effective when they become law, however, until October 1, 2012, the provisions of those sections shall apply only to the North Carolina State Crime Laboratory, and on or after October 1, 2012, the provisions of Sections 7 and 8 shall apply to all laboratories conducting forensic or chemical analysis for admission in the courts of this State. Nothing in this act is intended to amend or modify either the statutory or common law applicable to discovery in criminal cases which was applicable prior to the effective date of this act. Prosecutions for offenses committed before the effective date of this act are not abated or affected by this act, and the statutes that would be applicable but for this act remain applicable to those prosecutions."

SECTION 10. Sections 5, 6, and 7 of this act are effective when they become law and apply to willful refusals to accept post-release supervision or to comply with the terms of post-release supervision that occur on or after that date. Sections 8, 9, and 10 of this act are effective when they become law. The remainder of this act becomes effective December 1, 2011, and applies to offenses committed on or after that date.

In the General Assembly read three times and ratified this the 17th day of June, 2011.

s/ Walter H. Dalton
President of the Senate

s/ Thom Tillis
Speaker of the House of Representatives

s/ Beverly E. Perdue
Governor

Approved 10:38 a.m. this 27th day of June, 2011

Appendix E

N.C. Session Law 2011-412, Prison Maintenance/Justice Reinvestment/ Technical Corrections

GENERAL ASSEMBLY OF NORTH CAROLINA
SESSION 2011

SESSION LAW 2011-412
HOUSE BILL 335

AN ACT TO DIRECT THE DEPARTMENT OF CORRECTION AND THE DEPARTMENT OF PUBLIC SAFETY TO STUDY CONTRACTING FOR MAINTENANCE SERVICES AT PRISON FACILITIES AND TO TEMPORARILY LIMIT EXPANSION OF PRIVATE MAINTENANCE CONTRACTS AT PRISON FACILITIES; TO MAKE CLARIFYING CHANGES TO CERTAIN PROBATION STATUTES AND TO THE JUSTICE REINVESTMENT ACT; TO MAKE CLARIFYING CHANGES TO THE LAW RELATING TO PROVISIONAL DRIVERS LICENSES, MAKING A CHANGE TO THE BUDGET TECHNICAL CORRECTIONS BILL AND A TECHNICAL CHANGE TO S.L. 2011-313; TO PROVIDE BONDSMAN ACCESS TO CRIMINAL COURT RECORDS; TO AUTHORIZE ADDITIONAL CONNECTIONS TO WATER SUPPLY LINES FUNDED BY THE CLEAN WATER AND NATURAL GAS CRITICAL NEEDS BOND ACT OF 1998; AND TO CLARIFY THE QUALIFICATIONS OF PUBLIC MEMBERS OF THE NORTH CAROLINA HOME INSPECTOR LICENSURE BOARD.

The General Assembly of North Carolina enacts:

PART I. MAINTENANCE OF PRISONS
      SECTION 1.1. The Department of Correction shall study the potential benefits and costs of contracting for maintenance services at prison facilities and report its findings to the 2013 Session of the General Assembly. The Department shall not expand private maintenance contracts to additional prison facilities unless authorized by the 2013 Session of the General Assembly.
      SECTION 1.2. Effective January 1, 2012, Section 1.1 of this act reads as rewritten:
"**SECTION 1.1.** The Department of ~~Correction~~ Public Safety shall study the potential benefits and costs of contracting for maintenance services at prison facilities and report its findings to the 2013 Session of the General Assembly. The Department shall not expand private maintenance contracts to additional prison facilities unless authorized by the 2013 Session of the General Assembly."

PART II. JUSTICE REINVESTMENT/CLARIFICATIONS
      SECTION 2.1. Effective December 1, 2011, G.S. 15A-1343(b)(2), as amended by Section 1 of S.L. 2011-62, reads as rewritten:
    "(b)   Regular Conditions. – As regular conditions of probation, a defendant must:
          …
          (2)   Remain ~~accessible to the probation officer by making the defendant's whereabouts known to the officer and not leave the county of residence or the State of North Carolina~~ within the jurisdiction of the court unless granted written permission to leave by the court or his probation officer.
          …."
      SECTION 2.2. Effective December 1, 2011, Section 4 of S.L. 2011-62 reads as rewritten:
      "**SECTION 4.** This act becomes effective December 1, ~~2011, and applies to persons placed on probation on or after that date.~~2011. Sections 1 and 2 of this act apply to offenses committed on or after December 1, 2011. Section 3 of this act applies to persons placed on probation on or after December 1, 2011."
      SECTION 2.3.(a)   G.S. 15A-1343(a1)(3), as enacted by Section 1(c) of S.L. 2011-192, reads as rewritten:

H335-v-4

"(a1) Community and Intermediate Probation Conditions. – In addition to any conditions a court may be authorized to impose pursuant to G.S. 15A-1343(b1), the court may include any one or more of the following conditions as part of a community or intermediate punishment:

...

    (3)   Submission to a period or periods of confinement in a local confinement facility for a total of no more than six days per month during any three separate months during the period of probation. The six days per month confinement provided for in this subdivision may only be imposed as two-day or three-day consecutive periods. When a defendant is on probation for multiple judgments, confinement periods imposed under this subdivision shall run concurrently and may total no more than six days per month.

...."

SECTION 2.3.(b)   G.S. 15A-1343.2(e)(5), as enacted by Section 1(d) of S.L. 2011-192, reads as rewritten:

"(e)   Delegation to Probation Officer in Community Punishment. – Unless the presiding judge specifically finds in the judgment of the court that delegation is not appropriate, the Division of Community Corrections in the Department of Correction may require an offender sentenced to community punishment to do any of the following:

...

    (5)   Submit to a period or periods of confinement in a local confinement facility for a total of no more than six days per month during any three separate months during the period of probation. The six days per month confinement provided for in this subdivision may only be imposed as two-day or three-day consecutive periods. When a defendant is on probation for multiple judgments, confinement periods imposed under this subdivision shall run concurrently and may total no more than six days per month.

...."

SECTION 2.3.(c)   G.S. 15A-1343.2(f)(6), as enacted by Section 1(e) of S.L. 2011-192, reads as rewritten:

"(f)   Delegation to Probation Officer in Intermediate Punishments. – Unless the presiding judge specifically finds in the judgment of the court that delegation is not appropriate, the Division of Community Corrections in the Department of Correction may require an offender sentenced to intermediate punishment to do any of the following:

...

    (6)   Submit to a period or periods of confinement in a local confinement facility for a total of no more than six days per month during any three separate months during the period of probation. The six days per month confinement provided for in this subdivision may only be imposed as two-day or three-day consecutive periods. When a defendant is on probation for multiple judgments, confinement periods imposed under this subdivision shall run concurrently and may total no more than six days per month.

...."

SECTION 2.3.(d)   G.S. 15A-1344(d2), as enacted by Section 4(c) of S.L. 2011-192, reads as rewritten:

"(d2)   Confinement in Response to Violation. – When a defendant has violated a condition of probation other than G.S. 15A-1343(b)(1) or G.S. 15A-1343(b)(3a), the court may impose a 90-day period of confinement for a defendant under supervision for a felony conviction or a period of confinement of up to 90 days for a defendant under supervision for a misdemeanor conviction. The court may not revoke probation unless the defendant has previously received a total of two periods of confinement under this subsection. A defendant may receive only two periods of confinement under this subsection. If the time remaining on the defendant's maximum imposed sentence is ~~less than 90 days,~~ 90 days or less, then the term of confinement is for the remaining period of the sentence. Confinement under this section shall be credited pursuant to G.S. 15-196.1.

If a defendant is arrested for violation of a condition of probation and is lawfully confined to await a hearing for the violation, then the judge shall first credit any confinement time spent awaiting the hearing to any confinement imposed under this subsection; any excess time shall be credited to the activated sentence. The period of confinement imposed under this subsection on a defendant who is on probation for multiple offenses shall run concurrently on all cases related to the violation. Confinement shall be immediate unless otherwise specified by the court.

A defendant shall serve any confinement imposed under this subsection in the correctional facility where the defendant would have served an active sentence."

SECTION 2.3.(e) Subsection (d) of this section becomes effective December 1, 2011, and applies to probation violations occurring on or after that date. The remainder of this section becomes effective December 1, 2011, and applies to offenses committed on or after that date.

SECTION 2.4.(a) G.S. 15A-1340.17(e), as amended by Section 2(f) of S.L. 2011-192, reads as rewritten:

"(e) Maximum Sentences Specified for Class B1 through Class E Felonies for Minimum Terms up to 339 Months. – Unless provided otherwise in a statute establishing a punishment for a specific crime, for each minimum term of imprisonment in the chart in subsection (c) of this section, expressed in months, the corresponding maximum term of imprisonment, also expressed in months, is as specified in the table below for Class B1 through Class E felonies. The first figure in each cell of the table is the minimum term and the second is the maximum term.

15-30	16-32	17-33	18-34	19-35	20-36	21-38	22-39
23-40	24-41	25-42	26-44	27-45	28-46	29-47	30-48
31-50	32-51	33-52	34-53	35-54	36-56	37-57	38-58
39-59	40-60	41-62	42-63	43-64	44-65	45-66	46-68
47-69	48-70	49-71	50-72	51-74	52-75	53-76	54-77
55-78	56-80	57-81	58-82	59-83	60-84	61-86	62-87
63-88	64-89	65-90	66-91	67-93	68-94	69-95	70-96
71-98	72-99	73-100	74-101	75-102	76-104	77-105	78-106
79-107	80-108	81-110	82-111	83-112	84-113	85-114	86-115
87-117	88-118	89-119	90-120	91-122	92-123	93-124	94-125
95-126	96-128	97-129	98-130	99-131	100-132	101-134	102-135
103-136	104-137	105-138	106-140	107-141	108-142	109-143	110-144
111-146	112-147	113-148	114-149	115-150	116-152	117-153	118-154
119-155	120-156	121-158	122-159	123-160	124-161	125-162	126-164
127-165	128-166	129-167	130-168	131-170	132-171	133-172	134-173
135-174	136-176	137-177	138-178	139-179	140-180	141-182	142-183
143-184	144-185	145-186	146-188	147-189	148-190	149-191	150-192
151-194	152-195	153-196	154-197	155-198	156-200	157-201	158-202
159-203	160-204	161-206	162-207	163-208	164-209	165-210	166-212
167-213	168-214	169-215	170-216	171-218	172-219	173-220	174-221
175-222	176-224	177-225	178-226	179-227	180-228	181-230	182-231
183-232	184-233	185-234	186-236	187-237	188-238	189-239	190-240
191-242	192-243	193-244	194-245	195-246	196-248	197-249	198-250
199-251	200-252	201-254	202-255	203-256	204-257	205-258	206-260
207-261	208-262	209-263	210-264	211-266	212-267	213-268	214-269
215-270	216-271	217-273	218-274	219-275	220-276	221-278	222-279
223-280	224-281	225-282	226-284	227-285	228-286	229-287	230-288
231-290	232-291	233-292	234-293	235-294	236-296	237-297	238-298
239-299	240-300	241-302	242-303	243-304	244-305	245-306	246-308
247-309	248-310	249-311	250-312	251-314	252-315	253-316	254-317
255-318	256-320	257-321	258-322	259-323	260-324	261-326	262-327
263-328	264-329	265-330	266-332	267-333	268-334	269-335	270-336
271-338	272-339	273-340	274-341	275-342	276-344	277-345	278-346
279-347	280-348	281-350	282-351	283-352	284-353	285-354	286-356
287-357	288-358	289-359	290-360	291-362	292-363	293-364	294-365
295-366	296-368	297-369	298-370	299-371	300-372	301-374	302-375
303-376	304-377	305-378	306-380	307-381	308-382	309-383	310-384
311-386	312-387	313-388	314-389	315-390	316-392	317-393	318-394
319-395	320-396	321-398	322-399	323-400	324-401	325-402	326-404
327-405 ~~328-408~~328-406	329-407	330-408	331-410	332-411	333-412	334-413
335-414	336-416	337-417	338-418	339-419".			

SECTION 2.4.(b) This section becomes effective December 1, 2011, and applies to offenses committed on or after that date.

SECTION 2.5. Section 4(d) of S.L. 2011-192 reads as rewritten:

"**SECTION 4.(d)** ~~This~~Subsection (a) of this section ~~is~~becomes effective December 1, 2011, and applies to offenses committed on or after that date. Subsections (b) and (c) of this section become effective December 1, 2011, and apply to probation violations occurring on or after that date."

SECTION 2.6.(a) G.S. 15A-145.2(c), as amended by Section 5(b) of S.L. 2011-192, reads as rewritten:

"(c) Whenever any person who has not previously been convicted of (i) any felony offense under any state or federal laws; (ii) any offense under Chapter 90 of the General Statutes; or (iii) an offense under any statute of the United States or any state relating to controlled substances included in any schedule of Chapter 90 of the General Statutes or to that paraphernalia included in Article 5B of Chapter 90 of the General Statutes, pleads guilty to or has been found guilty of ~~(i)~~ a misdemeanor under ~~this~~Article 5 of Chapter 90 of the General Statutes by possessing a controlled substance included within Schedules I through VI of Chapter 90, or by possessing drug paraphernalia as prohibited by G.S. 90-113.22 or ~~(ii)~~pleads guilty to or has been found guilty of a felony under G.S. 90-95(a)(3), the court may, upon application of the person not sooner than 12 months after conviction, order cancellation of the judgment of conviction and expunction of the records of the person's arrest, indictment or information, trial, and conviction. A conviction in which the judgment of conviction has been canceled and the records expunged pursuant to this subsection shall not be thereafter deemed a conviction for purposes of this subsection or for purposes of disqualifications or liabilities imposed by law upon conviction of a crime, including the additional penalties imposed for second or subsequent convictions of Article 5 of Chapter 90 of the General Statutes. Cancellation and expunction under this subsection may occur only once with respect to any person. Disposition of a case under this subsection at the district court division of the General Court of Justice shall be final for the purpose of appeal.

The granting of an application filed under this subsection shall cause the issue of an order to expunge from all official records, other than the confidential files retained under G.S. 15A-151, all recordation relating to the petitioner's arrest, indictment or information, trial, finding of guilty, judgment of conviction, cancellation of the judgment, and expunction of records pursuant to this subsection.

The judge to whom the petition is presented is authorized to call upon a probation officer for additional investigation or verification of the petitioner's conduct since conviction. If the court determines that the petitioner was convicted of (i) a misdemeanor under Article 5 of Chapter 90 of the General Statutes for possessing a controlled substance included within Schedules I through VI of Article 5 of Chapter 90 of the General Statutes or for possessing drug paraphernalia as prohibited in G.S. 90-113.22 or (ii) a felony under G.S. 90-95(a)(3), that the petitioner has no disqualifying previous convictions as set forth in this subsection, that the petitioner was not over 21 years of age at the time of the offense, that the petitioner has been of good behavior since his or her conviction, that the petitioner has successfully completed a drug education program approved for this purpose by the Department of Health and Human Services, and that the petitioner has not been convicted of a felony or misdemeanor other than a traffic violation under the laws of this State at any time prior to or since the conviction for the offense in question, it shall enter an order of expunction of the petitioner's court record. The effect of such order shall be to restore the petitioner in the contemplation of the law to the status the petitioner occupied before arrest or indictment or information or conviction. No person as to whom such order was entered shall be held thereafter under any provision of any law to be guilty of perjury or otherwise giving a false statement by reason of the person's failures to recite or acknowledge such arrest, or indictment or information, or conviction, or trial in response to any inquiry made of him or her for any purpose. The judge may waive the condition that the petitioner attend the drug education school if the judge makes a specific finding that there was no drug education school within a reasonable distance of the defendant's residence or that there were specific extenuating circumstances which made it likely that the petitioner would not benefit from the program of instruction.

The court shall also order all law enforcement agencies, the Department of Correction, the Division of Motor Vehicles, and any other State or local agencies identified by the petitioner as bearing records of the conviction and records relating thereto to expunge their records of the conviction. The clerk shall notify State and local agencies of the court's order as provided in G.S. 15A-150."

SECTION 2.6.(b) This section becomes effective January 1, 2012, and applies to persons entering a plea or who are found guilty of an offense on or after that date.

SECTION 2.7. Effective January 1, 2012, G.S. 15A-1340.18(c), as enacted by Section 5(c) of S.L. 2011-192, reads as rewritten:

"(c)   ~~The~~ When imposing an active sentence for an eligible defendant, the court, in its discretion and without objection from the prosecutor, may ~~include a risk reduction incentive or incentives in sentencing an eligible defendant to an active sentence.~~order that the Department of Correction admit the defendant to the ASR program. The Department of Correction shall admit to the ASR program only those defendants for which ASR is ordered in the sentencing judgment."

SECTION 2.8. Effective January 1, 2012, G.S. 15A-1340.18(e), as enacted by Section 5(c) of S.L. 2011-192, reads as rewritten:

"(e)   The defendant shall be notified at sentencing that if the defendant completes the risk reduction incentives as identified by the Department, then he or she will be released on the ASR ~~date.~~ date, as determined by the Department pursuant to the provisions of subsection (d) of this section. If the Department determines that the defendant is unable to complete the incentives by the ASR date, through no fault of the defendant, then the defendant shall be released at the ASR date."

SECTION 2.9.   Except as otherwise provided, this Part becomes effective December 1, 2011.

PART III. TECHNICAL CORRECTIONS AND CLARIFICATION

SECTION 3.1. G.S. 68-25(b1), as enacted by S.L. 2011-313, is repealed.

SECTION 3.2. Section 6 of S.L. 2011-385 reads as rewritten:

"**SECTION 6.** ~~Sections 1, 2, and 3 of this act become effective October 1, 2011, and apply to limited learner's permits and limited provisional licenses issued on or after that date.~~ Section 1 of this act becomes effective October 1, 2011, and applies to persons issued a limited provisional license on or after that date. Section 2 of this act becomes effective January 1, 2012, and applies to persons issued a limited learner's permit on or after that date. Section 3 of this act becomes effective January 1, 2012, and applies to persons issued a limited provisional license on or after that date. Section 4 of this act becomes effective ~~October 1, 2011,~~ January 1, 2012, and applies to offenses committed on or after that date. The remainder of this act becomes effective October 1, 2011."

SECTION 3.3. Section 20 of S.L. 2011-391 is repealed.

PART IV. BAIL BONDSMEN

SECTION 4.1. Article 71 of Chapter 58 of the General Statutes is amended by adding a new section to read:

"**§ 58-71-200. Bondsman access to criminal court records.**

(a)   In order to assist licensed sureties and their agents in evaluating potential and current clients for the purposes of bail, the Administrative Office of the Courts shall provide any individual with a current license to act as professional bondsman, surety bondsman, or runner with access to search criminal records in the Administrative Office of the Courts' real-time criminal information systems.

(b)   Access granted under subsection (a) of this section shall be limited to information systems containing general criminal case information, as maintained by the clerks of superior court. Access shall not include systems for the production of criminal process by law enforcement officials and judicial officials under G.S. 15A-301.1 or other information not subject to public disclosure.

(c)   Access provided pursuant to subsection (a) of this section shall be without charge for individual searches of the Administrative Office of the Courts' criminal information systems. In order to defray the costs of establishing access, the Administrative Office of the Courts shall charge initial setup fees equivalent to its fees for governmental agencies granted access to its systems to each individual granted access pursuant to subsection (a) of this section.

(d)   All hardware, software, telecommunications charges, or other expenditures required for such access shall be the sole responsibility of the individual bondsman or runner. No State funds may be expended for any such expenses.

(e)   The Commissioner shall coordinate the access granted under subsection (a) of this section by providing all information requested by the Administrative Office of the Courts for the establishment of access. The Administrative Office of the Courts shall not provide access to any bondsman or runner who fails to provide all information requested by the Commissioner.

(f)   The Commissioner shall notify the Administrative Office of the Courts within 24 hours of any action to suspend or revoke a bondsman's or runner's license or authority to act as a bondsman or runner. The Administrative Office of the Courts shall immediately revoke access of the suspended or revoked bondsman or runner to its criminal information systems.

(g)   The Administrative Office of the Courts shall provide to the Commissioner copies of its current policies for access to court information systems for users outside the Judicial Branch. Any bondsman or runner granted access pursuant to subsection (a) of this section shall adhere to all such policies. The Administrative Office of the Courts shall revoke access of any bondsman or runner who violates such policies.

(h)   It is unlawful for any person to willfully do any of the following:

(1)   For any person to access information systems of the Administrative Office of the Courts by means of an online identifier, as defined in G.S. 14-208.6(1n), that was assigned to another individual by the Administrative Office of the Courts pursuant to subsection (a) of this section.

(2)   For any bondsman or runner granted access pursuant to subsection (a) of this section to allow any other person, directly or indirectly, to make use of access granted to the bondsman or runner pursuant to subsection (a) of this section.

(3)   For any bondsman or runner granted access pursuant to subsection (a) of this section to make use of that access at any time when the bondsman or runner knows or has reason to know that his or her license issued under this Article is in a state of suspension or revocation.

(4)   For any bondsman or runner granted access pursuant to subsection (a) of this section to distribute, in any medium or manner, information obtained from the information systems of the Administrative Office of the Courts to any person for any reason not directly related to the evaluation of the individual to whom the information pertains for the purposes of bail.

Unless the conduct is covered under some other provision of law providing for a greater punishment, any violation of this subsection shall be a Class H felony."

SECTION 4.2.(a) Section 8 of S.L. 2011-377 is repealed.

SECTION 4.2.(b) G.S. 15A-544.5(d)(4) reads as rewritten:

"(4)   If neither the district attorney nor the board of education has filed a written objection to the motion by the twentieth day after the motion is ~~served,~~ served by the clerk of superior court pursuant to Rule 4 of the Rules of Civil Procedure, the clerk shall enter an order setting aside the ~~forfeiture.~~ forfeiture, regardless of the basis for relief asserted in the motion, the evidence attached, or the absence of either."

SECTION 4.2.(c) G.S. 15A-544.5(d)(4), as amended by Section 4.2(b) of this act, reads as rewritten:

"(4)   If neither the district attorney nor the attorney for the board of education has filed a written objection to the motion by the twentieth day after a copy of the motion is ~~served,~~ served by the clerk of superior court pursuant to Rule 4 of the Rules of Civil Procedure, the clerk shall enter an order setting aside the forfeiture, regardless of the basis for relief asserted in the motion, the evidence attached, or the absence of either."

PART V. WATER SUPPLY LINES

SECTION 5. Notwithstanding Section 5.1(b) of S.L. 1998-132, the Secretary of Environment and Natural Resources shall grant a waiver to allow additional connections to a bond-funded waterline within an area designated as WS-I or the critical area of any area that has been designated as WS-II, WS-III, or WS-IV by the Environmental Management Commission pursuant to G.S. 143-214.5, provided the design capacity and size of the existing bond-funded waterline can accommodate the additional connections and the purpose of the additional connection is for either of the following reasons:

(1) To address an existing threat to public health or water quality.
(2) To provide water to a habitable structure located on a lot zoned for a single-family residence. There is no requirement that the habitable structure existed on the lot at the time of the construction of the bond-funded waterline.

PART VI. HOME INSPECTOR LICENSURE BOARD CLARIFICATION
SECTION 6. G.S. 143-151.46(a)(1) reads as rewritten:
"(a) Membership. – The North Carolina Home Inspector Licensure Board is established in the Department of Insurance. The Board shall be composed of the Commissioner of Insurance or the Commissioner's designee and seven additional members appointed as follows:
(1) A public member who is not actively engaged in one of the professional categories in subdivisions (2) through (4) of this subsection, appointed by the General Assembly upon the recommendation of the Speaker of the House of Representatives.
...."

SECTION 7. Except as otherwise provided herein, this act is effective when it becomes law.
In the General Assembly read three times and ratified this the 14th day of September, 2011.

s/ Walter H. Dalton
President of the Senate

s/ Thom Tillis
Speaker of the House of Representatives

This bill having been presented to the Governor for signature on the 15th day of September, 2011 and the Governor having failed to approve it within the time prescribed by law, the same is hereby declared to have become a law. This 15th day of October, 2011.

s/ Karen Jenkins
Enrolling Clerk

N.C. Session Law 2012-188, Justice Reinvestment Clarifications

GENERAL ASSEMBLY OF NORTH CAROLINA
SESSION 2011

SESSION LAW 2012-188
HOUSE BILL 1021

AN ACT TO CLARIFY CERTAIN PROVISIONS OF THE JUSTICE REINVESTMENT ACT.

The General Assembly of North Carolina enacts:

SECTION 1.(a) G.S. 15A-1343.2(e) reads as rewritten:
"(e)   Delegation to Probation Officer in Community Punishment. – Unless the presiding judge specifically finds in the judgment of the court that delegation is not appropriate, the Section of Community Corrections of the Division of Adult Correction of the Department of Public Safety may require an offender sentenced to community punishment to do any of the following:

(1)	Perform up to 20 hours of community service, and pay the fee prescribed by law for this supervision.
(2)	Report to the offender's probation officer on a frequency to be determined by the officer.
(3)	Submit to substance abuse assessment, monitoring or treatment.
(4)	Submit to house arrest with electronic monitoring.
(5)	Submit to a period or periods of confinement in a local confinement facility for a total of no more than six days per month during any three separate months during the period of probation. The six days per month confinement provided for in this subdivision may only be imposed as two-day or three-day consecutive periods. When a defendant is on probation for multiple judgments, confinement periods imposed under this subdivision shall run concurrently and may total no more than six days per month.
(6)	Submit to a curfew which requires the offender to remain in a specified place for a specified period each day and wear a device that permits the offender's compliance with the condition to be monitored electronically.
(7)	Participate in an educational or vocational skills development program, including an evidence-based program.

If the Section imposes any of the above requirements, then it may subsequently reduce or remove those same requirements.

The probation officer may exercise authority delegated to him or her by the court pursuant to subsection (e) of this section after administrative review and approval by a Chief Probation Officer. The offender may file a motion with the court to review the action taken by the probation officer. The offender shall be given notice of the right to seek such a court review. However, the offender shall have no right of review if he or she has signed a written waiver of rights as required by this subsection. The Section may exercise any authority delegated to it under this subsection only if it first determines that the offender has failed to comply with one or more of the conditions of probation imposed by the court or the offender is determined to be high risk based on the results of the risk assessment in G.S. 15A-1343.2, except that the condition at subdivision (5) of this subsection may not be imposed unless the Section determines that the offender failed to comply with one or more of the conditions imposed by the court. Nothing in this section shall be construed to limit the availability of the procedures authorized under G.S. 15A-1345.

The Division shall adopt guidelines and procedures to implement the requirements of this section, which shall include a supervisor's approval prior to exercise of the delegation of authority authorized by this section. Prior to imposing confinement pursuant to subdivision (5) of this subsection, the probationer must first be presented with a violation report, with the

alleged violations noted and advised of the right (i) to a hearing before the court on the alleged violation, with the right to present relevant oral and written evidence; (ii) to have counsel at the hearing, and that one will be appointed if the probationer is indigent; (iii) to request witnesses who have relevant information concerning the alleged violations; and (iv) to examine any witnesses or evidence. ~~Upon the signing of a waiver of rights by the probationer, with both the probation officer and a supervisor signing as witnesses, the~~The probationer may be confined for the period designated on the violation ~~report.~~report upon the execution of a waiver of rights signed by the probationer and by two officers acting as witnesses. Those two witnesses shall be the probation officer and another officer to be designated by the Chief of the Community Corrections Section in written Division policy."

   SECTION 1.(b) G.S. 15A-1343.2(f) reads as rewritten:

 "(f) Delegation to Probation Officer in Intermediate Punishments. – Unless the presiding judge specifically finds in the judgment of the court that delegation is not appropriate, the Section of Community Corrections of the Division of Adult Correction of the Department of Public Safety may require an offender sentenced to intermediate punishment to do any of the following:

(1)	Perform up to 50 hours of community service, and pay the fee prescribed by law for this supervision.
(2)	Submit to a curfew which requires the offender to remain in a specified place for a specified period each day and wear a device that permits the offender's compliance with the condition to be monitored electronically.
(3)	Submit to substance abuse assessment, monitoring or treatment.
(4)	Participate in an educational or vocational skills development program, including an evidence-based program.
(5)	Submit to satellite-based monitoring pursuant to Part 5 of Article 27A of Chapter 14 of the General Statutes, if the defendant is described by G.S. 14-208.40(a)(2).
(6)	Submit to a period or periods of confinement in a local confinement facility for a total of no more than six days per month during any three separate months during the period of probation. The six days per month confinement provided for in this subdivision may only be imposed as two-day or three-day consecutive periods. When a defendant is on probation for multiple judgments, confinement periods imposed under this subdivision shall run concurrently and may total no more than six days per month.
(7)	Submit to house arrest with electronic monitoring.
(8)	Report to the offender's probation officer on a frequency to be determined by the officer.

If the Section imposes any of the above requirements, then it may subsequently reduce or remove those same requirements.

 The probation officer may exercise authority delegated to him or her by the court pursuant to subsection (f) of this section after administrative review and approval by a Chief Probation Officer. The offender may file a motion with the court to review the action taken by the probation officer. The offender shall be given notice of the right to seek such a court review. However, the offender shall have no right of review if he or she has signed a written waiver of rights as required by this subsection. The Section may exercise any authority delegated to it under this subsection only if it first determines that the offender has failed to comply with one or more of the conditions of probation imposed by the court or the offender is determined to be high risk based on the results of the risk assessment in G.S. 15A-1343.2, except that the condition at subdivision (6) of this subsection may not be imposed unless the Section determines that the offender failed to comply with one or more of the conditions imposed by the court. Nothing in this section shall be construed to limit the availability of the procedures authorized under G.S. 15A-1345.

 The Division shall adopt guidelines and procedures to implement the requirements of this section, which shall include a supervisor's approval prior to exercise of the delegation of authority authorized by this section. Prior to imposing confinement pursuant to subdivision (6) of this subsection, the probationer must first be presented with a violation report, with the alleged violations noted and advised of the right (i) to a hearing before the court on the alleged violation, with the right to present relevant oral and written evidence; (ii) to have counsel at the hearing, and that one will be appointed if the probationer is indigent; (iii) to request witnesses who have relevant information concerning the alleged violations; and (iv) to examine any witnesses or evidence. ~~Upon the signing of a waiver of rights by the probationer, with both the probation officer and a supervisor signing as witnesses, the~~The probationer may be confined for the period designated on the violation ~~report.~~report upon the execution of a waiver of rights signed by the probationer and by two officers acting as witnesses. Those two witnesses shall be the probation officer and another officer to be designated by the Chief of the Community Corrections Section in written Division policy."

      SECTION 2. G.S. 15A-1344(d2) reads as rewritten:

    "(d2) Confinement in Response to Violation. – When a defendant under supervision for a felony conviction has violated a condition of probation other than G.S. 15A-1343(b)(1) or G.S. 15A-1343(b)(3a), the court may impose a 90-day period of ~~confinement for a defendant under supervision for a felony conviction or a period of confinement of up to 90 days for a defendant under supervision for a misdemeanor conviction.~~confinement. The court may not revoke probation unless the defendant has previously received a total of two periods of confinement under this subsection. A defendant may receive only two periods of confinement under this subsection. If the time remaining on the ~~defendant's~~maximum imposed sentence on a defendant under supervision for a felony conviction is 90 days or less, then the term of confinement is for the remaining period of the sentence. Confinement under this section shall be credited pursuant to G.S. 15-196.1.

    When a defendant under supervision for a misdemeanor conviction has violated a condition of probation other than G.S. 15A-1343(b)(1) or G.S. 15A-1343(b)(3a), the court may impose a period of confinement of up to 90 days. The court may not revoke probation unless the defendant has previously received a total of two periods of confinement under this subsection. A defendant may receive only two periods of confinement under this subsection. Confinement under this section shall be credited pursuant to G.S. 15-196.1.

    If a defendant is arrested for violation of a condition of probation and is lawfully confined to await a hearing for the violation, then the judge shall first credit any confinement time spent awaiting the hearing to any confinement imposed under this subsection; any excess time shall be credited to the activated sentence. The period of confinement imposed under this subsection on a defendant who is on probation for multiple offenses shall run concurrently on all cases related to the violation. Confinement shall be immediate unless otherwise specified by the court.

    A defendant shall serve any confinement imposed under this subsection in the correctional facility where the defendant would have served an active sentence."

      SECTION 3. G.S. 15A-1343(a1) reads as rewritten:

    "(a1) Community and Intermediate Probation Conditions. – In addition to any conditions a court may be authorized to impose pursuant to G.S. 15A-1343(b1), the court may include any one or more of the following conditions as part of a community or intermediate punishment:

        (1)   House arrest with electronic monitoring.
        (2)   Perform community ~~service.~~service and pay the fee prescribed by law for this supervision.
        (3)   Submission to a period or periods of confinement in a local confinement facility for a total of no more than six days per month during any three separate months during the period of probation. The six days per month confinement provided for in this subdivision may only be imposed as two-day or three-day consecutive periods. When a defendant is on probation for multiple judgments, confinement periods imposed under this subdivision shall run concurrently and may total no more than six days per month.
        (4)   Substance abuse assessment, monitoring, or treatment.
        (5)   Participation in an educational or vocational skills development program, including an evidence-based program.
        (6)   Submission to satellite-based monitoring, pursuant to Part 5 of Article 27A of Chapter 14 of the General Statutes, if the defendant is described by G.S. 14-208.40(a)(2)."

      SECTION 4. G.S. 15A-1368.3(c) reads as rewritten:

    "(c) Effect of Violation. – If the supervisee violates a condition, described in G.S. 15A-1368.4, at any time before the termination of the supervision period, the Commission may continue the supervisee on the existing supervision, with or without modifying the conditions, or if continuation or modification is not appropriate, may revoke post-release supervision as provided in G.S. 15A-1368.6 and reimprison the supervisee for a term consistent with the following requirements:

(1) Supervisees who were convicted of an offense for which registration is required under Article 27A of Chapter 14 of the General Statutes and supervisees whose supervision is revoked for a violation of the required controlling condition under G.S. 15A-1368.4(b) or for absconding in violation of G.S. 15A-1368.4(e)(7a) will be returned to prison up to the time remaining on their maximum imposed terms. All other supervisees will be returned to prison for three months and may be returned for three months on each of two subsequent violations, after which supervisees who were Class B1 through E felons may be returned to prison up to the time remaining on their maximum imposed terms. Reimprisonment for a violation under this subdivision tolls the running of the period of supervised release, except that a supervisee shall not be rereleased on post-release supervision if the supervisee has served all the time remaining on the supervisee's maximum imposed term.

(2) The supervisee shall not receive any credit for days on post-release supervision against the maximum term of imprisonment imposed by the court under G.S. 15A-1340.13.

(3) Pursuant to Article 19A of Chapter 15, the Division of Adult Correction of the Department of Public Safety shall award a prisoner credit against any term of reimprisonment for all time spent in custody as a result of revocation proceedings under G.S. 15A-1368.6.

(4) The prisoner is eligible to receive earned time credit against the maximum prison term as provided in G.S. 15A-1340.13(d) for time served in prison after the revocation."

SECTION 5. G.S. 90-95(h) reads as rewritten:

"(h) Notwithstanding any other provision of law, the following provisions apply except as otherwise provided in this Article.

(1) Any person who sells, manufactures, delivers, transports, or possesses in excess of 10 pounds (avoirdupois) of marijuana shall be guilty of a felony which felony shall be known as "trafficking in marijuana" and if the quantity of such substance involved:

    a. Is in excess of 10 pounds, but less than 50 pounds, such person shall be punished as a Class H felon and shall be sentenced to a minimum term of 25 months and a maximum term of 30–39 months in the State's prison and shall be fined not less than five thousand dollars ($5,000);

    b. Is 50 pounds or more, but less than 2,000 pounds, such person shall be punished as a Class G felon and shall be sentenced to a minimum term of 35 months and a maximum term of 42–51 months in the State's prison and shall be fined not less than twenty-five thousand dollars ($25,000);

    c. Is 2,000 pounds or more, but less than 10,000 pounds, such person shall be punished as a Class F felon and shall be sentenced to a minimum term of 70 months and a maximum term of 84–93 months in the State's prison and shall be fined not less than fifty thousand dollars ($50,000);

    d. Is 10,000 pounds or more, such person shall be punished as a Class D felon and shall be sentenced to a minimum term of 175 months and a maximum term of 219–222 months in the State's prison and shall be fined not less than two hundred thousand dollars ($200,000).

(1a) For the purpose of this subsection, a "dosage unit" shall consist of 3 grams of synthetic cannabinoid or any mixture containing such substance. Any person who sells, manufactures, delivers, transports, or possesses in excess of 50 dosage units of a synthetic cannabinoid or any mixture containing such substance, shall be guilty of a felony, which felony shall be known as "trafficking in synthetic cannabinoids," and if the quantity of such substance involved:

      a.   Is in excess of 50 dosage units, but less than 250 dosage units, such person shall be punished as a Class H felon and shall be sentenced to a minimum term of 25 months and a maximum term of 30 39 months in the State's prison and shall be fined not less than five thousand dollars ($5,000);

      b.   Is 250 dosage units or more, but less than 1250 dosage units, such person shall be punished as a Class G felon and shall be sentenced to a minimum term of 35 months and a maximum term of 42 51 months in the State's prison and shall be fined not less than twenty-five thousand dollars ($25,000);

      c.   Is 1250 dosage units or more, but less than 3750 dosage units, such person shall be punished as a Class F felon and shall be sentenced to a minimum term of 70 months and a maximum term of 84 93 months in the State's prison and shall be fined not less than fifty thousand dollars ($50,000);

      d.   Is 3750 dosage units or more, such person shall be punished as a Class D felon and shall be sentenced to a minimum term of 175 months and a maximum term of 219 222 months in the State's prison and shall be fined not less than two hundred thousand dollars ($200,000).

  (2)   Any person who sells, manufactures, delivers, transports, or possesses 1,000 tablets, capsules or other dosage units, or the equivalent quantity, or more of methaqualone, or any mixture containing such substance, shall be guilty of a felony which felony shall be known as "trafficking in methaqualone" and if the quantity of such substance or mixture involved:

      a.   Is 1,000 or more dosage units, or equivalent quantity, but less than 5,000 dosage units, or equivalent quantity, such person shall be punished as a Class G felon and shall be sentenced to a minimum term of 35 months and a maximum term of 42 51 months in the State's prison and shall be fined not less than twenty-five thousand dollars ($25,000);

      b.   Is 5,000 or more dosage units, or equivalent quantity, but less than 10,000 dosage units, or equivalent quantity, such person shall be punished as a Class F felon and shall be sentenced to a minimum term of 70 months and a maximum term of 84 93 months in the State's prison and shall be fined not less than fifty thousand dollars ($50,000);

      c.   Is 10,000 or more dosage units, or equivalent quantity, such person shall be punished as a Class D felon and shall be sentenced to a minimum term of 175 months and a maximum term of 219 222 months in the State's prison and shall be fined not less than two hundred thousand dollars ($200,000).

  (3)   Any person who sells, manufactures, delivers, transports, or possesses 28 grams or more of cocaine and any salt, isomer, salts of isomers, compound, derivative, or preparation thereof, or any coca leaves and any salt, isomer, salts of isomers, compound, derivative, or preparation of coca leaves, and any salt, isomer, salts of isomers, compound, derivative or preparation thereof which is chemically equivalent or identical with any of these substances (except decocainized coca leaves or any extraction of coca leaves which does not contain cocaine) or any mixture containing such substances, shall be guilty of a felony, which felony shall be known as "trafficking in cocaine" and if the quantity of such substance or mixture involved:

      a.   Is 28 grams or more, but less than 200 grams, such person shall be punished as a Class G felon and shall be sentenced to a minimum term of 35 months and a maximum term of 42 51 months in the State's prison and shall be fined not less than fifty thousand dollars ($50,000);

      b.   Is 200 grams or more, but less than 400 grams, such person shall be punished as a Class F felon and shall be sentenced to a minimum term of 70 months and a maximum term of ~~84~~ 93 months in the State's prison and shall be fined not less than one hundred thousand dollars ($100,000);

    c.   Is 400 grams or more, such person shall be punished as a Class D felon and shall be sentenced to a minimum term of 175 months and a maximum term of ~~219~~ 222 months in the State's prison and shall be fined at least two hundred fifty thousand dollars ($250,000).

(3a)   Repealed by Session Laws 1999-370, s. 1, effective December 1, 1999.

(3b)   Any person who sells, manufactures, delivers, transports, or possesses 28 grams or more of methamphetamine or any mixture containing such substance shall be guilty of a felony which felony shall be known as "trafficking in methamphetamine" and if the quantity of such substance or mixture involved:

    a.   Is 28 grams or more, but less than 200 grams, such person shall be punished as a Class F felon and shall be sentenced to a minimum term of 70 months and a maximum term of ~~84~~ 93 months in the State's prison and shall be fined not less than fifty thousand dollars ($50,000);

    b.   Is 200 grams or more, but less than 400 grams, such person shall be punished as a Class E felon and shall be sentenced to a minimum term of 90 months and a maximum term of ~~117~~ 120 months in the State's prison and shall be fined not less than one hundred thousand dollars ($100,000);

    c.   Is 400 grams or more, such person shall be punished as a Class C felon and shall be sentenced to a minimum term of 225 months and a maximum term of ~~279~~ 282 months in the State's prison and shall be fined at least two hundred fifty thousand dollars ($250,000).

(3c)   Any person who sells, manufactures, delivers, transports, or possesses 28 grams or more of amphetamine or any mixture containing such substance shall be guilty of a felony, which felony shall be known as "trafficking in amphetamine", and if the quantity of such substance or mixture involved:

    a.   Is 28 grams or more, but less than 200 grams, such person shall be punished as a Class H felon and shall be sentenced to a minimum term of 25 months and a maximum term of ~~30~~ 39 months in the State's prison and shall be fined not less than five thousand dollars ($5,000);

    b.   Is 200 grams or more, but less than 400 grams, such person shall be punished as a Class G felon and shall be sentenced to a minimum term of 35 months and a maximum term of ~~42~~ 51 months in the State's prison and shall be fined not less than twenty-five thousand dollars ($25,000);

    c.   Is 400 grams or more, such person shall be punished as a Class E felon and shall be sentenced to a minimum term of 90 months and a maximum term of ~~117~~ 120 months in the State's prison and shall be fined at least one hundred thousand dollars ($100,000).

(3d)   Any person who sells, manufactures, delivers, transports, or possesses 28 grams or more of MDPV or any mixture containing such substance shall be guilty of a felony, which felony shall be known as "trafficking in MDPV," and if the quantity of such substance or mixture involved:

    a.   Is 28 grams or more, but less than 200 grams, such person shall be punished as a Class F felon and shall be sentenced to a minimum term of 70 months and a maximum term of ~~84~~ 93 months in the State's prison and shall be fined not less than fifty thousand dollars ($50,000);

    b.   Is 200 grams or more, but less than 400 grams, such person shall be punished as a Class E felon and shall be sentenced to a minimum term of 90 months and a maximum term of ~~117~~ 120 months in the State's prison and shall be fined not less than one hundred thousand dollars ($100,000);

        c.   Is 400 grams or more, such person shall be punished as a Class C felon and shall be sentenced to a minimum term of 225 months and a maximum term of ~~279~~ 282 months in the State's prison and shall be fined at least two hundred fifty thousand dollars ($250,000).

(3e)   Any person who sells, manufactures, delivers, transports, or possesses 28 grams or more of mephedrone or any mixture containing such substance shall be guilty of a felony, which felony shall be known as "trafficking in mephedrone," and if the quantity of such substance or mixture involved:

        a.   Is 28 grams or more, but less than 200 grams, such person shall be punished as a Class F felon and shall be sentenced to a minimum term of 70 months and a maximum term of ~~84~~ 93 months in the State's prison and shall be fined not less than fifty thousand dollars ($50,000);

        b.   Is 200 grams or more, but less than 400 grams, such person shall be punished as a Class E felon and shall be sentenced to a minimum term of 90 months and a maximum term of ~~117~~ 120 months in the State's prison and shall be fined not less than one hundred thousand dollars ($100,000);

        c.   Is 400 grams or more, such person shall be punished as a Class C felon and shall be sentenced to a minimum term of 225 months and a maximum term of ~~279~~ 282 months in the State's prison and shall be fined at least two hundred fifty thousand dollars ($250,000).

(4)   Any person who sells, manufactures, delivers, transports, or possesses four grams or more of opium or opiate, or any salt, compound, derivative, or preparation of opium or opiate (except apomorphine, nalbuphine, analoxone and naltrexone and their respective salts), including heroin, or any mixture containing such substance, shall be guilty of a felony which felony shall be known as "trafficking in opium or heroin" and if the quantity of such controlled substance or mixture involved:

        a.   Is four grams or more, but less than 14 grams, such person shall be punished as a Class F felon and shall be sentenced to a minimum term of 70 months and a maximum term of ~~84~~ 93 months in the State's prison and shall be fined not less than fifty thousand dollars ($50,000);

        b.   Is 14 grams or more, but less than 28 grams, such person shall be punished as a Class E felon and shall be sentenced to a minimum term of 90 months and a maximum term of ~~117~~ 120 months in the State's prison and shall be fined not less than one hundred thousand dollars ($100,000);

        c.   Is 28 grams or more, such person shall be punished as a Class C felon and shall be sentenced to a minimum term of 225 months and a maximum term of ~~279~~ 282 months in the State's prison and shall be fined not less than five hundred thousand dollars ($500,000).

(4a)   Any person who sells, manufactures, delivers, transports, or possesses 100 tablets, capsules, or other dosage units, or the equivalent quantity, or more, of Lysergic Acid Diethylamide, or any mixture containing such substance, shall be guilty of a felony, which felony shall be known as "trafficking in Lysergic Acid Diethylamide". If the quantity of such substance or mixture involved:

        a.   Is 100 or more dosage units, or equivalent quantity, but less than 500 dosage units, or equivalent quantity, such person shall be punished as a Class G felon and shall be sentenced to a minimum term of 35 months and a maximum term of ~~42~~ 51 months in the State's prison and shall be fined not less than twenty-five thousand dollars ($25,000);

        b.   Is 500 or more dosage units, or equivalent quantity, but less than 1,000 dosage units, or equivalent quantity, such person shall be punished as a Class F felon and shall be sentenced to a minimum term of 70 months and a maximum term of ~~84~~ 93 months in the

State's prison and shall be fined not less than fifty thousand dollars ($50,000);

    c.   Is 1,000 or more dosage units, or equivalent quantity, such person shall be punished as a Class D felon and shall be sentenced to a minimum term of 175 months and a maximum term of ~~219~~ 222 months in the State's prison and shall be fined not less than two hundred thousand dollars ($200,000).

(4b)   Any person who sells, manufactures, delivers, transports, or possesses 100 or more tablets, capsules, or other dosage units, or 28 grams or more of 3,4-methylenedioxyamphetamine (MDA), including its salts, isomers, and salts of isomers, or 3,4-methylenedioxymethamphetamine (MDMA), including its salts, isomers, and salts of isomers, or any mixture containing such substances, shall be guilty of a felony, which felony shall be known as "trafficking in MDADMA." If the quantity of the substance or mixture involved:

    a.   Is 100 or more tablets, capsules, or other dosage units, but less than 500 tablets, capsules, or other dosage units, or 28 grams or more, but less than 200 grams, the person shall be punished as a Class G felon and shall be sentenced to a minimum term of 35 months and a maximum term of ~~42~~ 51 months in the State's prison and shall be fined not less than twenty-five thousand dollars ($25,000);

    b.   Is 500 or more tablets, capsules, or other dosage units, but less than 1,000 tablets, capsules, or other dosage units, or 200 grams or more, but less than 400 grams, the person shall be punished as a Class F felon and shall be sentenced to a minimum term of 70 months and a maximum term of ~~84~~ 93 months in the State's prison and shall be fined not less than fifty thousand dollars ($50,000);

    c.   Is 1,000 or more tablets, capsules, or other dosage units, or 400 grams or more, the person shall be punished as a Class D felon and shall be sentenced to a minimum term of 175 months and a maximum term of ~~219~~ 222 months in the State's prison and shall be fined not less than two hundred fifty thousand dollars ($250,000).

(5)   Except as provided in this subdivision, a person being sentenced under this subsection may not receive a suspended sentence or be placed on probation. The sentencing judge may reduce the fine, or impose a prison term less than the applicable minimum prison term provided by this subsection, or suspend the prison term imposed and place a person on probation when such person has, to the best of his knowledge, provided substantial assistance in the identification, arrest, or conviction of any accomplices, accessories, co-conspirators, or principals if the sentencing judge enters in the record a finding that the person to be sentenced has rendered such substantial assistance.

(6)   Sentences imposed pursuant to this subsection shall run consecutively with and shall commence at the expiration of any sentence being served by the person sentenced hereunder."

SECTION 6. G.S. 15A-1368.1 reads as rewritten:

"§ 15A-1368.1. Applicability of Article 84A.

This Article applies to all felons sentenced to an active punishment under Article 81B of this ~~Chapter.~~ Chapter or G.S. 90-95(h), but does not apply to felons in Class A and Class B1 sentenced to life imprisonment without parole. Prisoners subject to Articles 85 and 85A of this Chapter are excluded from this Article's coverage."

SECTION 7. G.S. 143B-720 is amended by adding a new subsection to read:

"(f)   The Commission may conduct the following proceedings by videoconference:

(1)   All hearings regarding the revocation or termination of post-release supervision and all hearings regarding revocation, termination, or suspension of parole.

(2)   All hearings regarding criminal contempt for willful refusal to accept post-release supervision or comply with the terms of post-release supervision by a prisoner whose offense requiring post-release supervision is

a reportable conviction subject to the registration requirement of Article 27A of Chapter 14 of the General Statutes."

SECTION 8. Section 4 of this act is effective when it becomes law and applies to supervisees violating the conditions of post-release supervision on or after that date. Sections 5 and 6 of this act become effective December 1, 2012, and apply to offenses committed on or after that date. Section 7 of this act becomes effective December 1, 2012. The remainder of this act is effective when it becomes law.

In the General Assembly read three times and ratified this the 28th day of June, 2012.

s/ Walter H. Dalton
    President of the Senate

s/ Thom Tillis
    Speaker of the House of Representatives

s/ Beverly E. Perdue
    Governor

Approved 3:50 p.m. this 16th day of July, 2012